SALLVSTIVS

CONCERNING THE GODS AND THE UNIVERSE

SALLVSTIVS
CONCERNING THE GODS AND THE UNIVERSE

Edited with Prolegomena & Translation

by

ARTHUR DARBY NOCK
Fellow of Clare College, Cambridge
Sometime Scholar of Trinity

CAMBRIDGE
AT THE UNIVERSITY PRESS
1926

CAMBRIDGE UNIVERSITY PRESS
Cambridge, New York, Melbourne, Madrid, Cape Town,
Singapore, São Paulo, Delhi, Mexico City

Cambridge University Press
The Edinburgh Building, Cambridge CB2 8RU, UK

Published in the United States of America by Cambridge University Press, New York

www.cambridge.org
Information on this title: www.cambridge.org/9781107645035

First published 1926
First paperback edition 2013

A catalogue record for this publication is available from the British Library

ISBN 978-1-107-64503-5 Paperback

PARENTIBVS · OPTIMIS

PREFACE

THE treatise here edited has come down to us under the name of Saloustios (here called Sallustius in accordance with the conventional Latinism) with no external evidence for its date or purpose. The suggestion that it was written by a friend of the Emperor Julian and in the service of his attempt to revive ancient paganism lent it a new interest, and in 1912 Professor Gilbert Murray gave it an English dress and drew public attention to it in his *Four Stages of Greek Religion* (now reissued in a revised form as *Five Stages of Greek Religion*). In his preface he expressed the view that 'an edition of Sallustius is urgently needed.' Some years later Professor Praechter said in the great German encyclopaedia of classical antiquity, 'A critical edition of the tractate is a pressing need,' and again, 'In addition to a convenient edition it needs a close linguistic and philosophic analysis; only by this can we learn where the writer stands, to what form of Neo-platonism he is attached, and in particular what are his relations with Iamblichus and Julian.' The present work seeks to meet this need. Muccio's discovery of the manuscript at Milan gives a trustworthy basis for the text: the Prolegomena are devoted to its exposition and to an attempt to place it in the right historical perspective. It is in truth not the least instructive or attractive document of the conflict of beliefs in the fourth century of our era, and the study of that conflict is surely of more than antiquarian interest.

My most sincere thanks are due to all those who have helped me, and in particular to the Managers of the Craven Fund, who by two grants enabled me to travel and to visit the libraries containing the manuscripts of Sallustius; to the Syndics of the Cambridge University Press for accepting financial responsibility for this book; to the Librarians of the Ambrosian Library at Milan and of the Vatican Library for facilitating my studies; to Professor Franz Cumont for putting his collation of the Vatican manuscript at my disposal and

for other help and advice; to Professor A. C. Pearson for his great kindness in reading the bulk of my work in manuscript and for many useful suggestions; to Mr E. Harrison for his vigilant reading of the proofs and for much assistance to me earlier in the preparation of the book; to Professor A. E. Housman for help in astrological matters; to Dr E. H. Minns for palaeographical aid; to Mr C. T. Seltman and the Rev. W. Telfer for valuable criticism and advice; and to Mr N. H. Baynes, Mr H. I. Bell, Mr A. B. Cook, Mr F. M. Cornford, Mr H. T. Deas, Mr H. Mattingly, Mr D. S. Robertson, and Mr F. H. Sandbach for assistance of one sort or another. In so far as this edition fails to answer the requirements of criticism it is not for want of friendly help. I should finally wish to express my indebtedness to Professor Murray, to whose book I owe my interest in the subject and whose translation has been of material service to me in the revision of my own.

A. D. NOCK.

CLARE COLLEGE,
25th September, 1925.

CONTENTS

ABBREVIATIONS

A. A. S. S. = *Acta Sanctorum*, the Bollandist edition, quoted by month, volume, and page.

Abh. = *Abhandlung* (in shortened references to Academy publications, with the place of the Academy).

A. J. A. = *American Journal of Archaeology*, 1885– .

Ann. épigr. = *Année épigraphique*, 1888– .

Arch. f. Pap. = *Archiv für Papyrusforschung.*

Arch. Jahrb. = *Jahrbuch des deutschen Archäologischen Instituts*, 1886– .

A. R. W. = *Archiv für Religionswissenschaft*, 1898– .

Ath. Mitth. = *Mittheilungen des deutschen Archäologischen Instituts: athenische Abteilung*, 1876– (and *Röm. Mitth.* = *römische Abteilung*, 1886–).

B. C. H. = *Bulletin de correspondance hellénique*, 1877– .

Berl. klass. T. = *Berliner klassiker Texte.*

B. ph. W. = *Berliner philologische Wochenschrift*, 1885– .

Ber. sächs. Ges. Wiss. = *Berichte über die Verhandlungen der königlich sächsischen Gesellschaft der Wissenschaften zu Leipzig, philologisch-historische Klasse*, 1848– .

B. M. C. = *Catalogue of Greek Coins in the British Museum* (followed by the name of the region, as *B. M. C. Ionia*).

Burs. = *Bursians Jahresberichte über die Fortschritte der classischen Altertumswissenschaft*, 1873– .

Byz. Zeit. = *Byzantinische Zeitschrift*, 1892– .

C. C. A. G. = *Catalogus codicum astrologicorum graecorum* (ed. F. Cumont, F. Boll, A. Olivieri, W. Kroll), 1898– .

Christ-Schmid = W. v. Christ, *Geschichte der griechischen Litteratur*, ed. VI. by W. Schmid, the Jewish and Christian sections revised by O. Stählin (cited as Christ-Stählin), Munich, 1912–1924.

C. I. G. = *Corpus Inscriptionum Graecarum*, ed. Boeckh, 1828–1877.

Cl. Phil. = *Classical Philology*, 1906– .

C. Q. = *Classical Quarterly*, 1907– .

C. R. = *Classical Review*, 1887– .

C. R. Ac. Inscr. = *Comptes Rendus de l'Académie des Inscriptions et Belles-Lettres*, Paris, 1859– .

Dar. S. = *Dictionnaire des antiquités grecques et romaines*, Ch. Daremberg et E. Saglio, Paris, 1877–1919.

Dessau = H. Dessau, *Inscriptiones latinae selectae*, Berlin, 1892–1916 (inscriptions quoted by number).

Diss. acad. Cracov. = *Dissertationes academiae Cracoviensis* (now published as *Rozprawy Akademii Umiejętności*).

Ditt. *O. G. I.* = W. Dittenberger, *Orientis graeci inscriptiones selectae*, Leipzig, 1903–1905.

Ditt. *Syll.*^{3} = W. Dittenberger, *Sylloge inscriptionum graecarum*, ed. III., Leipzig, 1915–1924, with the help of various scholars, by F. Hiller von Gärtringen.

D. L. Z. = *Deutsche Litteraturzeitung.*

F. H. G. = C. Müller, *Fragmenta Historicorum Graecorum*, Paris, 1841–1873.

Fleck. Jahrb. = *Jahrbücher für classische Philologie*, ed. A. Fleckeisen, 1855–1897.

Frazer, *G. B.*^{3} = J. G. Frazer, *The Golden Bough*, ed. III., London, 1911–1914 (quoted by volume).

Geffcken, *Apologeten* = J. Geffcken, *Zwei griechische Apologeten*, Leipzig, 1907.

Geffcken, *Ausgang* = J. Geffcken, *Der Ausgang des griechisch-römischen Heidentums*, Heidelberg, 1920.

G. G. A. = *Göttingische gelehrte Anzeigen*, 1753– .

G. G. N. = *Nachrichten von der Gesellschaft der Wissenschaften zu Göttingen, philologisch-historische Klasse.*

Head, *H. N.*^{2} = B. V. Head, *Historia Numorum*, ed. II., Oxford, 1911.

I. G. I. etc. = *Inscriptiones Graecae*, edited by the Berlin Academy, 1873– .

I. G. Rom. = *Inscriptiones Graecae ad res Romanas pertinentes*, ed. Cagnat, etc., Paris, 1901– .

Jahresh. = *Jahreshefte des österreichischen archäologischen Instituts in Wien*, 1898– .

J. Eg. Arch. = *Journal of Egyptian Archaeology*, 1914– .

J. H. S. = *Journal of Hellenic Studies*, 1880– .

J. T. S. = *Journal of Theological Studies*, 1899– .

Kaibel, *Epigr. gr.* = *Epigrammata Graeca ex lapidibus conlecta*, edidit Georgius Kaibel, Berlin, 1878.

Keil-von Premerstein I, II, III = J. Keil und A. von Premerstein, *Bericht über eine erste, zweite, dritte Reise, in Lydien*, in *Wien. Denkschr.* LIII. ii., LIV. ii., LVII. i.

Krumbacher^{2} = Krumbacher, *Geschichte der byzantinischen Litteratur*, ed. II., Munich, 1897.

ABBREVIATIONS

L. and S. *ed. nov.* = Liddell and Scott, *Greek-English Lexicon*, a new edition by H. S. Jones, 1925– .

Lebas-Waddington = Ph. Le Bas et W. H. Waddington, *Voyage archéologique en Grèce et en Asie Mineure*, II. Partie, Inscriptions grecques et latines, iii. 5 Asie Mineure, 6 Syrie proprement dite, Paris, 1847–1876 (quoted by number of inscription).

Mitteil. schles. Ges. Volkskunde = *Mitteilungen der schlesischen Gesellschaft für Volkskunde*, 1896– .

Mon. Ant. = *Monumenti antichi pubblicati per cura della Reale Accademia dei Lincei*, Milan, 1889– .

Neue Jahrb. = *Neue Jahrbücher für die klassische Altertumsgeschichte und deutsche Litteratur und für Pädagogik*, 1898– .

Notizie = *Notizie degli scavi di Antichità*, Rome, 1876– .

Philol. = *Philologus*, 1847– .

Philol. Unters. = *Philologische Untersuchungen*, 1880– .

Phil. Woch. = *Philologische Wochenschrift*, 1921– .

P. Oxy. = Oxyrhynchus Papyri, published by B. P. Grenfell and A. S. Hunt (quoted by number of papyrus).

Preisigke, *S. B.* = F. Preisigke, *Sammelbuch griechischer Urkunden aus Ägypten*, I.– , 1913– .

P. W. = Pauly-Wissowa, *Real-Encyclopädie der classischen Altertumswissenschaft*, Stuttgart, 1893– .

Rev. arch. = *Revue archéologique.*

Rev. phil. = *Revue de philologie*, 1877– .

R. G. V. V. = *Religionsgeschichtliche Versuche und Vorarbeiten*, 1903– .

Rh. Mus. = *Rheinisches Museum für Philologie*, Neue Folge, 1842– .

Roscher = *Ausführliches Lexikon der griechischen und römischen Mythologie*...herausgegeben von W. H. Roscher, 1884– .

Sitz. Ber. Ak. Wien = *Sitzungsberichte der Akademie der Wissenschaften*, Wien, *philosophisch-historische Klasse.*

Sitz. Ber. München = *Sitzungsberichte der bayerischen Akademie der Wissenschaften*, 1861– , *philosophisch-philologische und historische Klasse.*

Sitz. Ber. preuss. Akad. = *Sitzungsberichte der preussischen Akademie der Wissenschaften zu Berlin*, 1882– .

Steph. *Thes.* = *Thesaurus Graecae linguae, ab Henrico Stephano constructus*...ediderunt C. B. Hase, G. Dindorfius et L. Dindorfius, Paris, 1831–1865.

Suppl. = *Supplementband* (as of Fleckeisen's *Jahrbücher*).

Suppl. epigr. gr. = *Supplementum epigraphicum graecum*, 1923– .

ABBREVIATIONS

Wien. Denkschr. = *Denkschriften der Akademie der Wissenschaften*, Wien, 1850– , *philosophisch-historische Klasse.*

Woch. klass. Phil. = *Wochenschrift für klassische Philologie*, 1884– .

Y. W. = *Year's Work in Classical Studies*, 1907– (quoted as 1906/7–).

Zeller, III. i., ii. = E. Zeller, *Die Philosophie der Griechen in ihrer geschichtlichen Entwicklung*, vierte Auflage, dritter Teil, erste, zweite Abteilung, Leipzig, 1909, 1903.

In references a numeral above, as Friedländer, *Sittengeschichte*^{10}, denotes the edition used; a numeral below indicates a footnote, the number 0 being so used for footnotes which extend under a page beyond that below the text of which they start.

Julian's speeches are quoted by Spanheim's pagination, which is printed in the margin by Hertlein in the Teubner text, his *In Christianos* by Neumann's pagination (1880), his letters and decrees by the number and page of the edition by J. Bidez and F. Cumont (*Collection Budé, Textes et documents*, Paris, 1922); Hertlein's numeration is sometimes added with the letter H. For the *Protrepticus* of Iamblichus the pagination of H. Pistelli's Teubner edition (1888) is used, for the *De mysteriis* Parthey's (Berlin, 1857). Stobaeus is quoted by the pagination of Wachsmuth and Hense (Berlin, 1884–1923), abbreviated as W. or as H.: Hermetic fragments preserved by him have commonly also a reference to Scott's *Hermetica*, I. (Oxford, 1924), abbreviated as S. The *Corpus Hermeticum* has sometimes a page-reference to Scott, sometimes to Reitzenstein, *Poimandres*, abbreviated as R.: in every case number of document and paragraph are given. Patristic texts other than Clement of Alexandria are usually quoted from Migne, hagiographical texts from O. von Gebhardt, *Ausgewählte Märtyreracten* (Berlin, 1902), abbreviated as G., and from Ruinart, *Acta Martyrum*, in the second edition, published at Verona in 1731: its pagination, here given as R.^{2}, is unfortunately not reproduced in later reprints. The works of Maximus Tyrius are quoted as numbered in Hobein's Teubner edition (1910), those of various rhetorical writers by the volume and page of Walz, *Rhetores Graeci* (1832–6), and the commentaries of Eustathius by the pages of the Roman edition, as indicated in the outside margin of Stallbaum's text (1827–8).

PROLEGOMENA

PROLEGOMENA

CHAPTER I

THE INTELLECTUAL BACKGROUND

§ I

In the fourth century two rival systems of education present themselves in sharp opposition. There is on the one side philosophic training, which aims at imparting definite and scientific knowledge and thereby forming the mind; this conception is Plato's. Opposed to it is rhetorical training; this strives to give general rather than specialised knowledge and to produce men of good intelligence and wide range. Its great exponent is Isocrates. This opposition weakened during the Hellenistic age. Philosophers busied themselves more with rhetorical theory; thus Philo of Larisa expounded a broad conception of the art which may well have inspired, directly or indirectly, Cicero's picture of the perfect orator[1]. On the other hand, Hermagoras in the second century B.C. claimed for rhetoric the right to treat general questions, ζητήματα πολιτικά or θέσεις as they were called[2].

Such θέσεις became a regular feature of rhetorical training. Theon of Alexandria, who remarks that the great rhetoricians of the past thought philosophy a necessary preliminary to the study of oratory, suggests as a subject for discussion the

[1] Cf. H. von Arnim, *Leben und Werke des Dio von Prusa*, 87 ff., Christ-Schmid, II. 342 f. Von Arnim's contention that Cicero followed Philo closely in *De oratore* III. 54–143 has been greatly weakened by W. Kroll's paper, *Rh. Mus.* LVIII. 552 ff.; Kroll suggests Antiochus of Ascalon as the original employed.

[2] Cf. L. Radermacher, *P.W.* VIII. 692 ff. Posidonius seems to have contested this claim, cf. Plut. *Pomp.* 42.

view of Euripides that the mind of each individual is a god[3]. Theon's teaching enjoyed great authority in later times. On this subject it repeats what Quintilian had maintained. The latter, while disliking contemporary philosophers, pleaded for the necessity of philosophical studies and professed a warm regard for Plato and Aristotle[4]. His main interests in this direction were ethical; he wished his orator to be a wise Roman[5].

This theory corresponded with practice. Aristides received philosophical training at Athens, and professed a high admiration for Plato[6]. His attacks on false philosophers find parallels in Dio of Prusa and Epictetus[7]. The rhetorician Menander says that the special glory of Athens lies in language and philosophy[8], and Hermogenes mentions as occupations for which a man can be praised, philosophy, rhetoric, and the profession of arms[9]. The work of Callinicus *Against the schools of philosophers*[10] may have been aimed at particular schools or at philosophical dogmatism; in any case, it stands by itself. Later we find Themistius and Himerius keenly interested in abstract thought. Himerius knew Plato well at first hand[11]. So did Libanius, though to him Plato counted as a writer rather than as a thinker; at the same time, he praised philosophers in general and Iamblichus in particular[12]. Meanwhile, if we except Sextus Empiricus,

[3] *Progymn.* I. pp. 145, 212 Walz; elsewhere he quotes as models of fine writing Plato, *Rep.* I. II., *Sympos.*, *Phaed.*, *Tim.*, *Phaedr.*, condemns the style of Epicurus (p. 169), and refers to the *Zopyrus* of Phaedo (p. 177). He is dated at the end of the first or the beginning of the second century of our era (Christ-Schmid, II. 460 f.).

[4] *Inst. orat.* XII. 2. 8: cf. B. Appel, *Das Bildungs- und Erziehungsideal Quintilians und die Institutio oratoria* (Diss. München, 1914), 14.

[5] *Romanus sapiens*, cf. Appel, 32, 34, 39 ff. The orator is not to be *philosophus* (*Inst.* XII. 2. 6).

[6] For his training, cf. W. Schmid, *P.W.* II. 886 f.: for his admiration of Plato, *Or.* XLVI. p. 397 Dindorf.

[7] Boulanger, *Aelius Aristide*, 263, quotes well Dio Prus. XXXII. 10, XXXIV. 2; cf. Epictet. *Diss.* IV. 8, 4.

[8] IX. p. 201 Walz.

[9] I. p. 38 Walz, cf. Theon, p. 246, 251, Nicolaus, p. 274, Nicephorus, p. 466 (also Quintil. VII. I. 38, 4. 39).

[10] Πρὸς τὰς φιλοσόφους αἱρέσεις (Suid. *s.v.* Καλλίνικος: II. i., p. 47, Bernhardy).

[11] Richtsteig, *Byzantinisch-neugriechische Jahrbücher*, II. (1921) I ff.

[12] Geffcken, *Ausgang*, 165, 302, *Anm.* 40, 41, using Richtsteig's Breslau Dissertation of 1918.

there is not much antipathy shown by philosophers to rhetoric.

There was, then, little or no antagonism between rhetoric and philosophy under the Empire. Further, rhetorical training tended to include some philosophy. At the same time, in the first two centuries of our era real philosophers continued to give to many some philosophical teaching. The evidence on this point is not easy to use; we can, however, draw inferences from Galen's complaint that most of those who in his day pursued the study of medicine or philosophy lacked the necessary propaedeutic and could not even read well[13]. This remark excludes the hypothesis that only a chosen few then received such teaching. It may often have been very casual: pupils seem to have heard single lectures without staying through the course[14]. Some, however, like Galen's father, took the subject seriously[15]. Its study was not confined to those who could visit the great universities, if we may so call them, of Athens and Alexandria. There were many private teachers of philosophy, and it would appear from the number of impostors who embraced this profession that it was remunerative[16]. Further, the evidence of inscriptions indicates that philosophers were men of consequence in their cities[17].

[13] *Περὶ τῶν ἰδίων βιβλίων*, II. p. 91 Müller = XIX. p. 9 Kühn (for this propaedeutic cf. Norden, *Kunstprosa*, II. 670). Paulus Aegineta, writing in the seventh century, assumes the study of some philosophy as normal (I. 14). It could of course be learnt as part of general knowledge. For the habit of going to philosophers cf. Philostr. *Vit. Apoll.* VI. 36, *εἰ μὲν γὰρ παῖδά σε ἑώρων ἔτι, ξυνεβούλευον ἂν φοιτᾶν ἐπὶ φιλοσόφων τε καὶ σοφιστῶν θύρας καὶ σοφίᾳ πάσῃ τὴν οἰκίαν τὴν σεαυτοῦ φράττειν.*

[14] Plut. *Pomp.* 55 mentions that Pompey's wife listened *usefully* to discourses.

[15] *Περὶ ψυχῆς παθῶν* 8, i. p. 31 Marquardt = V. p. 41 Kühn. We find a philosophic family (father, daughter and her husband) at Apollonia in Mysia, *J.H.S.* XVII. 269, n. 6.

[16] Cf. Galen, *Περὶ τῆς τάξεως τῶν ἰδίων βιβλίων* I, ii. p. 81 Müller = XIX. p. 50 Kühn.

[17] So at Athens, *I.G.* III. 772*a*, at Ancyra, *J.H.S.* XLIV. 42, n. 76, at Chaeronea, Ditt. *Syll.*³ 844, at Samos, *I. G. Rom.* IV. 997, at Delphi, Ditt. *Syll.*³ 843, 868, at Dorylaeum, *I. G. Rom.* IV. 527, at Hadriani, *B.C.H.* XXXIII. (1909) 409, n. 409, at Panamara, Ditt. *Syll.*³ 900, at Pergamum (?), *I. G. Rom.* IV. 468, at Rhodes, *B.C.H.* XXXVI. (1912) 230, at Tichiussa, Lebas-Waddington 239, in the Hellenistic period at Samos, *Suppl. epigr. gr.* I. 368, and, to turn to the West, at Brundisium, Ditt. *Syll.*³ 1227, and at Madaura, *Ann. épigr.* 1919, n. 36 (Apuleius). The memory of earlier philosophers was also honoured; we find Chrysippus on Imperial coins of Soli-Pompeiopolis in Cilicia (Imhoof-Blumer, *J.H.S.* XVIII. 167 f., pl. XII. 13, 17),

Such oral teaching hardly existed outside Greece, Asia Minor, Syria, and Alexandria. There is no evidence for it in the Greek colonies in South Russia. The philosopher Sphaerus, a Bosporan by birth, taught at Alexandria, and Bion did not remain in his native Olbia[18]. From the third century B.C. onwards the Greeks of this region, like their brothers in the Danube valley, were engaged in a continual struggle for existence[19]. Again, in Egypt outside Alexandria philosophical instruction was probably not to be obtained, although elementary schools were frequent and the normal rhetorical training was readily available. At the same time it should be remembered that the reading which formed part of the latter included Plato and probably other philosophical texts[20]. Moreover, ideas were spread by books as well as by teaching; we may recall the letter in which Hierax of Oxyrhynchus is bidden by his father Cornelius to persevere in his reading[21]. Our extant papyri include much Plato, some Aristotle, the elementary Stoic treatise of Hierocles, an anonymous anti-Stoic brochure, anonymous Epicurean fragments, and the like[22]. These works were read, or at least handled, in the outposts of Greek culture.

Heraclitus on coins of Ephesus struck under Philip Senior (*B. M. C. Ionia*, 98, n. 340 f., pl. XIV. 12) and Anaxagoras on coins of Clazomenae (*ib.* 28, n. 102–4, pl. VII. 4, and 33, n. 125, pl. VII. 9). Lucian's phrase concerning impostors, *Pisc.* 31, *ὁρῶν δὲ πολλοὺς οὐκ ἔρωτι φιλοσοφίας ἐχομένους ἀλλὰ δόξης μόνον τῆς ἀπὸ τοῦ πράγματος*, confirms our view of the reputation enjoyed by philosophers. On their general position, and the benefits conferred on them by Marcus Aurelius cf. J. H. Walden, *The Universities of Ancient Greece*, 162 ff. In the fourth century they were for the most part private teachers, cf. A. Müller, *Philol.* LXIX. 297.

[18] Cf. E. H. Minns, *Scythians and Greeks*, 626, on the literary poverty of the region.

[19] Cf. V. Pârvan, *La pénétration hellénique et hellénistique dans la vallée du Danube*, 22 [=Acad. Rouman., Bull. sciences hist., X. (1923) 44].

[20] Cf. W. Schubart, *Einführung in die Papyruskunde*, 381 ff., and C. H. Oldfather, *The Greek Literary Texts from Greco-Roman Egypt* (*University of Wisconsin Studies in the Social Sciences and History*, IX. 1923), 50 f., with the modifications of the latter's conclusions on p. 62 ff. made by J. U. Powell, *J.H.S.* XLV. 143 f.

[21] *P. Oxy.* 531. 10, *τοῖς βιβλίοις σου αὐτὸ μόνον πρόσεχε φιλολογῶν.*

[22] Cf. Schubart, *op. cit.* 482, and the catalogue of a library at Memphis in Mitteis-Wilcken, *Grundzüge und Chrestomathie der Papyruskunde*, I. ii. 182 ff. n. 155; it included collections of Socratic letters, Aristotle Περὶ ἀρετῆς, excerpts from Posidonius Περὶ ὀργῆς α″, Theophrastus Περὶ σωφροσύνης, Dio Περὶ ἀπιστίας, Eratosthenes Περὶ ἀλυπίας, Cebes etc. But at Oxyrhynchus Plato was probably

In the East, indeed, advanced studies, as later theological controversies, radiate from a number of great centres, such as Antioch and Alexandria, and from various minor cities[23]. In the West we have Rome, where Plotinus taught, and there is evidence for the existence of teachers of philosophy in Sicily, which had a legacy of Greek tradition[24]; for the rest we find some seats of culture, such as Carthage, Burdigala, Lugdunum, and Corduba, but no distinguished home of abstract thought. The typical Roman point of view was that of Agricola's mother; her son might dabble in philosophy, but he must not take it seriously. In spite of distinguished exceptions, like the Sextii, the upper classes at Rome showed themselves averse from deep speculations. Their philosophical interests were primarily ethical, and these were the province of the domestic philosophers kept by men of wealth[25].

The training of most men of education fell into three stages. 'The first bowl,' says Apuleius, 'stimulates us with the elementary teaching of the primary master, the second equips us with the learning of the grammarian, the third arms us with the eloquence of the rhetorician. This is as much as most drink; I have drunk other bowls also at Athens[26].' It was indeed only the few who could go to Athens[27], and even at Athens philosophy did not enjoy an unchallenged supremacy. When Gellius arrived, it was assumed by the philosopher Taurus that he had come there to study rhetoric[28].

read as a writer rather than as a thinker; apart from fragments of his dialogues and one of the Προτρεπτικός of Aristotle, few philosophic texts have been found there (F. G. Kenyon, *J. Eg. Arch.* VIII. 136).

[23] Tarsus, Emesa etc., cf. Christ-Schmid, II. ii. 948 f. These and other centres of Greek culture in Asia Minor exercised no little influence in the direction of substituting in daily use Greek for the native dialects (cf. K. Holl, *Hermes*, XLIII. 248).

[24] Aristocles of Messina taught Alexander of Aphrodisias, cf. Vitanza, *Athenaeum*, 1923, 249.

[25] For these cf. Friedländer, *Sittengeschichte*[10], III. 283 ff.; one would like to know more about the place which they filled in the household. This preoccupation with ethics is in a measure general.

[26] *Florida*, 20. At this time the grammarian was concerned with language and with the reading of poetry only (in the East certainly), prose authors coming within the rhetorician's province; cf. Christ-Schmid, II. ii. 926 f.

[27] Cf. E. Rohde, *Kleine Schriften*, II. 51.

[28] *Noctes atticae*, XVII. 20. 4; Aristides is said to have studied rhetoric at Athens

For the intellectual condition of the Western half of the Empire the evidence is adequate. The *Florida* of Apuleius shows us what suited the taste of prosperous and cultured Africa, where Greek was till the third century of our era almost as familiar as Latin[29], while the inscription FILOSOFI LOLOCVS on the charming mosaic representing a garden in the baths of Pompeiana shows how vague a conception of *philosophia* there prevailed[30]. From Spain came the younger Seneca and the Stoic Decianus, but there is no evidence for philosophical studies in these provinces. For Gaul our information is most full in the fourth century and is due chiefly to the tedious verses which Ausonius wrote about his colleagues at Bordeaux. It would appear that the philosophers he praises were not distinguished by the depth of their studies[31]. In Britain and Belgium no trace of these studies appears; it has been truly observed that we do not know the name of an author of any sort born in the latter during the Roman occupation[32]. An inscription in the Rhineland records the death of a philosopher[33]. As he is described as the friend of Salvius Julianus, probably the consul of 174 A.D., we may reasonably infer that he was a domestic philosopher.

This distinction between the East and the West appears clearly in the history of medicine under the Empire. Greek medicine was from its beginnings greatly influenced by Greek

(Schol. in *Panath.* p. 306. 6 Dindorf). At the same time it will be remarked that he ridicules the exaggerated esteem there paid to Plato (*Orat.* XXVII. p. 548 Dindorf = 51, § 60 Keil).

[29] Cf. W. Thieling, *Der Hellenismus in Kleinafrika*, 20, 29; even later we read of Fulgentius that he knew Homer and Menander by heart, and spoke Greek perfectly (*Vita*, LXV. 119 Migne).—On Apuleius as typical of the age cf. P. Vallette, *L'Apologie d'Apulée* (1908), 185 ff.

[30] *Dar. S.* v. 887, fig. 7491, 888. *Philosophus* is used in the sense of 'architect' in *Passio quattuor coronatorum*.

[31] Cf. Haarhoff, *Schools of Gaul*, 79 f.

[32] Cumont, *Comment la Belgique fut romanisée*[2], 93.

[33] Riese, *Das rheinische Germanien in den antiken Inschriften*, p. 48, n. 363 = *C.I.L.* XIII. 8159. For Salvius Julianus cf. *Prosop. Imp. Rom.* III. p. 166, n. 104. The mosaic portraits of Socrates, Chilo, Cleobulus at Köln and Trier (Reinach, *Rép. peint. gr. rom.* p. 262 f.) prove nothing, and the 'philosopher' mosaic at Trier may represent the Muse and poets (F. Drexel, *Germania Romana*, p. x, on pl. XXI. 6).

philosophy, and even under the Empire doctors prided themselves on their philosophical attainments[34]. At Rome itself most practitioners were Greek[35]; the evidence for the Western provinces as a whole is inconclusive, but Greek doctors were certainly employed in the army[36]. We see therefore that in an occupation commonly associated with some philosophical knowledge the East far outshines the West.

Nevertheless, the excellence of the former is only relative. Philosophy was dying, and that largely because of the weak humanism of rhetorical training and the increasing dislike of intellectual effort. The shallow eclecticism of Plutarch was succeeded by the shallower eclecticism of Apuleius and by the intellectual bankruptcy of Philostratus. The decline was marked in the third century. Porphyry, in his *Life of Plotinus*, quotes a striking saying of the rhetorician Longinus, 'There were many philosophers when I was a boy, but now it is impossible to say how utterly this subject is neglected[37].' Neoplatonism brought a fresh stimulus to thought, but brought it too late; if its first expression was the serious metaphysics of Plotinus, in fifty years it became theosophy[38]. Material causes hastened the decay of philosophic studies. The economic fabric of the Empire was shaken by barbarian inroads, by plague, and by inefficient administration; the prosperity of the cities suffered grievously[39]. The Εἰς βασιλέα,

[34] Galen is the most striking example; among his treatises is one entitled "Ὅτι ὁ ἄριστος ἰατρὸς καὶ φιλόσοφος. Cf. *I. G. Rom.* III. 733 (Heraclitus of Rhodiapolis ποιητὴς ἔργων φιλοσοφίας), *I.G.* XIV. 942 (doctor at Ostia πάνσοφος), and *C.I.G.* 3311, 6607, *I. G. Rom.* III. 534, [Soran.] *Isag.* in Rose, *Anecdota*, II. p. 244. 16, *C.R.* 1919, 2 (doctor in the fourth century A.D. at Antioch in Pisidia as eloquent as any of the ten Attic orators, skilled in philosophy and familiar with Hippocrates). Galen uses such phrases as (τῶν) ἰατρῶν τε καὶ φιλοσόφων. Unlearned practitioners did of course exist as early as Aristotle (*De sensu*, p. 436*a* 20).

[35] Friedländer, I. 191, Kaufmann, *Handb. altchr. Epigr.* 256.

[36] Friedländer, 192, argues from the Roman names of provincial practitioners, but cf. S. Reinach, *Dar. S.* III. 1672. For the army cf. *ib.* 1688_{12}, Cheesman, *The Auxilia of the Roman Army*, 44.

[37] *Vita*, 20, quoted by Walden, *op. cit.* 101.

[38] E. J. Thomas has remarked well on this, *J. T. S.* XXIV. 349.

[39] Cf. M. Rostovtzeff, *Musée Belge*, XXVII. (1923) 233 ff. With this decline in city life we may perhaps associate the revival of native languages in Asia Minor. We may note L. Weber's conclusions concerning Phrygian Hierapolis, *Philol.* LXIX. 238, 'Im Handel und Wandel des alltäglichen Lebens hat sich das Griech-

wrongly ascribed to Aristides and assigned with good cause to the third century, speaks of the evil plight of education[40]. Formal rhetoric and Roman law were useful studies; philosophy was not, and suffered accordingly. Even in the second century, when Antoninus Pius gave immunity from taxation to a number of professional men in each city, he remarked, 'No number of philosophers was fixed, because of their rarity[41].' Philosophers are not mentioned among the learned beneficiaries of Alexander Severus[42], or of Diocletian, when the latter restored the immunities just mentioned, or among instructors in the latter's Edict concerning prices[43]. At Constantinople in 425 A.D. the university had one professor of philosophy, eight of rhetoric, and twenty-two of other subjects[44]. The fourth century was one of much intellectual activity, but in its course rhetoric itself was gradually superseded by the more profitable study of law[45].

It must be remembered that this was in a measure the supersession of an exhausted culture, the representatives of which were and felt themselves to be the followers of greater men, whose like would not come again. An orator of the fourth century is glorified as 'a master of eloquence so incomparable in his own generation that he could be likened only to the ancients[46].' Even Galen held that, in view of the badness of education and of men's preference of gold to virtue, there was no hope of any doctor rivalling Hippocrates[47]. The

ische (zweifellos bis in die türkische Zeit hinein) in H. unangefochten als die allein herrschende Sprache behauptet.'

[40] IX. p. 105 Dindorf; on the date of this speech cf. Christ-Schmid, II. ii. 701_2.

[41] *Digesta*, XXVII. I. 6, § 7. Each town was allowed a number of privileged rhetoricians and other teachers, and a number of privileged doctors.

[42] *Vita*, 44 (in the *Historia Augusta*).

[43] Cf. Walden, *op. cit.* 106 f.

[44] *Cod. Theod.* XIV. 9, 3, G. Rauschen, *Das griechisch-römische Schulwesen zur Zeit des ausgehenden antiken Heidentums* (Progr. Bonn, 1900, n. 458), 18, and S. Dill, *Roman society in the last century of the Western Empire*², 409.

[45] Cf. L. Hahn, *Philol.* LXXVI. (1920) 188 ff.; this at Constantinople still required a knowledge of Latin. On fourth century education in general cf. Walden, *op. cit.* 109 ff., on the narrowing of intellectual interests in Egypt in particular H. I. Bell, *J. Eg. Arch.* IV. 104 ff.

[46] Dessau, 2951. A literary example of this *Epigonengefühl* (Christ-Schmid, II. 735_8) is Dio of Prusa, XXI. I; cf. on the other hand Lucian, *Demon.* I.

[47] Ὅτι ὁ ἄριστος 2, ii. 4 Müller = i. p. 57 Kühn. Cf. Pliny, *N.H.* II. 117, X. 20, for

activity of dogmatic philosophy was often limited to the interpretation of canonical texts; 'what was philosophy, has become scholarship,' says Seneca[48]. No wonder, then, if these studies dwindled till S. Jerome could exclaim, 'What a handful now reads Aristotle! How many know the books or the name of Plato? Hardly do old men at leisure study them in seclusion[49].' The closing of the Academy at Athens in 529 A.D. is not so remarkable as its continued existence till that date[50].

§ 2

If we ask ourselves what was the rhetorical and philosophic basis for the thought of the average well-educated citizen of the Empire the answer must be that it was in the nature of things eclectic. Galen records that his father warned him not to hurry to declare himself a member of any school, but rather to learn and test their teaching at leisure and to pursue the four great virtues, since all praise them[51].

For very many the teacher of rhetoric was the sole source

the failure to make scientific observations *in desidia rerum omnium*, and some good remarks thereon by W. Kroll, *Studien zum Verständniss der römischen Literatur*, 280 ff. On the other hand, Hermes, *ap.* Stob. I. 21. 9, p. 193 W., prophesies that posterity will name stars yet unnamed.

48 *quae philosophia fuit, facta philologia est* (*Ep.* 108. 23); cf. Galen, Περὶ τῆς ἀρίστης διδασκαλίας 2, i. p. 86 Marquardt = i. p. 45 Kühn, for the reverence which the Academics showed to the writings of Carneades.

49 *Ad Ep. ad Gal.* III. (XXVI. 401 B Migne), quoted by Dill, *op. cit.* 410_4.

50 Even this was not the end of philosophic studies at Athens; they lingered on till the seventh century (F. Schemmel, *Neue Jahrb.* XXII. 513). We know something of such pursuits at Alexandria in the second half of the fifth century (cf. H. I. Bell, *J. Eg. Arch.* VIII. 153 f.), and at Byzantium in the seventh century (cf. Usener, *Kleine Schriften*, III. 251 ff.); the tradition survives later in Theodoros Prodromos (cf. K. Praechter, *Byz. Zeit.* XIX. 314 ff.). A smattering of knowledge of the great thinkers perhaps survived in rhetorical training; Georgios Monos, who is dated in the fifth century, quotes Aristotle (wrongly, it appears) and Plato (L. Schilling, *Fleck. Jahrb. Suppl.* XXVIII. 690). On later Byzantine education cf. H. von Schubert, *Gothein-Festgabe*, 96 ff., and F. Schemmel, *Phil. Woch.* 1923, 1178 ff.: 1925, 236 ff. A comprehensive monograph on the subject would be of much value.

51 Περὶ ψυχῆς παθῶν 8, p. 32 Marquardt = V. p. 42 Kühn (on the 'four virtues' cf. p. lxxvi, n. 166 *infra*). Philostr. *Vit. Apoll.* I. 7, represents Apollonius as receiving instruction at Aegae in Cilicia from Platonists, followers of Chrysippus, Academicians, and Epicureans, while he understood Pythagorean ideas, there taught by an unsatisfactory representative, through special inspiration.

of higher education. This condition of affairs is reflected by a papyrus lamenting the death of a Platonising rhetorician of the fourth century:

τὸν δὲ μετὰ χρειὼ ζαθεὴ πόλις αὖθι κατασχεῖν
ἤθελε παρπεπιθοῦσα, νέων ἵνα πῶυ νομεύσῃ
ἀνθρώπων εὐηγενέων ἀγανόφρονας υἷας...
ἡ πάρος αἰὲν ἄδακρυς ἐδάκρυσεν τότε Ῥώμη[52].

('And him, in its need, the divine city would fain win and keep, that he might be shepherd to the flock of the young, the gentle-minded sons of noble men....Rome, that never wept before, wept then.') Monumental praise rises to such heights as ἀνὴρ προφερέστατος ἀνδρῶν, ῥητορικός, μέγα θαῦμα[53] and ἐνθάδε κ[εῖται] Τ(ίτος) Φάνεος Μόδεστος σοφιστὴς εἷς μετὰ τῶν ἑπτὰ σοφῶν, μὴ γεμίσας εἴκοσι πέντε ἔτη[54]. How easily rhetoricians and philosophers could be classed together is shown by a phrase of Aristides, τῷ τε ῥήτορι καὶ φιλοσόφῳ[55], and by S. Jerome's juxtaposition of *campum rhetorici eloquii, tendiculae dialect⟨ic⟩orum, Aristotelis spineta*[56].

Typical of the second century are such rhetorical philosophers or philosophic rhetoricians as Apuleius and Maximus Tyrius[57]; philosophical or semi-philosophical matter was cast in a rhetorical form, as in the fragment Περὶ Ἱππομάχου[58].

[52] *Berl. Klass. T.* v. i. p. 87, col. iii. 88 (Ῥώμη is Constantinople, as we see from l. 81 Κωνσταντινιάδος νεοθηλέος ἐν χθονὶ Ῥώμης), cf. Dess. 2951 *praeceptor...uniuersae patriciae suboli lectus*. The last line of the quotation above need not be taken too seriously, in view of the recurrent πᾶσα γῆ δακρυσάτω (Preisigke, *S.B.* 366, 373. 2, 391 *a*, *b*, 1996; cf. *Arch. f. Pap.* v. p. 169, 24. 8), πᾶσ' ἐδάκρυσε πόλις, Kaibel, *Epigr. gr.* 493 (at Larymna), and *mundo flente* (Diehl, *Inscr. lat. christ.* 83 at Milan).

[53] Kaibel, *Epigr. gr.* 591. For a glowing picture of the fame which a rhetorician might acquire cf. Lucian, *Somn.* 11 (speech of Παιδεία).

[54] *Mon. Ant.* XXIII. (1914) p. 31, n. 25 *a*, cf. Lebas-Waddington, 1696, for an eighteen year old of Heraclea Salbace. The usual age of students at what may be called the university of Athens was probably from fifteen to twenty, cf. Walden, *op. cit.* 292 f.

[55] Κατὰ τῶν ἐξορχουμένων, II. p. 567 Dindorf.

[56] *Contra Heluidium*, XXIII. p. 185 Migne; for *tendiculas dialecticorum* cf. *In Mich.* 2, 5, p. 497 Vallarsi = XXV. 1204 A Migne.

[57] Philostr. *Vit. Soph.* I. 8. 4, uses the phrase τῶν φιλοσοφησάντων ἐν δόξῃ τοῦ σοφιστεῦσαι of men like Dio of Prusa and Favorinus and, among earlier men, Carneades. Cf. an epitaph at Thugga, Dessau 7772, *sapiendo opimus et dicendo splendidus*, another at Athens, Kaibel, *Epigr. gr.* 106, οὔνεκ' ἦν ῥήτωρ μὲν εἰπεῖν, φιλόσοφος δ' ἃ χρὴ νοεῖν.

[58] J. A. Cramer, *Anecdota Parisina*, I. 165 f., cf. A. Bohler, *Sophistae anonymi*

How superficial such writing could be is exemplified by the letters attributed to famous philosophers; many of these were written in the first century of our era[59]. Philosophy, then, could be degraded, as history had been when compelled to give material for fine writing and elegant digressions[60]; science also suffered, as men's interest in truth waned before the desire to expatiate on the exciting rather than the real. The signs of the eclipse of the critical faculty under the Empire are manifest[61]. Even rhetoric was the poorer for the intellectual state of the times; the technical and narrow system of Hermogenes held the field, and the wider views maintained by Aristotle in his *Rhetoric* were generally disregarded[62].

§ 3

To the slender modicum of philosophic ideas acquired at school something might be added by the diatribe, a species of popular sermon or causerie. The originator of this literary form was Bion the Borysthenite; as a rule it was tinged with Cynicism and written in a pointed style, with considerable use of popular phraseology. We know it best from the remains of Teles[63]. Its influence in a greater or less degree

protreptici fragmenta (Diss. Strassburg, 1903), K. Münscher, *Burs.* CXLIX. (1911) 43 f. Wilamowitz-Moellendorff, *Hermes*, LVIII. 80 ff., dates it in the third century, thinking that the statement ὅτι μὴ χρὴ μεμερίσθαι περὶ τοὺς θεοὺς μηδὲ διαιρετὸν εἶναι θεὸν ἀπὸ θεοῦ alludes to Christianity. This seems very unlikely.

[59] Cf. J. Marcks, *Symbola critica ad epistolographos graecos* (Diss. Bonn, 1883), 9 ff.: the letters ascribed to Hippocrates can be dated at the beginning of our era thanks to papyrus finds, which also prove the interesting fact that more than one edition of the collection was published; it must therefore have been popular (Pohlenz, *Hermes*, LII. 348 ff., Diels, *ib.* LIII. 79). For the rhetorical teaching of epistolography cf. G. Przychocki, *Diss. acad. Cracov.* III. v. (1913) 251 ff.

[60] Cf. Quintilian, *Inst. orat.* XII. 4. Yet considerable interest was felt in history, cf. Christ-Schmid, II. 745: the work of Pausanias indicates clearly that history interested his contemporaries more than the study of art, as A. Trendelenburg remarks, *Pausanias' Hellenika* (Progr. Berlin, 1911, n. 65), 29.

[61] Cf. W. Kroll, *Mitteil. schles. Ges. Volkskunde*, XXIV. (1923) 9 ff.; he remarks on the light which the *Pseudodemocritea* throw on the mentality of the time in which they were written. For the decline of geographical study after Ptolemy cf. F. Gisinger, *P. W. Suppl.* IV. 670.

[62] So Christ-Schmid, II. 927, I. 760 (where it is remarked that some of the ideas of the treatise became common property).

[63] I quote by page and line from O. Hense's second edition (1909).

has been traced in numerous writers of the Hellenistic age and of the Empire, such as Phoenix of Colophon, Seneca, Musonius, Dio of Prusa (and his imitator Themistius), [Plutarch] *De liberis educandis*, S. Gregory Nazianzen, and again in Horace and in certain epigram-writers of the Anthology. Naturally, this influence can be exaggerated[64]; what is certain is that a marked style and a definite kind of imagery were used by men of various schools of thought in giving popular expression to their views. When Lucretius asks what answer man could give if Nature took voice and answered his complaints, when he puts the question (III. 938), *cur non ut plenus uitae conuiua recedis?*, he is using the style in question. Teles quotes from Bion a similar 'Should the world itself take voice...' (p. 68)[65], and himself says 'I leave life as if it were a banquet' (p. 16, 2). Again, Seneca has much in common with the diatribe. Not to stress coincidences of detail[66], we may note the comparison of life with a house from which the landlord removes doors and windows in default of payment (that is a parallel to our loss of limbs or senses)[67], the argument that it is absurd to regret the brevity of an existence which can fill only a moment in time[68], the recurrent illustrations from medicine[69], and the constant use of anecdotes[70]. So too Philo's writings show clear signs of the

[64] Cf. R. Hirzel, *Der Dialog*, II. 13, Pohlenz, *Χάριτες für Leo*, 76, W. Kroll, *Studien*, 85 f. Frequently what looks like a direct use of philosophical writings may be explained as the repetition of one of the old traditional reflections common in poetry. Pohlenz has made some good remarks on this subject, *Phil. Woch.* 1897, 1064 ff. A new fragment of moralising poetry is *P. Oxy.* 1795 (acrostic epigrams, some hedonistic, some improving).

[65] Prosopopoea is characteristic of the diatribe; cf. R. Weber, *Leipziger Studien*, X. 161 ff., esp. 166, H. Weber, *De Senecae philosophi dicendi genere Bioneo* (Diss. Marburg, 1895), 22.

[66] As Seneca, *Ep.* 85. 5, *quemadmodum apyrina dicuntur*~Teles, p. 55, 2, *ὃν τρόπον ἀπύρηνος ῥόα.* Cf. in general Albertini, *La composition dans les ouvrages philosophiques de Sénèque* (1923), 304 ff.

[67] Seneca, *Ep.* 120. 14~Teles, p. 15, 12.

[68] Seneca, *Ep.* 77. 11~[Plut.], *Consol. ad Apoll.* 17 etc.; cf. Geffcken, *Kynika und Verwandtes*, 13 f.

[69] Cf. H. Weber, *op. cit.* 10 f. Characteristic of the diatribe is also the insistence that man's spiritual need is to be healed, cf. [Epict.] fr. xxxii. p. 473 Schenkl (*ed. mai.*[2]), Lucian, *Demon.* 10, Julian, *Ep.* 89, p. 146, 2 Bidez-Cumont [=p. 305 B], *Ep.* 61, p. 73, 17 [=p. 424 B], also p. lxxx *infra*.

[70] Cf. H. Weber, *op. cit.* 47; cf. *ib.* 54 ff. for the use of Bion's style by Stoics in

influence of the diatribe[71], and there seem to be traces thereof in the Epistle of S. James and in the first Epistle to the Corinthians, as also markedly in Tertullian, *De pallio*, and again in the *Corpus Hermeticum*[72]. Further, in Boethius *De Consolatione* we find again the argument that we could make no answer to Fortune if she replied to our charges, the familiar address to the human race in its perplexities[73], the old contempt for worldly riches and insistence that man's need is healing. Much that Usener regarded as directly taken from Cicero's lost *Hortensius* is more plausibly explained by Fr. Klingner as in the tradition of the diatribe[74].

The influence of this kind of teaching was therefore wide. The anecdotes which it employed had a wide circulation outside it, as for instance as χρεῖαι in schools[75]. Two sayings of Diogenes, obviously written out as a school task, occur on an ostrakon recently published[76], while one given by Teles is found also in a *gnomologium*[77].

Nor was the influence exercised merely through books. Throughout antiquity the spoken word counted for more than the written word. In its nature the diatribe was a written record of oral teaching, and its personal exponents continued to be of importance[78].

general. Hausrath, *Phil. Woch.* 1924, 1216, remarks rightly that apophthegms and fables are the natural ornament of all popular eloquence.

[71] Cf. Wendland, *Philos Schrift über die Vorsehung*, 1892.

[72] Cf. Geffcken, *op. cit.* 45 ff., Christ-Stählin, II. 1135, 1141_0, 1169_1 (for references); for Tertullian cf. Geffcken, 58 ff., for the *Corpus*, *J. Eg. Arch.* XI. 128 ff.

[73] Cf. for this *Corp. Herm.* VII. i. ποῖ φέρεσθε, ὦ ἄνθρωποι, μεθύοντες;

[74] *De Boethii consolatione* (*Philol. Unters.* XXVII.), 12 ff.

[75] Theon, *Progymn.* V. p. 201 Walz, cf. Steph. *Thes.* VIII. 1629; Sen. *Epp.* 33. 6, 7. On the contact which existed between rhetoric and the diatribe cf. Villeneuve, *Essai sur Perse*, 166.

[76] H. Thompson, *Proc. Soc. Bibl. Arch.* XXXIV. (1912) 197 = Preisigke, *Sammelbuch*, 5730: cf. the Diogenes anecdotes on a papyrus published by Wessely, *Festschrift Gomperz*, 67 ff. The existence of such sayings helps to explain the genesis of such collections as the Λόγια Ἰησοῦ and the *Apophthegmata patrum*, or of the collections earlier than the latter postulated by E. C. Butler, *The Lausiac History of Palladius*, I. 208 ff.

[77] Hense, *ad.* p. 12. 8.

[78] Strictly speaking διατριβή is the written record, and διάλεξις the lecture (Christ-Schmid, II. 553_3). For Maximus Tyrius cf. K. Meiser, *Sitz. Ber. München*, 1909, vi., K. Hobein, Χάριτες *für Leo*, 188 ff., esp. 204 ff.

An example is Demonax of whom Lucian has given us so appreciative a sketch. In Lucian's pages he is the diatribe personified. He laid all philosophical schools under contribution, admiring Socrates and above all Diogenes (ch. 5). The fortunate he reminded of the brief duration of human prosperity; sufferers from poverty, exile, ill-health or bereavement he consoled (ch. 8, 25). Like Diogenes and unlike Socrates he refused to do sacrifice, holding that the gods need nothing from us (ch. 11). The emphasis he laid on freedom of soul (ch. 20) is Cynic in origin and a commonplace of Hellenistic and later thought[79].

The diatribe, like Demonax, has a markedly eclectic tendency. Further, the extensive consolation literature of antiquity draws upon it for material[80]. A minor point of contact is that Demonax knew most of the poets by heart (ch. 4). Poetic quotations are a constant feature of diatribes and consolations[81].

Lucian holds up Demonax as a model to all philosophers. For all his admiration of Epicurus he was at heart

nullius addictus iurare in uerba magistri.

Elsewhere he makes Teiresias say to Menippus: 'The life of ordinary men is the best and is more sensible: abandon the folly of high speculations and questions of ends and causes, despise these wise syllogisms: think all that sort of thing nonsense and make it your only aim that you may use the present well and run your course smiling for the most part and in earnest about nothing[82].' To this ideal picture drawn

[79] Cf. p. xciv *infra*.

[80] Cf. Geffcken, 15. At the same time, its fountain-head is Crantor's book Περὶ πένθους and its matter in large part still older. Diatribe influence is clearest in its style. For the use of ideas appropriate to these consolations cf. Dio Cass. XXXVIII. 19 ff. (Philistus consoles Cicero on his exile.)

[81] Cf. H. Weber, 26 f., 49 f., also [Hippocr.] *Praecepta*, 12 (I. 326 Jones = IX. 268 Littré: on quotations in popular lectures on medicine), also Philo, *De aeternitate mundi* passim (on the character of which work cf. p. lxi ff. *infra*), Menander, Rhetor, Περὶ ἐπιδεικτικῶν 9, IX. 282 Walz (on the familiarity of Eur. *Cresphont.* fr. 449 N.²).

[82] *Menipp.* 21, cf. *Icaromen.* 5, *Hermot.* 84, also Praechter, *Philol.* LI. 284 ff. (who assumes that L. uses a Sceptic source).

by Lucian there are distinct resemblances in a brief portrait Apuleius gives of Crates[83].

An interesting example of this type as transplanted in Christian surroundings is to be found in S. Gregory of Nyssa's life of S. Gregory Thaumaturgus. The author's rhetorical standpoint has perhaps caused him to sketch a type rather than an individual[84]. His hero utters what is substantially a diatribe on the needlessness of housing: 'Why do you feel confined, with heaven covering you? Why seek you any other inn? Let one house be a care to you, your own, which you build and raise on high with your virtues. Be grieved only with the fear that this house may be ill equipped[85].'

Further, Gregory represents the Thaumaturge as acting the diatribe. 'The mourner was consoled, the young man was moderated, the old was physicked with the proper words: slaves were taught to feel affectionately to their masters, those in power to be kind to their subjects, the poor to think virtue

[83] *Florida*, 22: cf. Luc. *Dem.* 63.

[84] I do not wish to deny that he has in general a local tradition before him.

[85] XLVI. p. 921 A Migne. *ἦ στενοχωρεῖσθε τῇ οὐρανίῳ σκέπῃ καὶ ζητεῖτε παρὰ τοῦτο καταγώγιον ἄλλο; εἷς οἶκος ὑμῖν ἔστω διὰ σπουδῆς ὁ ἑκάστου ἴδιος ὁ διὰ τῶν ἀρετῶν οἰκοδομούμενος καὶ εἰς ὕψος ἀνατεινόμενος. τοῦτο λυπείτω μόνον, μὴ τὸ τοιοῦτον ἡμῖν οἰκητήριον ἀπαράσκευον ᾖ.*

For the recommendation of heaven as a shelter and home we may compare Lucian, *Cyn.* 15, *οἶκον δὲ τὸν κόσμον νομίζειν*, Varro, *Men.* 92 B, *mundus domus est maxima homulli*, Diog. Oenoand. fr. XXIV. ii. 10, p. 30 William, *εἷς ὁ κόσμος οἶκος*, for homelessness Plut. *Sept. Sap. conu.* I. 12, p. 155 A (of Anacharsis, whose character, though fixed in its main lines in the fifth century, developed under Cynic influence, cf. P. von der Mühll, *Festgabe Blümner* (1914), 425 ff., Epictet. *Diss.* III. 22, 47, Musonius, p. 71 Hense). Men's complaints that they lack house room are answered by Teles, *Περὶ αὐταρκείας*, p. 8, Musonius, *Περὶ σκέπης*, p. 105 ff. For *στενοχωρία, στενοχωρεῖν* we have such instances as Teles, p. 60, 11, Hippodamus, *ap.* Stob. IV. 34. 71 (vol. V. p. 848. 5 Hense), Epictet. I. 6. 26, 25. 28, IV. I. 106: for the notion we may refer to Seneca, *Ep.* 25. 4, 74. 28, 119. 10, 120. 15, *Dial.* III. 21. 4, IX. 4. 7, Hor. *Carm.* II. 10. 21. The soul may be called an *οἰκία*, cf. p. xix, n. 13 *supra*, *καταγώγιον* is equivalent to *deuersorium* (S. Ambrose, *De Abraham*, II. 8. 48, *exire ex his deuersoriis*, Prudent. *Hamart.* 854, *animam post deuersoria carnis ...renarrantem*: *καταγωγεῖον* is used of the underworld by Antiphanes, *Ἀφροδίσιος* fr. ii. III. 29 Meineke). The contrast of a well-furnished house and an ill-furnished soul is familiar from Persius, IV. 52, *Tecum habita; noris quam sit tibi curta supellex.* In general, for the contrast of material wealth and spiritual poverty cf. G. A. Gerhard, *Phoinix von Kolophon*, 128 ff.

For *εἰς ὕψος ἀνατεινόμενος* cf. *Gnomol. Epicteteum*, 60, p. 491 Schenkl[2], *εὖ ποιήσεις σὺ τὰ μέγιστα τὴν πόλιν εἰ μὴ τοὺς ὀρόφους ὑψώσεις ἀλλὰ τὰς ψυχὰς αὐξήσεις.*

the only wealth, virtue that is set before all to gain to the best of their ability: he that was proud of his riches was likewise admonished and taught to regard himself as the steward and not the master of what he had[86].' This is very like Lucian, *Demonax*, ch. 8. Such giving of consolation and advice was regarded as the task of a Cynic philosopher[87]. It rested on the belief that any part which Fortune may give one in the drama of life can be played well[88]. Poverty may even be of assistance in the pursuit of virtue[89]; for our happiness or unhappiness we are alone responsible[90], since only virtue can give the former[91].

How clearly this section of S. Gregory is related to the diatribe is shown by a comparison with any ordinary description in scriptural language of a model Christian character[92].

§ 4

To this popular philosophy, communicated by oral or by written teaching, we may trace some of the reflections on life and death which recur continually in Greek and Latin metrical epitaphs. It has been shown that the source of not a few of them is that consolation-literature of which the ancients were so fond[93]; that is not to say that the majority of those responsible for funerary inscriptions knew this literature at first hand. Very often the monumental mason employed may have suggested a few suitable words or the bereaved had seen an epitaph which they wished to copy. An idiomatic *ταῦτα*, 'that's that,' recurs continually, sometimes with amplifications,

[86] p. 924 A Migne: for the last thought cf. its possible source, Eur. *Phoen.* 555 f. *οὔτοι τὰ χρήματ' ἴδια κέκτηνται βροτοί, | τὰ τῶν θεῶν δ' ἔχοντες ἐπιμελούμεθα.*

[87] Cf. *Demonax*, 25, Dio, XXVII. 9, II. p. 285, 16 von Arnim (people sending for a philosopher to console themselves in grief), Suid. *s.v.* *Σαλούστιος φιλόσοφος*, II. ii. p. 658, 18, *πᾶσιν ἐπιτιθέμενος τοῖς ἁμαρτάνουσιν*, Julian, p. 223 B, Greg. Naz. *Ep.* 76 (XXXVII. 141 A Migne) *ἐπειδὴ δύο ταῦτα οἶδε φιλοσοφία, εὐπραξίαν τε διαθέσθαι μετρίως καὶ συμφορὰν εὐσχημόνως*, Przychocki, *l.c.* p. 363 ff.

[88] Teles, p. 5, 52, Hense², p. cxiv f., E. R. Bevan in *The Hellenistic Age*, 89.

[89] Teles, p. 45, Dio of Prusa, VII. 103 (I. p. 208, 16 Arnim).

[90] Teles, p. 33 ff.

[91] Dio of Prusa, LXIX. 1 ff. (II. p. 174 Arnim).

[92] As for instance the life of S. Porphyry of Gaza written by Mark the Deacon; esp. ch. viii.

[93] Cf. B. Lier, *Philol.* LXII. 450 ff.

as *ταῦτα πάντα κόνις*, 'all this is dust[94].' Parallel to this is perhaps a Syrian inscription, *οὐκέτι οὐδ[έν]· βίος, τέλος, πόνος*, which was translated by its editor as 'Plus rien; vie, c'est mort et misère,' but may rather be rendered 'Nothing remains any longer; the sum of things is life, death and toil[95].' This pessimism is a feature frequently apparent in popular thought and poetry of Hellenistic and Imperial times[96].

A thought common in consolations and also in epitaphs is that life is enjoyed on loan. We meet with it as early as Alexis:

ἀλλοτρίαν ὅτι
ζωὴν ἔχομεν ἅπαντες, ἣν ὅταν δοκῇ
πάλιν παρ' ἑκάστου ῥᾳδίως ἀφείλετο (sc. *τὸ δαιμόνιον*[97]).

'Because the life we have is not ours: God takes it back from each one lightly when He thinks fit.' The creditor may be Nature, Time, Fate or the Fates, a god or gods; more often he is not specifically mentioned[98]. One expansion of the idea

[94] *ταῦτα* is equivalent to *ταῦτα οὕτως ἔχει ὁ βίος, τὸ τέλος ὑμῶν τοῦ βίου ταῦτα*, or *ὁ βίος ἔχει*. Among the amplifications used are *ταῦτα· ἐκ γῆς γὰρ εἰς γῆν τἀγαθά, ὁ βίος οὗτος· τί στήκις, ἄνθρωπε, ταῦτα βλέπων; ὅταν κάμῃς, τοῦτο τὸ τέλος*. Cf. Loch, *Festschrift Friedländer*, 294, *Indogerm. Forsch.* XXXIII. 128 ff. for the explanation of *ταῦτα*, and Dessau 8105, Keil-von Premerstein, II. n. 84 with their note, Cumont, *Studia Pontica*, III. 238 *ad* n. 263 for illustrations.

[95] Mouterde, *Syria*, II. 217. H. J. Rose, *Year's Work in Classical Studies* 1921/2, 50 suggests 'No more life, end, pain,' which seems to me less probable. For *τέλος* compare Lebas-Waddington, 2538, *πάντων δέ, φίλε, τέλος θάνατος καὶ βυθός, | πλούτου, πενίης, ἀλόγων τε καὶ ἀνδρῶν*, *Öst. Jahresh.* XVIII. (1915), *Beibl.* 57, *τὸν πάντα τοῦ ζῆν μόχθον εἰς τόδε κατεθέμην τέλος*.

[96] Cf. the epigram by Posidippus, *A. P.* IX. 359, discussed by Geffcken, *op. cit.* 7, also an epigram from Cyrrhus in Syria, beginning *πόσαι δὲ σφαλερὲ βιότου φροντίδες· ἄλγος γὰρ ἀνθρώποις ὁ πολὺς ἑὼν* (= *αἰὼν*) *βίου γενᾷ* (= *γεννᾷ*). *ἄχος τίθησι ὅσαις ὑποχεῖται* [?] (Cumont, *Études Syriennes*, 335, *inscr.* 39), and a mosaic representing a skeleton, with the motto ΓΝΩΘΙ ΣΑΥΤΟΝ, in the Museo dei Termi in Rome (R. Paribeni, *Le terme di Diocleziano*[4], 73 n. 33), and the Boscoreale cups (Cagnat et Chapot, *Manuel d'archéologie romaine*, I. 589 ff., fig. 317 f.).

[97] *P. Berol.* 11771 published by Wilamowitz-Moellendorff, *Sitz. Ber. preuss. Akad.* 1918, 743 ff., A. Körte, *Ber. sächs. Ges. Wiss.* 1919, vi. 37, Simonides, fr. 104, *Anth. Lyr.*[4]. *θανάτῳ πάντες ὀφειλόμεθα* (with the parallels quoted by Diehl, *Anth. Lyr.* II. 112 *ad* 139) is not quite the same thing. A philosophic form of the idea is given by Plato, *Tim.* 42 E (the elements needed to make man borrowed from the universe); for later adaptations cf. Wyttenbach's note on Plut. *Consol. ad Apoll.* 106 F (*Animadu.* 723).

[98] Cf. Rohde, *Psyche*[2], II. 394, W. Schulze, *Sitz. Ber. preuss. Akad.* 1912,

on an inscription in Serbia may be mentioned, *memoriam uiui fabrikabimus et quod nescientes accepimus inuiti reddemus.* ταῦτα[99].

Other commonplaces are οὐκ ἤμην · οὐκ ᾔδειν · ἐγενόμην · οὐκ οἶδα · οὐκ εἰμί · οὐ μέλει μοι with its numerous variants[100], and the Syrian favourite οὐδεὶς ἀθάνατος, which means 'No one is not subject to death,' and is not a denial of life hereafter[101], as also ὅσα γεννᾶτε (= γεννᾶται) τελεῖτε (= τελεῖται), 'All things that are born die[102],' and εἰς αὐτὸ ἐγεννήθης, 'Thou wast born to have this end[103].' These reflections served to generalise the experience of the individual; his sorrows took their place in the general order of things, when he remembered 'These things have happened even to great kings':

haec eadem et magnis regibus acciderunt[104].

6914, for illustrations. Christian examples are not rare, as *Vita Pauli*, § 14, p. 26 Bidez (debt to God); St Ambrose, *De excessu fratris Satyri*, XVI. 1347 Migne; *De obitu Valentiniani*, 1434 Migne; [August.] *De consolatione mortuorum*, 2, XL. 1159 Migne.

[99] *Öst. Jahresh.* XII. (1909), *Beibl.*, 154, n. 16.

[100] Cumont, *Festschrift Hirschfeld*, p. 273 (Pontus), G. Vollgraff, *Mnemos.* XLVII. 1919, p. 251 (Cyrene): οὐ μέλει μοι is a tag on gems (I have noted three at Naples in the Museum inscribed λέγουσιν ἃ θέλουσιν· λεγέτωσαν· οὐ μέλει μοι; cf. *C. I. G.* IV. 7293, 7295, *Cat. Wyndham Cook*, 82, n. 359, pl. XIX). *I. G. Rom.* I. 313 gives ὅστις οὐκ ἤμην καὶ ἐγενόμην οὐκ εἰμὶ καὶ οὐ λυποῦμαι; cf. Vettius Valens, *Anthol.* VI. 2, p. 248, 27 Kroll, τὰ τοῦ βίου πράγματα ἐν οἷς διαθλεύσας ποικίλως καὶ τὸ τῆς ἐγκρατείας στέφος λαβὼν ὅπερ ἦν οὐκ ὢν τοῦτο γίνεται. In Latin we have *non fui, fui, non sum, non desidero* (Dessau, 8162 ff.), and *quod fueram, non sum, sed rursum ero quod modo non sum; | ortus et occasus uitaque morsque itidest* (*C.L.E.* 1559. 15, cf. Dessau, 8156, *Rev. Arch.* 1922, XV. 233, and a Christian example in Kaufmann, *Handb. altchr. Epig.*, 134).

[101] So W. M. Ramsay, *Luke the Physician*, 273; he draws attention to instances of the use of this formula by Christians.

[102] *I. G. Rom.* I. 207.

[103] *Mélanges de la faculté orientale...Beyrouth*, I. 149, n. 18.

[104] *Carm. lat. epigr.* 970. 14 Buecheler; cf. Vollmer *ad* Stat. *Silu.* II. 7. 90. Two more specimens of popular reflection may be noted, one from Lycia, *J.H.S.* XXXIV. 18 ff., n. 26, l. 20, παῖζε, γέλα, παροδεῖτα, βλέπων ὅτι καὶ σὲ θανεῖν δεῖ, and one from Antium, *I. G.* XIV. 2131, εἰπεῖν τίς δύναται σκῆνος λιπόσαρκον ἀθρήσας, | εἴπερ Ὕλας ἢ Θερσείτης ἦν, ὦ παροδεῖτα.

§ 5

At the same time there is evidence for a certain dissemination of more clearly philosophical ideas. Some years ago there was found at Philadelphia in Lydia a slab inscribed

οὐ γενόμαν Σάμιος κεῖνος ὁ Πυθαγόρας,
ἀλλ' ἐφύην σοφίη (= η?), τἀτὸ (= ταὐτὸ) λαχὼν ὄνομα,
τὸν πόνον ἐνκρείνας αἱρετὸν ἐν βιότῳ....

('I was not the famous Pythagoras of Samos, but I was a Pythagoras in wisdom and in name, and I regarded toil as the thing to choose in life'), and accompanied by a relief representing the Pythagorean Υ (symbolical of the Two Ways), with a man in repose on one side, a man toiling on the other, and a youth accompanied by *Asotia* or Debauchery matching one accompanied by *Arete* or Virtue[105]. Brinkmann, who was the first to notice the Υ, showed that Neopythagorean influence was here to be recognised[106]. Prof. Weinreich has recently explained the arrangement of studs in the shape ∴∵∴ on the front of a statuette of Cybele found at Pergamum as due to the Pythagorean view that 10 is the sum of 1, 2, 3, 4: this conclusion, if accepted, would be important, since the statuette has been dated in the second century B.C., which would make it an early indication of the Neopythagorean movement[107].

Certain recollections of philosophic thought are probably to be explained as literary reminiscences[108]. At the same time, there is reason to believe that much philosophic propaganda was carried on under the Empire. This is one of the new features of the Greek world after Alexander. The older philosophers had in general been more akin to professors than to missionaries, seeking in fact to teach those who would learn and not striving to save mankind from the danger of error.

105 Keil-von Premerstein, I. 34, n. 55; for this use of consecutive pentameters cf. the hymn quoted by Heliodor. *Aeth.* III. 2.

106 *Rhein. Mus.* LXVI. (1911) 622 ff. On the Two Ways cf. also *J. Eg. Arch.* XI. 129.

107 *Röm. Mitth.* XXXVI/XXXVII. (1921/2) 153.

108 Thus the Stoicism of *C.I.L.* XIII. 8371 (= Riese, *Das rheinische Germanien*, 2353), *spiritum mouere cuncta, spiritum esse quod deum*, is probably due to a recollection of Virg. *Georg.* IV. 221 ff., *Aen.* VI. 724 ff.

Epicurus struck a different note. In his letter to Menoeceus we read, 'Let no one young delay the pursuit of philosophy, let no one old grow weary thereof; no one is too young or too old for that which is healthful in the soul[109].' We find a like enthusiasm in Lucretius, and in the confession of faith which Diogenes of Oenoanda caused to be inscribed in a portico, at some date in the second or third century of our era, 'Being now by reason of old age at the setting of life and all but on the point of leaving it with a fair hymn of praise, for the perfect enjoyment of all pleasant things, I wished to give help now to all men of parts, lest death should come on first[110],' and a little later 'Since as I have said most men suffer alike from false opinions as if in a plague, and the number of sufferers increases, since by copying one another they catch the disease like sheep and it is right to give help to future generations, for they are ours even if they are yet unborn, having regard further to the love of mankind and the duty of giving help to strangers who are at hand, forasmuch as the benefits conferred by the written word are spread abroad I decided to use this colonnade and set forth in it the means of safety for all to see[111].' The phrase translated 'means of safety' is *τὰ τῆς σωτηρίας φάρμακα*, perhaps a reminiscence of Euripides *Phoen.* 893, where *φάρμακον σωτηρίας* is 'a means of saving Thebes'; it signifies here a remedy able to deliver from the peril of false opinions[112]. Diogenes says later 'I say

[109] *Ep. tertia*, p. 59 Usener (=p. 44 Von der Mühll). Epicurus was eager to convert men; this is perhaps why he was content with *any* explanation of physical phenomena which avoided the danger of *δεισιδαιμονία*; cf. E. Reitzenstein, *Theophrast bei Epikur und Lucrez* (*Orient und Antike*, II. 1924), 78 f.

[110] *Fragm.* II. col. ii. 7, p. 5 William (cf. fr. I. col. ii. 7, p. 3). *εὐσυνκρίτοις* I have, as William (p. 72), understood to mean 'well compounded of the elements,' rather than, as Usener, *Rh. Mus.* XLVII. 431, 'competent to judge.' For this Epicurean view of old age cf. *Gnomol. Vatican.* 17, p. 62. 9 Von der Mühll, *ὁ δὲ γέρων καθάπερ ἐν λιμένι τῷ γήρᾳ καθώρμικεν τὰ πρότερον δυσελπιστούμενα τῶν ἀγαθῶν ἀσφαλεῖ κατακλείσας χάριτι*, *ib.* 76, p. 68. 17 (cf. Metrodor. fr. 41 Körte). For *ἐπὶ δυσμαῖς τοῦ βίου* cf. Iambl. *De myst.* V. 22, p. 231. 1.

[111] Fr. II. col. iv. 3, p. 6 William.

[112] *σωτηρίας* is genitive of description, as in *σωτηρίας ἄκος* Eur. *Hel.* 1055. Prof. Pearson kindly drew my attention to these passages of Euripides. Porphyry, *Ad Marcellam* 8, has *τῆς σωτηρίας τὴν ὁδὸν* of philosophy; *σωτηρία, σῴζεσθαι* are words of wide range in the Imperial age, thus *σῴζεσθαι* in Diog. *ap.* Plut. *De disc. am. et adul.* xxxvi. 74[c] (cf. Wyttenbach *ad loc.*, *Animadv.* I. 549, on the Platonic origin

now as always as loudly as I can to Greeks and barbarians that pleasure is the aim of the best life[113].'

A similar enthusiasm marked the Cynic preachers of the early Empire, of whom Dio of Prusa is our most familiar example[114]. Their teaching was of the nature of the diatribe, which we have considered earlier. The Stoicism of Musonius and Epictetus possessed similar aims and carried on a similar propaganda, while the importance of Neopythagorean teaching is becoming more and more manifest. A prominent representative is Apollonius of Tyana, in whom this element stands out as clearly historical amidst the wild vagaries of the imagination of Philostratus[115]. It has recently been shown by Prof. Cumont that Alexander of Abonotichus belonged to the same school of thought[116].

All this earnest activity was bound to disseminate some philosophical conceptions. It was no doubt promoted by the compilation of convenient summaries of dogma, like the *Λόγος διδασκαλικὸς τῶν Πλάτωνος δογμάτων* of Albinus passing under the name of Alcinous and the kindred *De Platone et eius dogmate* of Apuleius[117]; a similar epitome of Platonism seems to lie behind Diogenes Laertius III. 70 ff., many of the *Dialexeis* of Maximus Tyrius[118], and the *Epitome*

of the use), Cebes, *Tabula*, IV. 3, XI. 2, etc., means *ad fructum bonum peruenire*; in inscriptions noted *C.R.*, 1925, 639, it is used of deliverance from the sea or from other pressing dangers.

[113] Fr. XXV. col. ii. 9, p. 32.

[114] Cf. Dill, *Roman Society from Nero to Marcus Aurelius*[2], 334 ff.

[115] E. Meyer's study, *Hermes*, LII. (1917), 371–424 (cf. esp. p. 390) is of great value.

[116] *Revue de l'histoire des religions*, LXXXVI. (1922) 202 ff. There was perhaps also some anti-Pythagorean propaganda, cf. Lucian, *Alex.* 4, ἀλλ' εἴ τις τὰ χείριστα καὶ βλασφημότατα τῶν ἐπὶ διαβολῇ περὶ τοῦ Πυθαγόρου λεγομένων, οἷς ἔγωγε οὐκ ἂν πεισθείην ὡς ἀληθέσιν οὖσιν, ὅμως συναγάγοι ἐς τὸ αὐτό, πολλοστὸν ἂν μέρος ἅπαντα ἐκεῖνα γένοιτο τῆς Ἀλεξάνδρου δεινότητος.

[117] The Λόγος is assigned to Albinus by Freudenthal, *Hellenistische Studien*, III. p. 297 ff. That it is based on the same source as the work of Apuleius is demonstrated at length by Th. Sinko, *De Apulei et Albini doctrinae Platonicae adumbratione* (*Diss. phil. class. Ac. Litt. Cracou.* XLI. (1905) 131 ff.), 3 ff. (he argues p. 13, 22, that Apuleius also used Plato, which is reasonable, and p. 41 f. that the *Liber περὶ ἑρμηνείας* also is closely related to Albinus). On Gaius as a fountainhead of such thought cf. K. Praechter, *Hermes*, LI. (1916) p. 510 ff., *P. W. Suppl.* III. 535, and on this literature in general G. C. Field, *C.Q.* XIX. (1925) 6 ff.

[118] Cf. H. Hobein, *De Maximo Tyrio quaestiones philologicae selectae*, 1895, p. 39 ff. (a very useful monograph).

of Arius Didymus[119]. Traces of this doxographical knowledge are frequent[120]. It has been observed that the Platonism of the Platonic summaries is not identical with that of Plato. Thus Apuleius and Alcinous deny that the world ever came into being[121]: the definition of the three parts of the soul, and their localisation in the body, the substitution of the Stoic φρόνησις for σοφία as the virtue of the reason, the definition of σωφροσύνη as the virtue of Desire, all belong to the school tradition[122]. This school tradition is of more importance for the later history of Greek thought than is the original teaching: its existence seems to account for a curious habit of quoting inherited arguments in a kind of shorthand[123].

[119] Cf. H. Diels, *Doxographi graeci*, 76 f.

[120] Cf. Diels, pp. 1 ff.; and lists of *placita philosophorum* as Diog. Oen. frag. v. col. i. 10, p. 10, Himer. *Orat.* XIV. 23 ff., Philo, *De somniis*, I. 22.

[121] I. viii. p. 91. 12 Thomas: xiv. p. 169 Hermann (so Sallustius, chs. vii, xiii, xvii): *contra* Plat. *Tim.* p. 28 B.

[122] Albin. xxiv. p. 176: Apul. I. xiii. p. 97: [Plut.] *De uit. et poes. Hom.* 129, p. 1163 B–C: Max. Tyr. XVI. 4, cf. Hobein, p. 53: for φρόνησις, σωφροσύνη, cf. Sall. x, K. Praechter, *P.W.* VIII. p. 1484. 10 ff. Hobein, p. 52, Freudenthal, p. 271, have discussed the Aristotelian elements in these Platonic summaries.

As for the school tradition, it may be noted that one work of Albinus was named Τῶν Γαΐου σχολῶν ὑποτυπώσεων Πλατωνικῶν δογμάτων βίβλοι ι'. Bousset, *Jüdisch-christliche Schulbetrieb in Alexandria und Rom*, p. 3, refers to the Ποσειδώνειαι σχολαί of Phanias and to the σχολαὶ Ζήνωνος used by Philodemus in his Περὶ ἠθῶν καὶ βίων: the emphasis Bousset lays on the intellectual background of Philo and of Clement of Alexandria makes his book very valuable. The school tradition, again, is the basis of the philosophic thought of Origen's adversary Celsus (K. W. Schmidt, *Jahrb. phil. Fak. Gött.* (1922), II. p. 69 ff.).

[123] As Sallustius gives the arguments against astral fatalism in IX. (cf. p. lxxii ff. *infra*). His τινες (p. 4. 28), τις (p. 22. 20, 24), οἱ τὸν κόσμον φθείροντες (p. 26. 4: cf. Arist. *De caelo*, p. 283, b. 31, τῶν γεννώντων, sc. τὸν οὐρανόν) may be explained as Philo's ἤκουσα, τινές φασιν, οἱ δὲ λέγουσιν (E. Bréhier, *Les idées philosophiques et religieuses de Philon d'Alexandrie*[2], 55_2, 56), παρειλήφαμεν (Bousset, 135, and cf. p. lxii, n. 110 *infra*). E. Reitzenstein, *Theophrast bei Epikur und Lucrez* 8, notes that Epicurus is the first philosopher to quote *placita* without naming their authors, and quotes the remark of W. W. Jaeger, *Nemesios von Emesa* 33, 'Es gehört zur Stil der Doxographie, den Namen zu nennen, zum Stil des Abschreiben, ihn zu verschweigen.' Similar references to τινές, τινὲς τῶν νεωτέρων, τινὲς (πολλοί) τῶν ἡμετέρων, τινὲς τῶν παρ' αὐτοῖς θεολόγων occur in Ioannes Philoponus *De aeternitate mundi contra Proclum* (cf. H. Rabe, *index*, p. 653). Proclus alludes to οἱ διαλεκτικοί, ἐξηγηταί, οἱ ὑπομνηματισταί, οἱ νεώτεροι, οἱ παλαιοί, οἱ πρεσβύτεροι (Diehl, index to Comm. in *Tim.* III. pp. 362–3–4–5–8, 377, cf. p. xciv, n. 223 *infra*). οἱ ἀρχαῖοι in astrological texts generally refers to Nechepso and Petosiris (F. Dornseiff, *Das Alphabet in Mystik und Magie*, ΣΤΟΙΧΕΙΑ, VII. 15_1). The Christian apologists used philosophical handbooks (Geffcken, *Apol.* 111, 170 f., 211 f.): so Athenagoras

The tradition represented by these epitomes is of considerable importance for the study of Sallustius[124]. It contains as fixed components:

the requirement of natural attainments (φύσις) and their development (Albin. i., Sallust. i.):
the assertion of the perfect nature of the Supreme Being (Albin. x., Apul. I. 5, Max. T. VIII. 10, XVII. 9, Sall. i.), under whom are set two inferior classes of gods (Apul. I. 11, cf. Albin. xv., Sall. ii. vi.):
the doctrine that the universe has neither beginning nor end in time (Albin. xiv., Apul. I. viii., Sall. vii. xiii. xvii.),
the description of the four elements, the seven planetary spheres and the surrounding immobile sphere (Albin. xiv. f., Apul. I. 11, cf. Sall. vii.):
the assertion of the soul's supremacy over the body (Albin. xxiii., Apul. I. 13, Sall. viii.), of its tripartite nature (p. xxxviii, *supra*), the explanation thence of virtues and vices (Albin. xxix., Apul. II. 6, cf. Sall. x.: they agree that virtues are perfect only when found together):
the discussion of Providence: the view that God cannot be credited with evil or our moral responsibility denied, the functions of Fate and Fortune (Albin. xxvi., Apul. I. 12, Sall. ix.):
the mention of daemones as intermediaries between God and man (Albin. xv., Apul. I. 12, *De deo Socratis* VI. p. 13, Thomas, Sall. xiii.[125]).

Such conceptions were popularised by little handbooks. By noting these ideas as they occur in the treatise of Sallustius we may make some attempt to isolate the more characteristic elements in his thought and to seek their source[126].

uses the phrase ὡς οἱ τὰ ἐκείνου ἀκριβοῦντες μνημονεύουσιν (xxiii. p. 141. 17 Geffcken) in mentioning a view ascribed to Thales.

[124] I follow a hint given by Hobein, *op. cit.* 40.

[125] Cf. Plut. *De def. orac.* 13, p. 411 E, R. Heinze, *Xenokrates*, 109. To mention details, there are these further points of contact. The universe is ageless (Albin. xii., Apul. I. viii., Sall. xvii.), circular motion is appropriate to νοῦς (Albin. xii., Apul. I. viii., Sall. vii.). Apul. II. viii. as Sall. xi. discusses the state after virtues and vices; Albinus treats it after virtues and friendship (xxxiv.), and Apuleius returns to the subject later, II. xxiv.

[126] In stressing the element of school tradition in Sallustius and in others we do not necessarily deny that they made what they thus inherited their own. It may be of service to quote E. Meyer's dictum on Cicero, *De re publica*, 'das überkommene Gut ist durchaus sein geistiges Eigentum geworden' (*Caesars Monarchie*³, 180_0).

CHAPTER II

THE CONTENT OF THE TREATISE

We may now proceed to analyse the Περὶ θεῶν καὶ κόσμου section by section[1].

i. Those who would learn about the gods must be men of parts and well educated, so that they may have in themselves something akin to what they are to learn. They must be free from popular errors; they must also know those true conceptions which are common to all mankind. Such are the goodness, the impassibility, and the changelessness of every god.

The demand for natural gifts and training in the learner is common to all introductory treatises[2]. Sallustius improves on the commonplace with ἵν' ὅμοιόν τι ἔχωσι τοῖς λόγοις[3].

[1] Most of the parallel passages quoted from other Neoplatonic texts are borrowed from Orelli or his predecessors.

[2] Cf. Albin. i., Galen, Ὅτι ὁ ἄριστος 4, ii. p. 8 Müller = i. p. 62 K. The view that natural gifts, teaching, and practice are necessary is traced back to Protagoras by A. Burk, *Die Pädagogik des Isokrates* (*Stud. Gesch. Kult. Alt.* XII. 3/4, 19 f.); cf. B. Appel, *op. cit.* 46 ff., for its popularity.

Julian states his view of education, *Ep.* 61 (= 42 H.), παιδείαν ὀρθὴν εἶναι νομίζομεν οὐ τὴν ἐν τοῖς ῥήμασιν καὶ τῇ γλώττῃ πολυτελῆ εὐρυθμίαν ἀλλὰ διάθεσιν ὑγιῆ νοῦν ἐχούσης διανοίας καὶ ἀληθεῖς δόξας ὑπέρ τε ἀγαθῶν καὶ κακῶν, καλῶν τε καὶ αἰσχρῶν, and gives a summary of what he regards as necessary truth, *Ep.* 89 *b*, p. 141 Bidez-Cumont [= p. 301 A Spanheim] ὅσα...διδάσκει περὶ θεῶν πρῶτον μὲν ὡς εἰσίν, εἶτα ὡς προνοοῦσι τῶν τῇδε, καὶ ὡς ἐργάζονται μὲν οὐδὲ ἓν κακὸν οὔτε ἀνθρώπους οὔτε ἀλλήλους.... For ἀνοήτοις δόξαις, popular errors, cf. Plat. *Phil.* 12 D, Philodem. Περὶ θεῶν α', xvi. 19, τὴν ἐκ ψευδοδοξίας περὶ θεῶν ταραχήν, xx. 4, Liban. *Ep.* 819. 2 F. (= 730 W.) καὶ γὰρ εἰ διέστηκεν ἡμῶν τῇ περὶ τὸ θεῖον δόξῃ, βλάπτοι μὲν ἂν αὐτόν, εἴπερ ἐξηπάτηται, παρὰ δὲ τῶν συνήθων οὐκ ἂν εἰκότως πολεμοῖτο. Sallustius clearly implies that the masses could not understand true theology; cf. Julian, VI. p. 188 D, 196 D, Iambl. *Protr.* vi. p. 40. 8, xii. p. 60. 8. W. C. Wright, *Julian*, II. 418 f. has rightly remarked on the limited nature of the field touched by Julian's revival.

[3] Cf. iii. p. 2. 25, πάντα τὰ ὄντα ὁμοιότητι μὲν χαίρει.

The importance assigned to *κοιναὶ ἔννοιαι*, universal ideas, is usual since the rise of Stoicism, which valued the argument from *consensus hominum*[4]; it may be noted that earlier Aristotle used it in maintaining the immortality of the soul; all men, he said, pour libations to the dead[5]. The rhetorician Theon states that all men have an *ἔννοια* that the gods have forethought for us[6]; the Epicureans did not deny that there was an *ἔννοια* of the existence of gods, and Lucretius explains its origin from two considerations perhaps due to Aristotle[7]. Julian regards this belief as one naturally possessed by men, and due in the first instance to the contemplation of the sky[8].

The definition of divine perfection given as among these *ἔννοιαι* is a Platonic commonplace as applied to the Supreme Being[9]. Sallustius extends it to the whole Pantheon, rejecting once and for all those attributes which critics of mythology, from Xenophanes onwards, attacked, while clinging, as we shall see, to a belief in that mythology as enshrining truths.

ii. **They must be taught that the gods never came into being (what is immortal, possessed of the first power, and impassive, cannot come into being), are incorporeal, are not limited by space, and are not separated from the First Cause or from one another any more than thoughts from the mind, knowledge from the soul, or perceptions from any living being.**

[4] Cf. E. V. Arnold, *Roman Stoicism*, 143, 223.

[5] Fr. 33, p. 1480*a*. 11, *ed. acad.*

[6] *Progymn.* 12, i. 250 Walz. Hermogenes, *Prog.* 11, i. p. 53 Walz, mentions 'the customs common to men' as considerations to use in closing one's case in support of a general proposition (*θέσις*).

[7] Usener, *Epicurea*, 59. 17, 232: Lucr. v. 1169 ff.: Arist. fr. 12, p. 1475 *b* 37 ff., *ed. acad.* (dreams, and observation of celestial bodies). Cf. also Philodem. *De signis*, fr. 8 (*Rh. Mus.* LXIV. 16).

[8] Cf. R. Asmus, *Julians Galiläerschrift* (Progr. Freiburg: 1904, n. 709), 6 f. Iambl. *De myst.* I. 3, p. 7. 13, says *συνυπάρχει γὰρ ἡμῶν αὐτῇ τῇ οὐσίᾳ ἡ περὶ θεῶν ἔμφυτος γνῶσις, κρίσεώς τε πάσης ἐστὶ κρείττων καὶ προαιρέσεως, λόγου τε καὶ ἀποδείξεως προϋπάρχει.*

[9] Cf. p. xxxix, *supra*. J. Geffcken, *Apologeten*, 36 ff. (Stoic sources), also Herm. Trism. *ap.* Stob. III. 11. 31 (III. 439 Hense = Scott, *Hermetica*, I. 384. 28), *πᾶν γὰρ τὸ ἀλλοιούμενον ψεῦδός ἐστι, μὴ μένον ἐν ᾧ ἐστι, φαντασίας δὲ μετατρεπόμενον ἄλλας καὶ ἄλλας ἐπιδείκνυται ἡμῖν*, Procl. *in Rep.* I. 35. 6 (on changelessness). On *ἀγαθός* cf. p. lvi, n. 81 *infra*.

That whatever comes into being must perish is a commonplace of Greek thought[10]. As applied to the gods, it involves a considerable change of traditional ideas, as most of them had birth-legends. The *first power* here mentioned is defined by Proclus as 'not controlling some things and not others, but having anticipated in itself the powers of all existing things alike[11].' Of incorporeality we hear more in xiii. (p. 24 ff.). The assertion that the gods are free from limitations of space is possibly meant to counter Christian polemic[12].

This view of the gods as functions of a First Cause had a certain popularity in the fourth century: it was a compromise which suited the tendency to monotheism[13]. As for *ἡ πρώτη αἰτία*, Plato speaks of the creator as *ἄριστος τῶν αἰτίων*[14], and Aristotle uses *αἰτία* of the generative impulse[15], of the moving impulse in the universe[16], and of the final cause[17]. Cicero uses *caussa* in a personal way[18], and Seneca says 'Juppiter is the first of all causes, and the others are dependent on him[19].' Proclus speaks commonly of *ἡ πρω-*

[10] Cf. Arist. *De caelo*, p. 279 *b* 17, Athenag. *Leg.* 19, Origen *Contra Celsum*, III. 43 (xviii. 308 Lommatzsch), Nemes. Em. II. 45, p. 104 Matthaei, Herm. Trism. *ap.* Stob. I. 49. 3, p. 320 W. (=p. 450. 6 Scott): *contra* Herm. Trism. *ap.* Stob. I. 41. 1, p. 275 W. (=p. 428. 15 Scott), *πᾶν τὸ γενόμενον μεταβλητόν· οὐ πᾶν τὸ γενόμενον φθαρτόν*, though in the same text we read later, p. 276 W. (=p. 430. 20 S.), as Heeren restores, *τὸ ἀπογιγνόμενον* <*καὶ ἐπιγίγνεται· τὸ ἐπιγιγνόμενον*> *καὶ ἀπογίγνεται*, and p. 278 W. (=p. 432. 31 S.) that if men prone to evil learn that the universe came into being they will despise it, as also, if they learn that all things happen in accordance with Providence and Necessity, they will plunge into every evil deed: on this last view cf. p. lxxii, n. 149 *infra*.

[11] *Inst. Theol.* 121, cf. Arist. *Met.* IV. 12, p. 1019 *a* 26, *ἔτι ὅσαι ἕξεις καθ' ἃς ἀπαθῆ ὅλως ἢ ἀμετάβλητα ἢ μὴ ῥᾳδίως ἐπὶ τὸ χεῖρον εὐμετακίνητα δυνάμεις λέγονται· δύναμις* can also approach *δαίμων* in meaning: cf. Diels, Philod. *Περὶ θεῶν α'* (*Abh. preuss. Ak.* 1915, ix.) p. 92, note on xxiv. 3.

[12] Cf. Aristid. *Apol.* 1, *Mart. SS. Iust. et Soc.* 3, p. 19. 14 Gebh. In general cf. Iambl. *De myst.* I. 8, p. 27. 13, 17, p. 50. 16, III. 17, p. 143. 3.

[13] Cf. *J.H.S.* XLV. 90 f., F. Heinemann, *Plotin*, 293 ff., H. J. Rose, *Roman Questions of Plutarch*, 61, also *P. Leid. W* ii. 33 (Dieterich, *Abraxas*, 176. 20), *οἱ ὑπὸ σοῦ φανέντες θεοί.*

[14] *Tim.* 29 A, cf. *Phil.* 27 B.

[15] *Phys.* 194 *b* 20, *Met.* 1003 *a* 31, *De anim. gen.* 732 *a* 4.

[16] *Meteor.* 339 *a* 23.

[17] *Eth. N.* 1112 *b* 19 (*αἴτιον*).

[18] *De fin.* V. 33.

[19] *Nat. quaest.* II. 45. 2, cf. *Ep.* 65. 12, Apul. *Apol.* 64, Arnob. I. 31 (*prima enim tu causa es*).

τίστη αἰτία[20], and the Christian Philoponus uses a similar phrase[21]. πρώτη αἰτία was therefore a familiar expression.

iii. **Why did the ancients leave these simple statements and use myths? This very enquiry is a useful exercise. Myths are divine as can be inferred from their use by inspired poets, the best philosophers, the founders of mysteries, and the gods speaking in oracles. They are divine because they must be like the gods if they are to please them and win their favour for us. Myths, then, imitate the gods and teach the foolish simply that the gods exist, the wise their nature and character. This saves the former from contempt, the latter from sloth. The universe can be called a myth; the outer shell veils the inner realities. Still, why are the myths so strange? Surely it is in order that man may regard the stories as mere cloaks wrapped round the secret truth.**

Sallustius faces a difficulty. Men can allegorise myths and reconcile them with Neoplatonic tenets; but why should the myths exist? The apologist Aristides said pertinently, 'If the histories of the gods are mythical, they are merely stories; if they refer to natural phenomena, it is no longer gods who have done and suffered these things; if they are allegorical, they are myths and nothing else[22].' The divergence of philosophic teaching and popular belief was recognised by Plutarch and by the rhetorician Alexander: the latter attempted a reconciliation[23].

The myths are θεῖοι because they are used by θεοί and the like, Sallustius argues[24]; his attribution of authority to in-

[20] As *Comm. in Tim.* I. p. 34. 26, 151. 21, 298. 24, 385. 2, III. p. 271. 19 Diehl. He speaks also of τὰ πρῶτα αἴτια, as I. p. 118. 7 (cf. Iambl. *De myst.* I. 18, p. 56. 16; *ib.* V. 9, p. 210, we have ἔτι δὲ τούτων πρεσβυτάτης μιᾶς αἰτίας ἐξηγουμένης), or τὰ δημιουργικὰ αἴτια as I. 191. 26.

[21] τῇ ἀγενήτῳ καὶ δημιουργικῇ αἰτίᾳ of God (*De aeternitate mundi contra Proclum*, I. 4, p. 13. 21 Rabe, cf. IV. 10, p. 80. 20, IV. 11, p. 84. 9, XVIII. 9, p. 636. 4).

[22] *Apol.* 13. Cf. St Aug. *Ciu. D.* VII. 27, *nihil uideo nisi ad temporalia terrenaque opera naturamque corpoream, uel etiamsi inuisibilem, tamen mutabilem potuisse reuocari: quod nullo modo est uerus Deus* (*ib.* VII. 25, he attacks Porphyry's explanation of the story of Attis; VI. 8, a rationalisation of the myth of Kronos). Firmicus Maternus, *De err. prof. rel.* ii., iii., v., rejects similar interpretations of the stories of Osiris, Attis, and the supposed consort of Mithras.

[23] *Amat.* XVIII. p. 763 C; IX. p. 336. 19 Walz. Cf. *J.H.S.* XLV. 90 f.

[24] Cf. Hermog. *Progym.* VII., I. p. 40 Walz, τὰ δὲ πράγματα ἐγκωμιάσεις ἀπὸ τῶν

spired poets is common enough[25]; founders of rites are so quoted by Julian[26]; poets, lawgivers and philosophers are adduced by Plutarch (*l.c.*) as supporting belief in the existence of the gods. As for the reference to oracles, it will be remembered that a collection of *Oracula Chaldaica* enjoyed great authority among Neoplatonists, as did the prophecies of Claros in the world at large[27]. Myths must be divine in order to please the gods and win their favour[28]. They reflect and reproduce the divine nature in every aspect and activity, and the universe can be called a myth. So Iamblichus says 'Just as Nature has in a way set the stamp of invisible thoughts on visible objects[29].' The belief that nature likes to be concealed is expressed by Julian[30].

The argument that myths cause man to use his wits, if any, rests on a familiar commonplace, known to us from Virgil. 'The great Father himself willed it that the path of cultivation should not be easy: he was the first to cause the fields to be tilled by skill, sharpening human intelligence by toil[31].'

εὑρόντων, οἷον τὴν θηρευτικὴν Ἄρτεμις ηὕρηκε καὶ Ἀπόλλων, καὶ ἀπὸ τῶν χρησαμένων, ὅτι οἱ ἥρωες αὐτῇ ἐχρήσαντο. (Cf. Theon, p. 233, Nicolaus, p. 334, 417, Georgius, p. 572.)

[25] Cf. Aphthonius, I. p. 77 Walz (Orpheus is no doubt included, cf. Ar. *Ran.* 1032, Pausan. IX. 30. 12, St Aug. *Ciu. D.* XVIII. 14).

[26] p. 148 B. The founders were the Curetes according to *Orph. H.* 38. 6, the Muses according to 76. 7. For the belief in personal founders cf. H. J. Rose, *The Roman Questions of Plutarch*, 60.

[27] p. lxviii, n. 135 *infra*.

[28] Cf. Athenae. 14 C (*sc.* ὁ Δημόδοκος) εἰδὼς ἐν τρυφερῷ τινι βίῳ τεθραμμένους κἀντεῦθεν ὁμοιότατα τοῖς τρόποις αὐτῶν τὰ πρὸς ἀνάπαυσιν προφέρων. For εὐμενεῖς cf. Julian, *Conu.* 336 C, ἡγεμόνα θεὸν εὐμενῆ καθιστὰς σεαυτῷ.

[29] *De myst.* VII. 1. p. 250, ὥσπερ καὶ ἡ φύσις τοῖς ἐμφανέσιν εἴδεσι τοὺς ἀφανεῖς λόγους διὰ συμβόλων τρόπον τινὰ ἀπετυπώσατο, I. 11, p. 37, καθάπερ δὴ καὶ ἡ γενεσιουργὸς φύσις τῶν ἀφανῶν λόγων ἐμφανεῖς τινας μορφώσεις ἀπετυπώσατο. Cf. earlier Plotin. *Enn.* VI. 9. 11, ταῦτα μὲν οὖν μιμήματα καὶ τοῖς οὖν (?) σοφοῖς τῶν προφητῶν αἰνίττεται ὅπως θεὸς ἐκεῖνος ὁρᾶται. σοφὸς δὲ ἱερεὺς τὸ αἴνιγμα συνιεὶς ἀληθινὴν ἂν ποιοῖτο ἐκεῖ γενόμενος τοῦ ἀδύτου τὴν θέαν. For the contrast of the inner meaning and the literal sense of myths cf. Heliodor. *Aeth.* IX. 9 (Osiris, Isis, really the Nile and earth).

[30] p. 216 C, φιλεῖ γὰρ ἡ φύσις κρύπτεσθαι, cf. Macrob. *Comm. in Somn. Scip.* I. ii. 17.

[31] *Georg.* I. 121 ff. Cf. K. Reinhardt, *Hermes*, XLVII. 503 ff. (Democritus perhaps author of idea that necessity was the mother of civilisation), and for a late example the note of Proclus preserved in the Scholia on Hes. *Op. et Di.* 42, p. 66. 9 Gaisford.

Origen makes a similar application thereof, saying 'God, wishing man's nature to be exercised everywhere, that it might not remain idle and without a conception of the arts, created him with needs, whereby his very need might compel him to invent arts, some to provide food, some to provide shelter; for in truth it was better for those who would not seek and ponder divine things to be in difficulty, that they might use their intelligence to discover arts, rather than to be at ease and therefore despise intelligence everywhere[32]'; in general his attitude towards difficult stories in the Bible presents a striking analogy to this view of myths[33]. The concluding idea, that the very incongruity of myths is of high value in that it reminds us that they conceal truth, occurs in Julian's *Speech against the Cynic Heraclius*[34], which presents a view of myths closely resembling that maintained above.

iv. **Some myths are theological and concerned with the actual natures of the gods; some are physical and concerned with their actual effluences in the universe; some are psychical and concerned with the activities of the soul itself; some are material; and there are mixed myths.**

This classification is perhaps peculiar to Sallustius, but constructed on the usual lines[35]. The allegorisation of myths

[32] *Contra Celsum*, IV. 76, xix. p. 116 Lommatzsch: *πανταχοῦ τὴν ἀνθρωπίνην σύνεσιν γυμνάζεσθαι βουλόμενος ὁ θεὸς ἵνα μὴ μένῃ ἀργὴ καὶ ἀνεπινόητος τῶν τεχνῶν, πεποίηκε τὸν ἄνθρωπον ἐπιδεῆ, ἵνα δι' αὐτὸ τὸ ἐπιδεὲς αὐτοῦ ἀναγκασθῇ εὑρεῖν τέχνας, τινὰς μὲν διὰ τὴν τροφήν, ἄλλας δὲ διὰ τὴν σκέπην· καὶ γὰρ κρεῖττον ἦν τοῖς μὴ μέλλουσι τὰ θεῖα ζητεῖν καὶ φιλοσοφεῖν τὸ ἀπορεῖν ὑπὲρ τοῦ τῇ συνέσει χρήσασθαι πρὸς εὕρεσιν τεχνῶν ἤπερ ἐκ τοῦ εὐπορεῖν πάντῃ τῆς συνέσεως ἀμελεῖν.* Cf. for the thought Iambl. *De myst.* III. 15, p. 136. 5, *καθάπερ οὖν δι' εἰκόνων γεννῶσι πάντα καὶ σημαίνουσιν ὡσαύτως διὰ συνθημάτων, ἴσως δὲ καὶ τὴν ἡμετέραν σύνεσιν ἀπὸ τῆς αὐτῆς ἀφορμῆς εἰς ὀξύτητα πλείονα ἀνακινοῦσι.*

[33] Cf. C. E. Bigg, *The Christian Platonists of Alexandria*², 176 f.

[34] p. 222 D; sometimes Julian says emphatically that myths are really suited to children, cf. R. Asmus, *op. cit.* 5. In illustration of the view that it is desirable that men of intelligence should be compelled to study philosophy we may note the statement in a Hermetic text (*ap.* Stob. I. 41. 1, p. 273 Wachsmuth, p. 390 Scott), *ὁ δὲ εὐσεβῶν ἄκρως φιλοσοφήσει· χωρὶς γὰρ φιλοσοφίας ἄκρως εὐσεβῆσαι ἀδύνατον.* For the contrast of the many and the few cf. Julian, IV. p. 157 D, *δοίη δ' ὁ μέγας Ἥλιος μηδὲν ἔλαττόν* (sc. *τοῦ Ἰαμβλίχου*) *με τὰ περὶ αὐτοῦ γνῶναι, καὶ διδάξαι κοινῇ τε ἅπαντας, ἰδίᾳ δὲ τοὺς μανθάνειν ἀξίους.*

[35] Aphthonius, analysing *μῦθοι* (=fables), gives as kinds *τὸ λογικόν, τὸ ἠθικόν, τὸ μικτόν* (p. 59 Walz), defines each, and illustrates the genus. The rhetorician

had become very common; popularised by the Stoics, it was spread abroad in such treatises as the *Homeric Allegories* of Heraclitus and a work *On the Life and Poetry of Homer* wrongly ascribed to Plutarch, and reached wide circles[36]. Porphyry's work *De antro nympharum* is an elaborate example.

The story of Kronos can be treated as belonging to any one of these three categories.

Theologically, **the god is intellectual, and the action of intellect is directed inwards[37]. Therefore he may be said to devour his children.**

Physically **Κρόνος is equated with Χρόνος, time[38]. Time devours his children, that is, his parts.**

Psychically, **Κρόνος is typical of the soul, whose activities remain within itself.**

Sallustius here seeks to make acceptable a myth which met with much criticism. So Pausanias, after recounting the Arcadian story that Rhea, after giving birth to Poseidon, offered Kronos a foal to swallow, remarks, 'When I began this work I used to look on these Greek stories as little better than foolishness; but now that I have got as far as Arcadia

Menander classifies hymns as *κλητικοί*, *ἀποπεμπτικοί*, *φυσικοί*, *μυθικοί*, *γενεαλογικοί*, *πεπλασμένοι*, *εὐκτικοί*, *ἀπευκτικοί*, and illustrates these categories (IX. 132, Walz). Cf. the account of the *εἴδη* of the healing art given by [Galen], "Ὅροι ἰατρικοί, xix. p. 351 K., also Artemidor. II. 39, p. 145 (he speaks of the *φυσικὸς λόγος* of Sarapis, Isis, Anubis, and Harpocrates), *Schol.* in Lucian. *Dial. Meretr.* II. p. 276. 24 Rabe (*μυθικὸς λόγος* and *φυσικὸς λόγος* of Thesmophoria), *Schol.* in Pind. *Pyth.* III. 177 *b*, *Isthm.* VII. 3, and p. cxx, n. 16 *infra*.

[36] Cf. Aphthon. I. p. 79 (story of Apollo and Daphne), *Confessio Sancti Cypriani* in *A.A.S.S. Sept.* VII. 222 (the Hieros Gamos at Argos is described as a union of air and ether, earth and water), and in general H. J. Rose, *op. cit.*, 57, W. Kroll, *Studien*, 81 ff. For the verb *αἰνίττεται* cf. O. Casel, *R.G.V.V.* XVI. 2. 114, 159, Lyd. *De mens.* I. 11, p. 2. 26 Wünsch.

[37] Cf. Julian, p. 249 B.

[38] So as early as Pherecydes, cf. M. Mayer, Roscher, II. 1546, Pohlenz, *P.W.* XI. 1986, 53: for *φυσικῶς* cf. *Schol.* in Apoll. Rh. *Argon.* I. 1098, p. 368 Merkel-Keil, *καὶ φυσικῶς ταύτης* (Ῥέας=γῆς) *ἄνδρα τὸν Κρόνον φασίν, οἱονεὶ τὸν χρόνον, μεταβολῇ τῶν ἀντιστοίχων· σύνεστι δὲ τῇ τῶν στοιχείων τάξει ἐξ ἀνάγκης ὁ χρόνος*: for *μέρη τοῦ χρόνου* Serv. *ad Aen.* III. 104, *dicitur deus esse aeternitatis et saeculorum. saecula autem annos ex se natos in se reuoluunt*: cf. also Chrysipp. fr. 1087, 1091, Arnim, St Aug. *Ciu. D.* VI. 8, *quod longinquitas temporis, quae Saturni nomine significatur, quidquid gignit ipsa consumit*, and for the idea that the parts of time or of a period are its children, Nonn. *Dion.* XL. 372, Cleobul. *A.P.* XIV. 101.

my opinion about them is this: I believe that the Greeks who were accounted wise spoke of old in riddles and not straight out, and accordingly I conjecture that this story about Kronos is a bit of Greek philosophy. In matters of religion I will follow tradition[39].' The Christians attacked this legend with vigour[40].

The worst way of interpreting myths is the materialistic, favoured by the Egyptians. To say that elements, plants, stones, animals belong to gods is reasonable: to identify them with those gods is madness.

The Greeks, as Prof. Geffcken has observed, vacillated between warm admiration and hearty contempt of Egyptian ways[41]. Iamblichus maintained the former attitude; his *De mysteriis* shows clearly that he would have accepted the description of Egypt as *mundi totius templum* in the Hermetic *Asclepius*, attributed to Apuleius (ch. 24). But the Julianic reaction was definitely Greek. Julian uses Ἑλληνισμός for 'paganism,' Ἕλλην, Ἑλληνικός, Ἑλληνιστής for 'pagan[42].' (It is perhaps to him that we must trace this linguistic usage, which was destined to a long life[43].)

39 VIII. 8. 3, translated by J. G. Frazer. Noteworthy is a phrase in a Cyprian *defixio* (L. Macdonald, *Proc. Soc. Bibl. Arch.* XVII. Feb. 1891), viii. 33, ἐξορκίζω ὑμᾶς τοὺς ἀπὸ Κρόνου ἐκτεθέντας θεούς.

40 Cf. Aristid. *Apol.* 9, Athenag. *Leg.* 22, Julian, *In Christianos*, p. 167 Neumann. Macrob., *Comm. in Somn. Scip.* I. ii. 11, mentions Saturn's treatment of Caelus and his worsting by his son as a typical example of a difficult myth.

41 *Apol.* p. ix.

42 *Ep.* 84 *a* (=49 H.), ὁ Ἑλληνισμὸς οὔπω πράττει κατὰ λόγον, and many references in Bidez-Cumont, *index*, 302 *b*. It will be remembered that Julian's philhellenism led him to send an account of his reasons for marching to seize power to the states of Athens, Sparta and Corinth. (But in his description of Sallustius, probably our author, as ἄνδρα εἰς τοὺς πρώτους τῶν Ἑλλήνων τελοῦντα (p. 252 A), Ἕλλην can hardly mean 'pagan,' as Constantius was still reigning: so Cumont, *Rev. phil.* XVI. 524.)

43 So Ἕλλην Eunap. fr. 80, *F.H.G.* IV. p. 49 (=p. 524 Boissonade), *Vita Aedesii*, p. 29 Boiss., Greg. Naz. *Orat.* IV. 30 (XXXV. p. 557 Migne), Sozomen, *H.E.* V. 4. 3, Damasc., *Vit. Isid. ap.* Phot. *Bibl.* 242, p. 342 *b* 6, 348 *b* 30, *Cod. Just.* I. I. 10, Marcus Diac. *Vita Porph.* xxi., Suid. s.v. Τριβωνιανός, II. ii, p. 1204. 12, Niceph. Blemm. Ode VII. l. 82, p. 130 Heisenberg, a prayer in A. Vassiliev, *Anecdota graecobyzantina*, I. p. 344, Lebas-Waddington, 638.

Ἑλληνικός, Phot. *Bibl.* cod. 163, p. 107 *a* 9 Bekker, Suidas s.v. Διοκλητιανός, I. i. p. 1384. 2, Niceph. Greg. *ap.* Lambec. *Bibl. Caes.* VIII. p. 140 A: a supposedly pagan settlement on Cythnus is called Ἑλληνικά to this day (Bürchner, *P. W.* XII.

Sallustius, like Julian, is chiefly concerned with saving the traditional Greek religion as interpreted by the later Neoplatonism. He could not prejudice his case by trying to defend Egyptian cults, which presented a vulnerable side to Christian polemic. In the latter it was continually stated that the pagans worshipped the elements, and the charge was not without foundation; it was certainly held by Greek thinkers that the Egyptians worshipped the elements[44]. Sallustius urges that the elements belong to the deities, just as wine belongs to Dionysus; but they are not the deities; wine is not Dionysus. He compares sacred animals, plants, and stones, which cannot be called gods except by a figure of speech. (It should, however, perhaps be observed that animals were worshipped in Egypt[45], plants invested with some measure of occult power in popular superstition[46], and sacred stones commonly adored[47].)

222. 47, to which fact Mr C. T. Seltman has drawn my attention), as are certain ruins between Astros and Sparta (J. G. Frazer, *Comm. on Pausanias*, III. 308: *-iko*).

Ἑλληνιστής, Sozomen, III. 17: Ἑλληνισμός, *ib.* V. 4.

Ἑλληνικῶς, Sozomen, III. 17. For the close association of Greek culture and paganism cf. p. l *infra*.

[44] Cf. Geffcken, *Apol.*, 49 f. (The Christians could use Epicurean polemic against Stoic allegorisation; cf. Philippson, *Hermes*, LV. 225 ff.) For the Greek views of Egyptian worship mentioned cf. Diod. Sic. I. 12, Plut. *Is. et Os.* 32, p. 363 D, also note *P. Leid.*, J. 384, col. vii. 23, ἐγώ εἰμι Ὄσιρις ὁ καλούμενος ὕδωρ, ἐγώ εἰμι Ἶσις ἡ καλουμένη δρόσος, ἐγώ εἰμι Ησενεφυς ἡ καλουμένη ἔαρ. For the identification of Kronos with water, p. 6. 5, cf. Chrysipp. fr. 1076, 1089 Arnim and note Philolaus, A 14 Diels, i. p. 305. 18. For Adonis as καρπός cf. Glotz, *Rev. Ét. grecques*, 1920, 214 f.

[45] Cf. Th. Hopfner, *Tierkult der alten Ägypter* (*Wien. Denkschr.* LVII. ii. 1913). Perdrizet, *Monuments Piot*, XXV. 367 ff. argues that it grew in importance in the Ptolemaic period. Of interest are two representations of the adoration of a sacred animal in the mural painting of the peristyle of the villa of Eutyches at Pompeii, *Notizie degli scavi*, 1922, 470 fig. 9.

[46] Cf. *Folklore*, XXXVI. (1925), 93 ff.

[47] Cf. Lucr. V. 1196, Theophr. *Char.* xvi., and for Minoan stone-cults, A. Evans, *J.H.S.* XXI. 99 ff. (add *ib.*, XLIV. 269: baetyl in sanctuary at Mallia in Crete), for Syrian baetyl-worship F. C. Conybeare, *Trans. III Congr. Hist. Rel.* II. 177, for a stone-cult on Latmos in the tenth century A.D. Usener, *Kl. Schr.* IV. 198: a curious statement is made by [Apul.] *Ascl.* 38, *Et horum, o Trismegiste, deorum, qui terreni habentur, cuius modi est qualitas? constat, O Asclepi, de herbis, de lapidibus, et de aromatibus diuinitatis naturam in se habentibus.* λίθοι could also refer to gems, some of which were sacred to particular deities, cf. A. Ludwich, *Maximus et Ammon*, 121. 8, Anon. ed. J. Mesk, *Wien. Stud.* XX. 320. 8.

Yet this rejection of Egyptian ideas is somewhat surprising, in view of the fact that Julian was a warm adherent of the cult of their gods; the latter appear frequently on his coins, and are mentioned with reverence in his writings[48].

Further, there is the mixed variety of myths, as for example that of the Judgment of Paris.

This contains

i. a theological element, since the supramundane powers of the gods are indicated by their being together[49]:

ii. a physical element, since the composition of the universe from united opposites is indicated by the statement that the apple was thrown by Strife, and the varied gifts of the deities are signified by their supposed rivalry for the apple[50]:

iii. a psychical element; the soul living in accordance with the senses sees beauty and none of the other powers in the universe[51].

The myth here defended had been much criticised[52].

Each kind of myth has its special appropriateness; theological myths suit philosophers, physical and psychical myths poets, mixed myths mysteries, the function of which is to give us union with the universe and with the gods.

So Julian, in the speech quoted earlier, states (p. 216 B) that myths are unbecoming to the parts of philosophy concerned with logic, natural science, and mathematics; at most, he says, they suit that branch of practical philosophy which

[48] Cf. G. Macdonald, *Coin Types*, 232; what Julian says of the Egyptian deities will be found conveniently collected in Th. Hopfner, *Fontes historiae religionis Aegyptiacae*, 538 ff.

[49] Cf. Procl. *Proleg. in Hesiodum*, p. 4. 15 Gaisford, *τῆς μὲν Πιερίας τὴν ὑπὲρ τὸν κόσμον τάξιν δηλούσης.*

[50] Cf. Pherecyd. B 3 Diels, ii. p. 203: (sc. ὁ Ζεύς = Ἔρως) *τὸν κόσμον ἐκ τῶν ἐναντίων συνιστάς*, Heraclit. B 67 Diels, i. p. 90, [Arist.] *De mundo*, p. 396 *b* 7. Νεῖκος played a leading part in the cosmogony of Empedocles (as A 33 Diels, i. p. 205).

[51] For *ἡ κατ' αἴσθησιν ζῶσα ψυχή* cf. Iambl. *De myst.* III. 4, also *κατὰ νοῦν*, *ap.* Stob. II. 8. 44, p. 173. 19, *κατ' ἀρετήν*, xxi. *infra*, Procl. ad Hes. *Op. et Di.* 288, p. 199. 11 Gaisford. Porphyry, *De abst.* III. 19, says *ἐπ' αἰσθήσει μόνον ζῶντας.*

[52] As by Agatharchides, *Geogr. Gr. min.* I. 116. 21 ff., and by the apologist Aristides, ch. 8. For earlier allegorisations cf. Türk, *Roscher*, III. 1591 f.

deals with the individual and that part of theological philosophy which relates to initiations and mysteries. This may well come from the source followed by Sallustius. The model myth given by Julian (p. 227 C ff.) might be classed as ψυχικός. This Oration and that in honour of the Mother of the Gods are coupled by Libanius in his funeral speech on the Emperor. Thinking, says he, that eloquence and piety were sisters, and seeing one completely destroyed and the other largely, he laboured that eloquence might prosper to the full and might regain its hold on men's affections; to this end he honoured those skilled in writing and himself wrote. Immediately he put forth two speeches, each the work of a single day, or, to be exact, of a single night; one of them smote hip and thigh a counterfeit imitator of Antisthenes, for defining Cynicism with unreasoning assurance, the other says many fine things about the Mother of the Gods[53].

To this notion of union with the gods (συναφή) we shall return[54].

Again, the story of Attis represents an eternal cosmic process, not an isolated event in the past. As the story is intimately related to the ordered universe, we reproduce it ritually to gain order in ourselves[55]. We, like Attis, have fallen from heaven; we die mystically with him and are reborn as infants. It is suitable that this festival should be celebrated at the vernal equinox, as also that the Rape of Proserpine, which symbolises the soul's descent to the underworld, should be said to have happened at the autumnal equinox.

[53] *Orat.* XVIII. 157, ii. p. 304 Förster = i. p. 574 Reiske, cf. for the association of Greek culture and paganism XIII. 1, *ἐπανήκει μετὰ τῶν ἱερῶν, ὦ βασιλεῦ,* [Julian], *καὶ τὸ τιμᾶσθαι τὴν τῶν λόγων τέχνην, οὐ μόνον ὅτι μέρος τῶν ἱερῶν οὐκ ἐλάχιστον ἴσως οἱ λόγοι, ἀλλ' ὅτι καὶ πρὸς τὴν τιμὴν τῶν θεῶν ὑπ' αὐτῶν ἐκινήθης τῶν λόγων.* For the suitability of myths to philosophy cf. Macrob. *Comm. in Somn. Scip.* I. ii. 11, *aut sacrarum rerum notio sub pio figmentorum uelamine honestis et tecta rebus et uestita nominibus enuntiatur, et hoc est solum figmenti genus quod cautio de diuinis rebus philosophantis admittit* (but Macrobius first rejects the story of the castration of Uranus by Saturn and the binding of the latter by his son as *quod genus totum philosophi nescire malunt*: he approves of myths like that of Er).

[54] p. xcviii *infra*.

[55] On the common notion, perhaps here implied, that man is a *μικρὸς κόσμος* cf. Lobeck, *Aglaophamus*, 920 ff.

This specimen myth is added as an awkward afterthought. It is a story which needed defence[56]. The explanation here given has the most obvious similarity to that given by Julian in his Oration in honour of the Mother of the Gods[57]. Sallustius has clear echoes of Julian's language[58], and the general sequence is the same in the two: myth, theological explanation, description of ritual, significance of time of rites, significance of the sacred season at Eleusis. Sallustius speaks of the myth, Julian, p. 173 A, of the rite. Julian gives a far more exhaustive treatment of the point and a different explanation, making the motive of the great mysteries in Boedromion the desire for defence when the Sun retires, the lesser mysteries being a preliminary rite in his presence. Moreover, Sallustius explains Cybele's love of Attis as arising when the primary gods were perfecting the secondary, and as resulting in the gift to him of the starry cap symbolical of heavenly powers[59]; Julian, p. 166 B, theorises more elaborately;

[56] K. Praechter, *P.W.* I. A, 1965. 30 ff., remarked that the story of Attis as here told has no connection with the classification of myths. For the criticism of the story by Christian writers cf. Geffcken, *Apol.*, 72.

[57] p. 161 C ff. The theory that Sallustius uses this passage directly, as Cumont urged, has been supported recently by R. Asmus, *Woch. klass. Phil.* 1904, 238 ff.

[58]

As Sall. iv. p. 8. 12, *ἔδει στῆναι τὴν γένεσιν*.	Julian { 167 B, *ἐχρῆν...στῆναι τὴν ἀπειρίαν*. 171 C, *στήσαντα δὲ αὐτὸν τῆς ἀπειρίας τὴν πρόοδον*. } (For *στῆναι* cf. Herm. *ap.* Stob. III. 11. 31, p. 441 W. = 386 S., *ἵνα μὴ στῇ ἡ γένεσις τῶν ὄντων*.)
p. 8. 14, *ταῦτα δὲ ἐγένετο μὲν οὐδέποτε, ἔστι δ' ἀεί*.	171 C, *καὶ οὐδέποτε γέγονεν ὅτε μὴ ταῦτα τοῦτον εἶχε τὸν τρόπον, ὅνπερ νῦν ἔχει, ἀλλ' ἀεὶ μὲν Ἄττις ἐστὶν ὑπουργὸς τῇ Μητρὶ καὶ ἡνίοχος, ἀεὶ δὲ ὀργᾷ εἰς τὴν γένεσιν, ἀεὶ δὲ ἀποτέμνεται τὴν ἀπειρίαν*...(cf. 169 D f.).
p. 8. 24, *ἐφ' οἷς ἱλαρεῖαι καὶ στέφανοι*.	p. 168 D, *ἐπὶ τούτοις Ἱλάρια, φασί, καὶ ἑορταί*.
p. 8. 28, *ἡμέρα δὲ μείζων γίνεται τῆς νυκτός*.	p. 172 C, *ὥστ' εἶναι τὴν ἡμέραν μείζω τῆς νυκτός*.

[59] For the starry cap cf. H. von Fritze, *Nomisma*, IV. 36 (Attis wearing it on coins of Pessinus), A. B. Cook, *Zeus*, I. 742, II. 385 f., M. Rostovtzeff, *J.H.S.* XXXIX. 89. It may be noted that *τελειῶ* (used p. 8. 8, *τελειούντων*) is a common verb in Iamblichus, as *ap.* Stob. I. 48. 8, p. 318. 10; he uses *τελείωσις ap.* Stob. I. 49. 65, p. 454. 21, *De myst.* V. 23, p. 232. This speculation is in the spirit of his school.

Cybele, the providence preserving things subject to birth and death, loves their creative cause, and bids it create in the world of things apprehended by the intellect and not sink to the material, which sinking is typified by the passion of Attis for a nymph. The discrepancy is comprehensible. Julian expatiates freely; Sallustius is writing for a world not initiated in the truths of Neoplatonism. He therefore simplifies, and incidentally explains a familiar attribute of Attis, the πῖλος. Other discrepancies are of less importance[60]. We must probably conclude that Sallustius used Julian's oration, but not without an independent exercise of his intelligence. How far Julian's treatment of the theme is original cannot be determined so easily. He claims as his own the identification of Attis, also called Gallos, with the Being of creative mind that makes all things down to the lowest grade of matter: yet even here he is applying the theories of Iamblichus to the story. He seems to have clothed in that philosopher's terminology a traditional belief very like that of the Naassenes, as recorded by Hippolytus, or that of the *Poimandres*[61]. Sallustius does not follow his more elaborate developments of the theme.

Some points of detail require discussion. Rhea, whose identification with the Phrygian Mother of the gods had long been commonly accepted, is in the *Oracula Chaldaica*, a Gnostic compilation probably of the end of the second century A.D., credited with possessing and disseminating the powers or δυνάμεις of all things, which illustrates Cybele's

[60] Julian adds an appendix (p. 174 A ff.) on fasting (for the religious importance of which custom cf. O. Kern, *Orphica*, 47, p. 118 = Diels, *Vors.*[4], 66 B 21, ii. p. 178). He mentions the time at which the festival occurs at an earlier point than Sallustius. Passamonti, *Rendiconti acc. Lincei*, 1892, 724 f., notes other differences in this section; they are probably to be explained as simplifications by Sallustius, who certainly had a mind of his own.

[61] *C.H.* I. 14: Julian's claim to originality is made p. 161 C. On this question I accept the conclusions of H. Bogner, *Philol.* LXXIX. (1923), 258 ff., esp. 260 f. He is hardly on safe ground in arguing Julian's independence in interpreting the nature of Attis from the fact that Macrob., *Sat.* I. 21. 9, explains Attis otherwise, as solar; though it is probable (it cannot be called certain) that Macrobius follows Iamblichus in this matter, yet we must reckon with the possibility that he may have given something like this explanation in a lost work. Still, the general probabilities are in favour of Julian's having himself made this application of philosophic theory to the myth.

gift of heavenly powers to Attis[62]. The view of Sallustius (p. 8. 7) that matter begins at the Milky Way occurs in Julian, but not, it seems, elsewhere[63]. The normal Greek idea was that the moon is the upper boundary of the world of Becoming (as opposed to the higher regions of Being); the Milky Way is commonly the path of the Sun, the path of the gods, or the path of the blessed dead[64]. The notion that the Nymphs preside over Becoming (p. 8. 10) may in part originate in cult; they are called γενέθλιαι in an inscription found at Phaleron[65]. Sallustius speaks cautiously of the way in which Attis left Cybele, possibly to avoid any suggestion of imperfection in the divine nature; Julian talks plainly of his παραφροσύνη or infatuation[66]. As for πεσόντες ἐξ οὐρανοῦ (p. 8. 19), the belief that man is a fallen god is an old one in Greece; we find it in Empedocles, in the Orphic tablets, and in other Neoplatonic texts[67]. The doctrine of the descent of the soul from heaven

[62] Cf. Kroll, *De oraculis Chaldaicis* (*Bresl. phil. Abh.* VII. i.), 30, and for its date and sources 66 ff. The fragment in question says (Ῥείη) πάντων γὰρ πρώτη δυνάμεις κόλποισιν ἀφράστοις | δεξαμένη γενεὴν ἐπὶ πᾶν(?) προχέει τροχάουσαν; cf. Hippol. *Refut.* V. 17. 2, p. 114. 20 Wendland, ἀναλαμβάνει τὰς δυνάμεις, and for the actual phrase δυνάμεις γονίμους cf. Iambl. *De myst.* II. 1, p. 67. 15 f. Julian, p. 166 A, agrees in sense. For the epithet ζωογόνος (p. 8. 3), cf. Cornut. *Theol.* 6, p. 6. 7 f. Lang, κωδίαν δ' ἀνατιθέασιν αὐτῇ (*sc.* τῇ Ῥέᾳ) παριστάντες ὅτι αἰτία τῆς ζωογονίας αὕτη ἐγένετο.

[63] Julian, p. 165 C, 171 A. H. Bogner, *l.c.* 275, suggests that this idea is due to the verbal similarity of Γάλλος and Γαλαξίας, and remarks well that Julian returns to the common view that the moon is the boundary in saying, p. 165 D, τὸν τῶν ἐνύλων καὶ ὑπὸ σελήνην εἰδῶν συνοχέα. Macrob., *Comm. in Somn. Scip.* I. xii., attributes to Pythagoras the notion that the realm of Dis begins at the Milky Way.

[64] Cf. Gundel, *P. W.* VII. 560 ff. In Iambl. *ap.* Stob. I. 49. 39, p. 378. 12, Heraclides Ponticus is credited with the view that souls descend to earth from the Milky Way.

[65] Ἐφημερὶς Ἀρχαιολογική, 1909, 244 ff., *fig.* 1: cf. also their function in mythology of nursing Dionysus. As for πᾶν γὰρ τὸ γινόμενον ῥεῖ (p. 8. 11), it is an obvious recollection of the Heraclitean ῥεῖν τὰ ὅλα ποταμοῦ δίκην (Diog. Laert. IX. 1. 8); it may be recalled that Geffcken, *Ausgang*, 284, has drawn attention to the frequency with which Iamblichus quotes Heraclitus.

[66] p. 167 D. For the possibility of divine overstepping of limits cf. Heraclit., B 94 Diels, i. p. 96, ἥλιος γὰρ οὐχ ὑπερβήσεται μέτρα, εἰ δὲ μή, Ἐρινύες μιν Δίκης ἐπίκουροι ἐξευρήσουσιν. Julian modifies the word, τῆς τοῦ Ἄττιδος λεγομένης π.

[67] Cf. for Empedocles, B 119 Diels, i. p. 268, B 115, p. 267 (he is a god on earth, B 112, p. 264); for the Orphics, B 18 Diels, ii. p. 176 (=Olivieri, *Lamellae aureae Orphicae*, A 3, p. 4=O. Kern, *Orphica*, 32 *c*, p. 106); for Neoplatonists, Porph.

is mentioned by the rhetorician Menander as a familiar commonplace[68]; its passage through the planetary spheres was embellished with much detail[69]. Its divinity might be recovered at death[70], or by appropriate ritual[71]. Gruppe concluded that it is probable, but not certain, that the rites of Attis were held to confer immortality; Prudentius clearly states that he who had received the *taurobolium*, that strange bedrenching in the blood of a bull, was adored by those

Sent. 32, πεσούσης δὲ εἰς σώματα (*sc.* τῆς ψυχῆς), Procl. *Inst. Theol.* 206, κατιέναι εἰς γένεσιν.

[68] Περὶ ἐπιδεικτικῶν 9, ix. p. 283. 17 Walz, συγγενὴς γὰρ οὖσα τοῦ θεοῦ ἡ ψυχὴ κἀκεῖθεν κατιοῦσα σπεύδει πάλιν ἄνω πρὸς τὸ συγγενές; cf. Kroll, *P.W.* VIII. 816.

[69] Cf. Lobeck, *Aglaophamus*, 932 ff., A. B. Cook, *J.H.S.* XV. 16.

[70] So we read in an Orphic inscription (B 19^a 4, ii. p. 177 Diels = Olivieri B^2 p. 18 = Kern, 32 g, p. 108) νόμῳ ἴθι δῖα γεγῶσα, in a tablet of gold-foil (B 17, p. 175 Diels = Olivieri ba^1 p. 12 = Kern, 32 a, p. 105) καὶ τότ' ἔπειτ' ἄλλοισι μεθ' ἡρώεσσιν ἀνάξεις. Cf. the oracle given to Julian (Eunap. *Hist.* fr. 26 Dindorf = *F. H. G.* IV. 25) ἥξεις δ' αἰθερίου φάεος πατρώιον αὐλήν, | ἔνθεν ἀποπλαγχθεὶς μεροπήιον ἐς δέμας ἦλθες.

[71] So possibly we should interpret the Orphic θεὸς ἐγένου ἐξ ἀνθρώπου B 20. 9, p. 177 Diels = Olivieri c A^2 p. 16 = Kern 32 f, p. 108). Zalmoxis is said to have taught the Getae a ritual to make themselves immortal (cf. Hdt. IV. 94, G. Kazarow, *Klio*, XII. 355 ff.). The question of how man could become god interested men deeply. In *P. Berol.* 13044, col. iii. 28 ff. (U. Wilcken, *Sitz. Ber. preuss. Akad.* 1923, 161 f.), Alexander asks a Gymnosophist τί ποιῶν ἄν τις γένοιτο θεός; and receives the unsatisfactory answer ὃ μὴ δυνατόν ἐστιν ἀνθρώπῳ ποιῆσαι εἰ ποιήσειέν τις (as we read later in Plut. *Alex.* 64). Religion might offer a solution; a Syrian dedication to Leucothea (Cumont, *Cat. Sculpt. Inscr. Mus. Cinquantenaire*^2, 166 ff., n. 141) has the phrase τοῦ ἀποθεωθέντος ἐν τῷ λέβητι, which refers to some ritual pretence of boiling in a cauldron of regeneration (cf. L. R. Farnell, *J.H.S.* XXXVI. 41 ff.). Magic also might help; an ἀπαθανατισμός is preserved in the great magical papyrus of Paris. Dieterich, indeed, called this a *Mithrasliturgie*, and his view has won the support of Th. Hopfner, *Griechisch-Ägyptischer Offenbarungszauber*, II. 58, § 116, but it is probably right to follow Cumont, *Revue de l'instruction publique en Belgique*, 1904, 1 ff., in regarding it as a product of syncretism in Egypt.

Religious ecstasy can of course produce a belief in the worshipper that he is identified with the god, cf. Dieterich, *Mithrasliturgie*^3, 97 f., 240, Rohde, *Psyche*^2, II. 14 ff., H. J. Rose, *Aberystwyth Studies*, IV. 26 (a probable explanation of Eur. *Bacch.* 580 f.: the character there called Dionysos in the MSS. is a votary who now feels that he is a Bakchos in the full sense, and has attained unity with the god). For the magical claim to be a particular deity cf. *P. Par.* l. 1018, *P. Lond.* 121, l. 334 Wessely = 326 Kenyon, 340 W. = 332 K., 506 W. = 498 K., Griffith and Thompson, *Demotic Magical Papyrus*, 47, 55, 83, 89, 105, 159, 185, 187, G. F. Abbott, *Macedonian Folklore*, 75 ('I am a Skantzos even as thou art'). For the Hermetic belief that man while still in the body can be or become divine cf. W. Kroll, *P. W.* VIII. 811.

present as divine[72]. The ideas of ritual rebirth and of the recommencement of life thereafter as a small child are to be found elsewhere in mystery religions of the Empire[73]. What is said about the fast (p. 8. 20) is important, as suggesting that enthusiastic devotees kept a fast from March 15th, when the solemnities began, till March 24th, probably with special austerity from March 22nd (the day against which *arbor intrat* is marked in the calendar); Sallustius distinguishes between abstinence from bread and other impure food, and *νηστεία*, or real fasting, after the cutting of the tree, ritually borne in on the 22nd. For the joyous celebrations which followed we have other evidence[74].

The argument on the seasons of festivals can be paralleled from Macrobius, who, in a section probably based on Iamblichus, infers that these rites are particularly connected with the Sun from the fact that the *Hilaria* is fixed at the vernal equinox[75]. Attis was so closely associated with the seasons that on a sarcophagus now in the Barberini collection his pine-crowned figure is substituted for that of Winter, and put with those of Summer, Autumn and Spring[76].

May my words give no offence to the gods or to the great dead who have written these tales!

So Sallustius closes his discussion of myths, as Herodotus his disquisition on Heracles[77].

[72] *Griechische Mythologie*, 1541_7; *Peristeph.* x. 1048, cf. Apul. *Met.* xi. 24 (Lucius, after initiation in the mysteries of Isis, is dressed as the Sun).

[73] Cf. *J.H.S.* xlv. 99, and on the ritual use of milk (p. 8. 24) also Procl. in *Rep.* ii., 129 Kroll (he connects the offerings of milk to the gods who purify souls with the belief that souls dwell in the Milky Way, and with the fact that milk is the first food of the newly born), A. B. Cook, *Zeus*, i. 785, S. Eitrem, *Opferritus und Voropfer der Griechen und Römer*, 102, 107.

[74] On the duration of the fast cf. H. Hepding, *Attis* (*R.G.V.V.* i.), 182 f., on the Hilaria, J. G. Frazer, *Golden Bough*[3], v. 272, D. S. Robertson, *J.H.S.* xxxix. 114.

[75] *Sat.* i. 21. 10: cf. *C.R.* 1924, 37, in support of Wissowa's view of this section (proposed in his Breslau dissertation of 1880, *De Macrobii Saturnaliorum fontibus*), and on the connection of festivals with phases of the year, M. P. Nilsson, *Griechische Feste*, iv. f.

[76] F. Cumont, *Rev. Arch.* 1916, iv. 7. Von Fritze, *Nomisma*, iv. 36 f., gives reason to believe that this conception of Attis is not a late product.

[77] ii. 45 *καὶ περὶ μὲν τούτων τοσαῦτα ἡμῖν εἰποῦσι καὶ παρὰ τῶν θεῶν καὶ παρὰ τῶν ἡρώων εὐμένεια εἴη.* This is an epilogue to the whole discussion of myths, not

v. **The reader must next learn of the First Cause and the divine hierarchy, of the nature of the universe, of mind and soul, of providence, fate, and chance, of virtue and vice, of the good and evil constitutions arising thence, and of the origin of evils. Each of these is a large subject; still, there is no harm in my treating them briefly, to the end that people may not be entirely ignorant of them.**

Sallustius here indicates the scope of his treatise from *τὴν πρώτην αἰτίαν* (p. 10. 14) to *ἀρκέσει ταῦτα* (p. 24. 15), after which come discussions of controversial points. He defines clearly his purpose in writing this epitome of necessary truth.

The First Cause must be one, for that is the supreme number, and all things must share in it. It is not soul or mind or being; it is good and superior to being: so the brave prefer the good to mere being.

The dignified position of the number One is a legacy from Pythagoras: we find it in the *Oracula Chaldaica* and in Neoplatonic texts[78]. Iamblichus describes the Supreme Being in a similar but more personal way[79]. The First Cause must be, says Sallustius, not mind[80] or soul, and must be superior to being. This last point is Platonic[81]; Sallustius supports it with an *argumentum ad homines*[82].

to the section about Attis (so Praechter rightly, *P.W.* IA, 1965. 61). A noteworthy parallel is Lucian, *Alex.* 4, ἀλλ' ἵλεως μὲν ὁ Πυθαγόρας εἴη.

[78] Cf. F. M. Cornford, *C.Q.* XVI. 140, XVII. 3 (he argues that the 'monad symbolises a primal undifferentiated unity,' cf. Hes. *Op. et Di.* 108). Kroll, *De oraculis Chaldaicis*, 15, Plut. *De uita et poesi Homeri*, § 145, p. 1183 A.

[79] *De myst.* VIII. 2, p. 262, ἀρχὴ γὰρ οὗτος καὶ θεὸς θεῶν, μονὰς ἐκ τοῦ ἑνός, προούσιος καὶ ἀρχὴ τῆς οὐσίας. ἀπ' αὐτοῦ γὰρ ἡ οὐσιότης καὶ ἡ οὐσία, διὸ καὶ οὐσιοπάτωρ καλεῖται. In *Corp. Herm.* V. 2, the Supreme Being is οὐχ εἷς ἀλλ' ἀφ' οὗ ὁ εἷς: *ib.* XVI. 3, p. 349 R., he is εἷς.

[80] Cf. Plotin. *Enn.* VI. 9. 2 f. on the Good, and E. Passamonti, *Rend. acc. Linc.*, 1892, 652 f.

[81] *Rep.* 509 B: cf. K. Schmidt, *Jahrb. phil. Fak. Univ. Götting.*, 1922, II. 72. Cf. Kroll, *P.W.* VIII. 805. 28 on the essential goodness of the Supreme Being in Hermetic texts. ἀγαθός implies moral perfection and in fact general perfection, cf. Philo, *Alleg. Leg.* I. 59, p. 54 M., ἡ γενικωτάτη ἀρετή, ἥν τινες ἀγαθότητα καλοῦσιν, ἀφ' ἧς αἱ κατὰ μέρος ἀρεταὶ συνίστανται, and Preuschen-Bauer, *Wörterb. N.T.*[2] *ss.vv.* ἀγαθός, ἀγαθότης.

[82] That is the meaning of σημεῖον, cf. *Rhet. ad Alex.*, *passim*: for the commonplace used cf. Liban. XXX. 41, etc.

vi. Next come the orders of gods:—(*a*) Those in the universe, twelve in number, three to create, three to animate, three to harmonise, three to guard the universe; a triad is necessary for each operation since each has a beginning, a middle, and an end; their duties are symbolised by the attributes of their cult statues. The other members of the Pantheon have a subordinate existence; so Dionysus exists in Zeus, Asclepius in Apollo, the Graces in Aphrodite. The twelve occupy the twelve celestial spheres.

(*β*) Those outside the universe: some make the being of the gods, some the mind, some the soul. They are treated in more recondite works.

The first division into mundane and transcendental deities is found earlier[83]. Sallustius refers for the latter to the treatises concerned with them: his interest lies in showing how the familiar pagan gods and goddesses find a place in the scheme, not in giving a complete exposition of philosophic dogma. For the three parts of each act we have a parallel in Iambl. *De myst.* II. 7, p. 85, but the triad is a natural combination of deities[84], and the number twelve as old as Pindar[85]. The

[83] Cf. Max. Tyr. XI. 12, and the distinction of *terreni* and *caelestes dei* in [Apul.] *Ascl.* 38, though the *caelestes* there do the work of our ἐγκόσμιοι: (cf. *unus quisque ordinem quem accepit complens atque custodiens* ∼ τρεῖς ἔχουσι τάξεις... οἱ δὲ ἡρμοσμένον φρουροῦσιν. Juppiter is merely the *dispensator* of the highest god, ch. 27 [cf. Kroll, *P. W.* VIII. 806. 19]; as here Zeus is one of the ἐγκόσμιοι, not the πρώτη αἰτία or even one of the ὑπερκόσμιοι). Comparable also is the distinction between πηγαί and ἀρχαί in the later Neoplatonism (cf. Kroll, *De orac. Ch.* 37). Iambl. *De myst.* VIII. 8, p. 271. 10, distinguishes περικόσμιοι and ὑπερκόσμιοι θεοί.

[84] Cf. Usener, *Rh. Mus.* LVIII. (1903), 1 ff., esp. 36, and add as further instances of triads Lykabas Sozon, Herakles, and Hermes on a coin of Thermisonium (*B. M. C. Phrygia*, 420. 10, pl. XLIX. 5), Apollo, Dionysos, and Demeter on a coin of Flaviopolis in Bithynia (*Recueil général des monnaies grecques d'Asie mineure*, I. 339. 38, pl. LIV. 16), a female triad on a terracotta figured by Winter, *Typenkatalog* (=*Die Antiken Terrakotten*, III.), I. 57. 10. The *Oracula Chaldaica* explained how the triad proceeded from the monad (Kroll, 18) and gave an arrangement of gods in four triads differing from ours (*ib.* 37). Proclus, *Theol. Plat.* VI. 10, p. 367, 22, p. 403, gives a similar account of the functions of the gods.

[85] *Ol.* X. 49, cf. Aristoph. *Au.* 95, Ditt. *Syll.*^{3} 180. 7, 181. 8, 589. 44, 961 n. 2, *Suppl. epigr. gr.* I. 468, B. Pace, *Annuario*, III. 71. 5: for *duodecim dei* cf. *C.I.L.* VI. 29848 *b*, Aust, *P.W.* IV. 910, and a Pompeian picture *Notizie degli scavi*, 1911, 420, fig. 2 *a*.

function of *harmonising* implies a survival of the belief held by Pythagoras and Heraclitus that the established order of things is a *ἁρμονία*[86]. Hephaestus here has a somewhat unusual eminence, for which Neoplatonic parallels exist[87].

The idea that divine character is indicated by the attributes of cult statues occurs in Julian and in Macrobius, and may therefore fairly be ascribed to Iamblichus[88]. It is important to note that the ancients conceived of the gods as thus represented; this is shown by various accounts of visions, and by a section of the *Oneirocritica* of Artemidorus dealing with the appearance of gods in sleep[89].

What is said of the subordination of deities is in accordance with tradition. The sonship of Dionysus was peculiarly intimate, and his cults blend with those of Zeus[90], as do those

[86] Cf. also *C.H.* XVIII. 14, p. 359. 27 R., *μίαν ἐργαζόμενος ἁρμονίαν τῶν πάντων*, Kroll, *De orac. Ch.*, p. 48.

[87] Cf. Orelli, *ad loc.* Chrysippus identified him with fire (Zeno, fr. 111, Pearson p. 156, cf. L. Malten, *P.W.* VIII. 338 ff.)

[88] Julian, p. 148 D: *Sat.* I. 17. 13; 19. 2, 8, 10; 21. 9. A point of contact may be remarked:

ὁ δὲ Ἀπόλλων λύραν ἁρμόζει...ἐπειδὴ ἁρμονία μὲν τὸ κάλλος ποιεῖ.	*Sat.* I. 19. 15, *ut lyra Apollinis chordarum septem tot caelestium sphaerarum praestat intellegi, quibus solem moderatorem natura constituit.*

(It need not be supposed that this type of argument was invented by Iamblichus.) With p. 12. 11, *γυμνὴ δὲ ἡ Ἀφροδίτη...τὸ δὲ κάλλος ἐν τοῖς ὁρωμένοις οὐ κρύπτεται*, we may compare Suidas *s.v.* *χάριτες*, II. ii., p. 1603, *καὶ παροιμία αἱ Χάριτες γυμναὶ ἤτοι ὅτι δεῖ ἀφελῶς καὶ φανερῶς χαρίζεσθαι* (a Stoic thought, cf. Sen. *De ben.* I. 3. 5). Sallustius argues from the Praxitelean type, which was used as a cult-type (cf. Lucian, *Amores* 13, Marcus Diaconus, *Vita Porph.* 59, *B. M. Guide to the antiquities of Roman Britain*, p. 122, fig. 136 [pipeclay copy of image in shrine], Lippold, *Gemmen*, 25. 8), not the conical stone of Paphos, or the older Greek types. At the same time, it should be remembered that the earlier types did under the Empire frequently surpass in popular esteem the finest products of Greek art (to the coin references given *C.R.*, 1925, 62, add Imhoof-Blumer, *Nomisma*, VIII. 1 ff. and C. T. Seltman, *Athens, its history and coinage*, 88 f.). How a fixed mode of representation was in fact part of the religious tradition is illustrated by an inscription in a Mithraeum at Ostia, *Notizie degli scavi*, 1924, 73, *deum uetusta religione in uelo formatum et umore obnubilatum* (*deum* probably being Juppiter-Caelus).

[89] Cf. Deubner, *De incubatione*, 9. 135, Artemidor. II. 37, p. 142 Hercher (the three chief art-types of Aphrodite mentioned): cf. *ib.* 39, p. 146, *κοινὸν δὲ λόγον ἔχουσιν οἱ θεοὶ καὶ τὰ ἀγάλματα αὐτῶν.*

[90] We have Ζεὺς Βάκχος at Pergamon (*C. I. G.* 3538 = *I. G. Rom.* IV. 360. 32),

of Asclepius and Apollo[91]; again, Aphrodite and the Graces are closely associated[92].

In assigning spheres to the gods Sallustius avoids the reproach of identifying deities with elements or planets[93]. Earth is the sphere of Hestia[94], water of Poseidon, air of Hera, fire of Hephaestus. We are not told by our author that Poseidon *is* water and Hera air, as Eustathius says[95], or that Hephaestus *is* fire, as the Stoics said. These four elements or *στοιχεῖα* are regarded as forming four zones or *σφαῖραι* beneath the planetary spheres, arranged thus:

FIRE
AIR
WATER
EARTH[96].

Above are the six planetary spheres assigned to their usual owners: Apollo has that of the Sun, Artemis that of the Moon; the places of Aphrodite, Hermes, Zeus, and Ares are obvious. The seventh and furthest from the earth, that of Saturn, is assigned not to Kronos but to Demeter, who in

Ζεὺς Ποτεύς by Lake Ascania (Ramsay, *C. B.* I. 337, *inscr.* 178), Ζεὺς κελαινεύς, hardly distinguishable from Διόνυσος κελαινεύς (*C. B.* II. 434), and Ζεὺς φίλιος represented as Dionysus (Pausan. VIII. 31. 4).

[91] Joint temple at Cyzicus, *I. G. Rom.* IV. 159. 17, joint cult elsewhere (K. Wernicke, *P. W.* II. 40).

[92] Cf. Pind. *Pae.* VI. 3, *Pyth.* VI. 1, Eustath. *ad Od.*, p. 1601. 5, Seneca, *De benef.* I. 3, 9; a possible joint cult at Paros (K. Tümpel, *P. W.* I. 2749): they were thought to be her daughters at Orchomenus (Serv. *ad Aen.* I. 720).

[93] There is no deviation from this in p. 12. 19 f. As Mr D. S. Robertson pointed out to me, Helios and Selene are the deities, not the heavenly bodies.

[94] Cf. Süss, *P. W.* VIII. 1293.

[95] *ad Il.*, p. 123. 24, 150. 41. The elements are personal in *Kore kosmou* (54, p. 403 W.=p. 486. 22 ff. Scott).

[96] A stele at Carnuntum (F. Cumont, *Jahreshefte* XII., *Beibl.*, 213, cf. *Études Syriennes*, 70. 101 f., Norden, *Aen.* VI.[2] 24 f.) depicts the soul's passage through air and water to fire: as an illustration of popular notions thereof cf. Aristid. εἰς Δία, I. p. 5 Dindorf (water and earth on a level: air above, fire still higher): for the way in which they took their positions, Manil. I. 149 ff., Philo, *De aeternitate mundi*, VII. 33. The physical doctrine involved and the use of σφαῖρα occur in Aristot. *Meteorologica*, p. 354 *b* 23, τοῦ γὰρ ὕδατος περὶ τὴν γῆν περιτεταμένου, καθάπερ περὶ τοῦτο ἡ τοῦ ἀέρος σφαῖρα καὶ περὶ ταύτην ἡ λεγομένη πυρός: for the conception we can go back as far as Anaximander 10, Diels i. p. 16, 18, φλογὸς σφαῖραν περιφυῆναι τῷ περὶ τὴν γῆν ἀέρι: whether he used the word we cannot say.

virtue of her identification with Rhea[97] was connected with him. Kronos might be one of the ὑπερκόσμιοι θεοί. The planets would probably be arranged thus:

SATURN
JUPPITER
MARS
SUN
VENUS
MERCURY
MOON

FIRE etc.[98].

The aether is assigned to Athena, not to Zeus, as is more common[99]. The heaven, that is here the sphere of the fixed stars, is shared by all the deities.

vii. **The universe itself must be uncreated and immortal. It is impossible that it should perish; therefore it cannot have had any beginning.**

There are, says Tzetzes, four views of the philosophers[100]:

(1) The universe is uncreated and imperishable.
(2) It is created and perishable (ascribed to Meton).
(3) It is uncreated, except for certain perishable parts.
(4) It is created, but by Divine Providence will not perish (ascribed to Plato and Pythagoras[101]).

The matter had long been disputed: Diodorus Siculus

[97] As early as the fifth century (O. Kern, *P. W.* IV. 2755), cf. Procl. *Theol. Plat.* V., p. 267. Porphyry *ap.* Euseb., *Praep. euang.* III. 11, distinguished Rhea and Demeter, which is of interest as illustrating the way in which Sallustius is not concerned with Neoplatonists earlier than Iamblichus. For ascription of planets to deities other than their homonyms cf. Roscher, III. 2527. 10 ff.

[98] Cf. F. Boll, *P. W.* VII. 2567 f.

[99] For αἰθήρ—Ζεύς cf. A. B. Cook, *Zeus*, I. 27 ff. (again, Porphyry maintained this, *Quaest. Hom.*, p. 200. 13 Schrader). For αἰθήρ—Athena, Muccio, *Studi Ital.* VII. 53, quotes Cornut. 20, Eustath. *ad Il.* I. 197, p. 83, Zeno *ap.* Diog. Laert. VII. 147: the aether had long been regarded as the home of the divine element in man (cf. Kaibel, *Epigr. gr.* 21. 5, [Plat.] *Axioch.* 366 A, and A. Fairbanks, *C. R.* XV. 431, A. C. Pearson *ad* Eur. *Hel.* 1014, *E. R. E.* I. 165), and Athena was connected with intelligence, cf. Julian, *In Galil.*, p. 179. 14 Neum.

[100] *Chil.* X. 527 ff., p. 384 Kiessling.

[101] Cf. Aetius II. 4. 2, *ap.* Stob. I. 20. 1, p. 170. 10 Wachsmuth (=p. 330. 18 Diels, *Doxogr. gr.*), where the view is ascribed to Plato, who does not use the word πρόνοια in *Tim.*, p. 41 B.

mentions views (1) and (2)[102], Philo in his treatise *De aeternitate mundi* (1), (2) and (4), quoting for (1) Aristotle and Ocellus, for (4) the *Timaeus* (at second hand[103]), Hesiod, and Moses. We may pause to analyse the earlier portion of this book.

Causes of destruction must be external or internal[104]. But there is nothing outside, as all things were put together to make the universe. The universe will continue to be one, because like matter will take the place of anything that fails[105]; whole, because all being has been spent to make it; unharmed by age and disease, because bodies attacked by age and disease are overthrown by heat or cold or other opposites from outside. Nor again will anything internal destroy it; the whole is stronger than the part, and what can face external perils is strong enough to endure internal also: so cattle, horses and men are liable to die of disease *because* they can also be destroyed by the sword[106]. This is corroborated by Plato, *Timaeus*, p. 32C. Since therefore the universe is imperishable, it must be uncreated; for dissolution is the fate of whatever has come into being, freedom therefrom of whatever has not; as the poet says,

τό τοι γενόμενον κατθανεῖν ὀφείλεται.

Again, when a compound perishes, it breaks up into its components. We men are composed of the four elements: on our death they return to their freedom, as the tragedian (Euripides, called ὁ τραγικός earlier, II. 6, as is Aeschylus in IX. 49) says. Such a compound is unnatural[107]. On the other hand, in the universe the elements occupy their right and proper places. Further, the nature of each object wishes to preserve it for ever: so must the nature of the universe.

[102] I. 6.

[103] This is indicated by φασιν, IV. § 13, and the passage is the famous θεοὶ θεῶν..., one of the commonest Platonic quotations in writers of the Empire. In quotations from this treatise the Roman figure gives the chapter in Cumont's edition, the Arabic the section as in the *editio minor* of Cohn and Reiter.

[104] So also Philolaus *ap.* Stob. I. 20. 2, p. 172. 13.

[105] This point is expressed more elaborately by Sallustius in ch. xvii.

[106] Cf. p. lvi *supra* for this style of reasoning.

[107] Here we have the old fifth-century antithesis of φύσις and νόμος. The source of the poetic fragment is unknown.

Now this nature is invincible and superior to all hostile forces.

There remains that argument on which very many pride themselves, thinking it irrefragable. Why should God destroy the universe? That He may not again make a universe or that He may make another? The first suggestion, that He makes disorder out of order and changes His plan, implies a defect of intellect in Him, and is unworthy of Him. As for the second, another universe would be worse than this, like it, or better. If it is worse, so is its Creator; if like, He has wasted labour in a childish way: if better, He has become better and therefore was imperfect when He made the present universe. But God is always like Himself and cannot become better or worse. We change and therefore what we make is perishable.

Stoic theories of the destruction of the universe by fire are untenable, for the destruction of the heavens involves the destruction of the stars, whom they regard as visible gods, and of Providence, the soul of the universe. Chrysippus is unconvincing. Since time has no beginning, neither has the universe[108].

This brief analysis shows a striking similarity to the discussion of the matter given by Sallustius here and in the excursus which forms ch. XVII. In the latter there are slight additions and omissions, but the essence of the argument and much of its detail is the same[109]. We have noted earlier that the core of Philo's thought is a school tradition, and this is particularly clear in the *De aeternitate mundi*[110]. It may

[108] Here follow detailed criticisms of some remarks of Critolaus, and later more objections to Stoic teaching: on these E. Norden, *Fleck. Jahrb. Suppl.* XIX., p. 440 ff., may be consulted. Since F. Cumont's edition (1891) there can hardly be any doubt of the authenticity of this work. Noteworthy in it is the similarity of XVI. 82 with Sallustius xvii. p. 32. 19; the relevant words are quoted in the critical note.

[109] Additions are:

(α) The destructive agent must be corporeal or incorporeal, but....

(β) The destructive agent must move in a circle or in a straight line, but....

(γ) Destruction must be in form or in matter, but....

(δ) Destruction must be natural or unnatural, but....

[110] As appears from its stock quotations, and from such phrases as ἔνιοι νομίζουσιν (17), φασιν (13, 79), οἱ φθείροντες αὐτὸν (sc. τὸν κόσμον) (72), τινες τῶν ἀίδιον ὑπολαμβανόντων τὸν κόσμον (113): conclusive testimony is afforded by § 39

even be, as Bousset argued, notes of a lecture taken down by Philo and written up by him[111].

The conclusion to be drawn is fairly clear. Though the tractate was known to S. Ambrose and to Zacharias of Mytilene, who show a knowledge of Philo's other writings, it is most unlikely that Sallustius was acquainted with it[112]. In him as in Philo we must recognise a school tradition, communicated by oral teaching or by a handbook. Some of its arguments were, it seems, used by Proclus in his lost work on the subject: but Proclus had learning beyond the range of handbooks[113]. The fixity of these traditional bodies of argument is further illustrated by the fact that Joannes Philoponus makes but seven Scriptural quotations in his reply to Proclus, a work which fills 646 pages in H. Rabe's edition. It is perhaps a fair inference that he found arguments ready to hand, and did no more than expand them[114].

The planetary spheres and the sphere of the fixed stars

ἀποδεικτικώτατός γε μὴν κἀκεῖνος ὁ λόγος ἐστίν, ἐφ' ᾧ μυρίους οἶδα σεμνυνομένους ὡς ἠκριβωμένῳ καὶ πάνυ ἀνεξελέγκτῳ, § 134 *ἔστι δ' οὔτε νέον τὸ λεγόμενον οὔτε ῥήμαθ' ἡμῶν, ἀλλὰ παλαιὰ σοφῶν ἀνδρῶν, οἷς οὐδὲν ἀδιερεύνητον τῶν εἰς ἐπιστήμην ἀναγκαίων ἀπολέλειπται*, and § 150 *ἃ μὲν οὖν περὶ ἀφθαρσίας τοῦ κόσμου παρειλήφαμεν, εἴρηται κατὰ δύναμιν*. In general cf. p. xxxviii, n. 123 *supra*.

111 *Jüdisch-christlicher Schulbetrieb*, 135 ff. I say 'written up,' since Cumont has shown that the language of the work is markedly Philonian, distinct as its thought is from his normal ideas (p. xv ff. of the Prolegomena to his edition).

112 Cf. Cumont, p. xv_6, xii ff. The isolated reminiscence of *Vit. Mos.* III. 24 in Heliodorus, *Aeth.* IX. 9, does not tell seriously against this view. Philo was later used by writers on the exegesis of the Old Testament, as Procopius of Gaza (Krumbacher[2], p. 126 f.) and in *Catenae* (*ib.* p. 215): he is mentioned by Arethas in his Commentary on the Apocalypse (*ib.* p. 130).

113 An attempted reconstruction of his treatise has been made by A. Vacherot, *Histoire critique de l'école d'Alexandrie*, II. 350 ff. With the words of Sallustius, p. 14. 1, *καὶ ὅτι ἀνάγκη διὰ τὴν τοῦ θεοῦ ἀγαθότητα...* cf. Procl. *in Tim.* 29 E (I. p. 367. 21) *ὡς γὰρ ὁ ἥλιος ἐν ὅσῳ ἐστί, πάντα καταλάμπει καὶ τὸ πῦρ θερμαίνει... οὕτω καὶ τὸ ἀεὶ ὂν ἀγαθὸν ἀεὶ βούλεται τὰ ἀγαθά. εἰ δὲ ἀεὶ τὰ ἀγαθὰ βούλεται, ἀεὶ δύναται τὰ ἀγαθά, ἵνα μὴ βουλόμενος μέν, ἀδυνατῶν δὲ τὸ τῶν φαυλοτάτων ὑπομένῃ πάθος. οὐδὲ γὰρ ὁ σπουδαῖος ἄλλα βούλεται ἢ ἃ δύναται, εἰ δὲ ἀεὶ δύναται τὰ ἀγαθά, ἀεὶ ἐνεργεῖ τὰ ἀγαθά, ἵνα μὴ ἀτελῆ τὴν δύναμιν ἔχῃ· εἰ δὲ ἀεὶ ἐνεργεῖ τὰ ἀγαθά, ἀεὶ ποιεῖ τὰ ἀγαθά. εἰ δὲ αὐτὸς ἀεὶ ποιεῖ, ἀεὶ γίνεται κόσμος. ἀΐδιος ὁ κόσμος ἄρα· ἀεὶ γὰρ ἀγαθὸς ὁ δημιουργός ἐστιν* (also *Corp. Herm.* XI. 17: *ib.* XVI. 19, p. 354 R., the universe is coeval with God since all things are parts of Him: this is a pantheistic view which Sallustius would avoid): cf. E. Passamonti, *l.c.* 654 ff., for references.

114 A. Gudeman, *P. W.* IX. 1789. 23, notes the fact, and prefers to conclude that Philoponus wished to defeat the enemy on his own ground.

imitate mind and have a circular motion, the former Eastward, the latter Westward. The four elements imitate soul and move in straight lines, fire and air ascend, earth and water descend. All this has a purpose. Moreover since the celestial bodies differ in mode of motion from the elements they must differ from them in nature also and be devoid of the ordinary physical properties of matter. The universe being a sphere, since gravitation takes place towards the earth, the earth must be its centre.

These observations on the motions of heavenly bodies are traditional. Sallustius sees a purpose in them, as in all the order of the universe, of which he speaks in ch. IX[115]. The sharp distinction which he draws between the physical qualities of the elements and of the celestial bodies agrees with the general Aristotelian and post-Aristotelian differentiation of the sublunar and the upper zones.

The universe is seen to be a sphere, because of the Zodiac[116]. That the centre of a sphere is its lowest part is a doctrine well attested in antiquity[117].

[115] For planetary imitation of mind and motion in circles cf. Plotin. *Enn.* II. 2: for the contrasted motion of the elements in straight lines cf. Aristot. *De caelo*, p. 310 *b* 16, 308 *b* 13 etc., Philo, *De aeternitate mundi*, VII. § 33 (fire going upwards), Aristot. *De caelo*, p. 383 *b* 26 (air going upwards), and *Phys.* p. 214 *b* 14, *De caelo*, p. 308 *b* 14 (earth going downwards), *De caelo*, p. 312 *a* 26 (water going downwards), Herm. *ap.* Stob. I. 49. 69, p. 471 f. [Scott p. 528. 27 ff.] (fire and air upwards, water and earth downwards).

For the opposed motions of the sphere of the fixed stars and the planetary spheres cf. Cic. *De re publica*, VI. 17 Müller, Macrob. *Comm. in Somn. Scip.* I. 17. 7 ff., Joannes Philoponus, *De aeternitate mundi*, VI. 24, p. 198. 17 ff. Rabe, also Julian, p. 131 A.

The purpose, that the process of becoming might not be imperfect, is illustrated by *C. H.* IX. 5, *ἡ κοσμικὴ φορὰ τρίβουσα* (?) *τὰς γενέσεις ποιὰς ποιεῖ*, 7, *τὸ δὲ τάχος αὐτοῦ τῆς φορᾶς τὴν ποικιλίαν τῶν ποιῶν γενέσεων ἐργάζεται* (cf. W. Kroll, *P. W.* VIII. 808. 17 ff.).

[116] Muccio quotes well Philopon. *De opificio mundi*, III. 9, p. 129. 5 Reichardt, *τούτων οὕτως ἐχόντων ὀφθαλμῶν ἄρα μόνων χρεία καὶ τηρήσεως ἀκριβοῦς ἐξ ὧν τὸ σφαιρικὸν τοῦ οὐρανοῦ σχῆμα διὰ τοῦ ζῳδιακοῦ μέσον τὸν ὅλον τέμνοντος οὐρανὸν προφανέστατα δείκνυται.*

[117] Cf. Cic. *N. D.* II. 84, *medium locum mundi qui est infimus*, and for other references A. E. Housman *ad* Manil. I. 170 f., E. Bickel, *Philol.* LXXIX. 363; the Pythagoreans regarded earth as a *πυθμήν* (*Vita Pythag. ap.* Phot. *Bibl.* 249, p. 439 *b* 31). Concerning the tendency of heavy bodies to occupy the centre cf. Aristot. *Phys.* p. 205 *b* 15, and as a parallel to this statement of the fact of gravitation cf. Philo, *De aet.* VII. 33, Muccio, *Studi Italiani*, VII. p. 554.

All these things are made by the gods, ordered by Mind, and set in motion by Soul.

For this Mind and this Soul we have abundant evidence[118].

viii. **Our human souls are perfected by a divine Mind as sight is by the Sun[119]. Some are reasoning and immortal, some unreasoning and mortal; the former come from the primary gods, the latter from the secondary.**

This Mind which perfects our souls is part of the system of Iamblichus, wherein it ranks after Being and before Soul[120]. We find also there as here the doctrine that there are two kinds of souls: this is a marked feature of Hermetism, in which it was taught that certain individuals have divine and immortal souls, while others, lacking *νοῦς*, have mortal souls[121]. This conception of a limited immortality has its roots in Hellenistic philosophy, and is found in Gnosticism; it is clearly expressed in a fragment of the *Oracula Chaldaica*, and again by Iamblichus[122]. Further, just as Sallustius derives the

[118] For Mind cf. Iambl. *De myst.* I. 7, p. 21. 18, *νοῦς τοίνυν ἡγεμὼν καὶ βασιλεὺς τῶν ὄντων*, VIII. 3, p. 263. 7, *ὁ γὰρ δημιουργικὸς νοῦς καὶ τῆς ἀληθείας προστάτης καὶ σοφίας*: for Soul Iambl. *De myst.* I. 7, p. 22. 5 and *ap.* Stob. I. 379. 13, and the Stoic doctrine of the world soul, in Virg. *Georg.* IV. 219 ff. and *Aen.* VI. 724 ff.: for the term *ψυχή* Cleanth. fr. 21 Pearson, M. Adler, *Stoic. Vet. frag.* IV. 166. *Ψυχή* is a deity in Greco-Egyptian syncretism, cf. Reitzenstein, *Sitz. Ber. Ak. Heidelb.* 1917, x., K. Preisendanz, *Deutsche Litt.-Z.*, 1917, 1427 ff.

[119] P. 14, 21, cf. O. Weinreich, *Hessische Blätter f. Volkskunde*, VIII. 168 ff., and the Egyptian hymn translated by Erman, *Sitz. Ber. preuss. Akad.* 1923, 66.

[120] Cf. Zeller, III. ii. 794_0; for this view as found in the *Oracula Chaldaica*, Kroll, *Orac.* 47, in the Hermetic Corpus, *P. W.* VIII. 809.

[121] Iambl. *De differentia descensus animarum*, *ap.* Stob. I. 49. 40, p. 379. 22, *De myst.* V. 22, p. 223. 9: Hermes *ap.* Stob. I. 49. 49, p. 417. 16, I. 47. 8, p. 304. 8. A belief arose that the attainment of Gnosis could confer immortality on any (cf. *Corp. H.* I. 22 for the idea that the virtuous are given *νοῦς*, *ib.* § 28, *ἔχοντες ἐξουσίαν τῆς ἀθανασίας μεταλαβεῖν*), and that *every* human soul contained a divine element (Hermes *ap.* Stob. I. 49. 5, p. 323. 17), but there remains clear evidence (as *C. H.* IX. 5) for the definite conviction that immortality depended entirely on the soul's nature as given at birth; Herm. *ap.* Stob. I. 49. 45, p. 407 ff. W. (=494 ff. Scott, cf. § 69, p. 463 W.=514 S.) explains the origin of kingly souls, of noble souls, and of male and female souls (as also the reason why the Egyptians are the most intelligent of men). In the *Kore Kosmou*, § 16 (*ap.* Stob. I. 49. 44, p. 390 W.=p. 466. 3 ff. Scott) we read that all souls are alike immortal, but differ in quality; they belong to sixty grades, determined by the order in which they were made from the original soul-stuff, of which the second portion was inferior to the first, and so on.

[122] For the Hellenistic precedent cf. Cic. *De rep.* VI. 16, W. Kroll, *P. W.* VIII.

superior souls from the primary gods, the inferior from the secondary, so the *Oracula* derive the truly blessed from the Sun and from Zeus[123].

Soul is that by which the animate differs from the inanimate. The unreasonable soul is subject to the passions of the body, the reasonable despises it and contends against the unreasonable.

ψυχή is here defined as vital principle[124]. It is not stated directly here, but follows from X., that reasonable and unreasonable soul exist simultaneously in a man; this is a commonplace of Hellenistic philosophy. In Iamblichus also it is complementary to the general belief in two kinds of soul[125]; so in the *Poimandres* man is assigned a dual nature[126]. The struggle of the reasonable soul and the unreasonable is again a commonplace[127].

The soul must be immortal, because it knows the gods. Every good soul has employed Mind, and this is not brought into being by bodies.

That nothing mortal can know what is immortal is a

810: for Gnostic examples W. Bousset, *P. W.* VII. 1518. 64: for the *Oracula Chaldaica* W. Kroll, *De oraculis Chaldaicis*, 59, οὐ γὰρ ὑφ' εἱμαρτὴν ἀγελὴν πίπτουσι θεουργοί, and τοῖς δὲ διδακτὸν ἔδωκε φάους γνώρισμα λαβέσθαι, | τοὺς δὲ καὶ ὑπνώοντας ἑῆς ἐνεκάρπισεν ἀλκῆς.

[123] Cf. Kroll 58; in Plato, *Tim.* 41 C, the inferior deities add the mortal part of man, and so produce him.

[124] Cf. Steph. *Thes.* VIII., p. 1944 A; for αἰσθήσει, φαντασίᾳ (p. 14. 25) cf. Iambl. *De myst.* III. 26, p. 162. 7 (both predicated of ζῷα), also *Protrept.* V., p. 35. 14 (αἴσθησις and νοῦς distinguish man from plant); Herm. *ap.* Stob. I. 41. 6, p. 288 (=400. 18 Scott) allows the existence of αἰσθήσεις in a restricted form even in τὰ ἄψυχα. Sallustius does not divide ἔμψυχα in two classes, φυτικά and αἰσθητά, as does Max. Tyr. XI. (=XVII. Dübner) 8. On φαντασία cf. P. Shorey, *Cl. Phil.* X. (1915), 483 f.

[125] Cf. *De myst.* VIII. 6, p. 269. 1, δύο γὰρ ἔχει ψυχάς, ὡς ταῦτά φησι τὰ γράμματα (the Hermetic writings), ὁ ἄνθρωπος. καὶ ἡ μέν ἐστιν ἀπὸ τοῦ πρώτου νοητοῦ, μετέχουσα καὶ τῆς τοῦ δημιουργοῦ δυνάμεως, ἡ δὲ ἐνδιδομένη ἐκ τῆς τῶν οὐρανίων περιφορᾶς εἰς ἣν ἐπεισέρπει ἡ θεοπτικὴ ψυχή (cf. Sall., p. 20. 14, ἡ λογικὴ τούτοις ἐφεστηκυῖα...).

[126] *C. H.* I. 15, ἀθάνατος γὰρ ὢν καὶ πάντων τὴν ἐξουσίαν ἔχων τὰ θνητὰ πάσχει ὑποκείμενος (-α MS. corr. Casaubon) τῇ εἱμαρμένῃ: cf. Herm. *ap.* Stob. I. 49. 5, p. 323. 17 = p. 404. 13 S.

[127] Cf. Plaut. *Trin.* 308 f., Theag. *ap.* Stob. III. I. 117, p. 77. 12, Julian, p. 142 D, and in particular Herm. *ap.* Stob. I. 41. 1, p. 274 W. = p. 392 S.

thought commonly expressed[128]. Such knowledge is in virtue of divine Nous, used by every good soul[129].

It is in antithesis to the body, best when that is failing using the body as an instrument, it does not dwell in it, any more than the mechanist is in the machine: yet the soul can err because of the body's defect, as arts can fail from injury to the instruments.

The antithesis of soul and body is treated here as by Plotinus[130]. The soul's mode of controlling the body was a disputed point. Iamblichus gives six views:

(1) The soul directs the body as a steersman steers a ship. This does not tie it to the body.
(2) The soul is like a charioteer driving his chariot, and participating in its motion.
(3) Soul and body share a joint activity.
(4) The soul is a part of the whole living being.
(5) The soul is like the art directing the tools, as it were a living rudder.
(6) The body is for creation the slave of the powers that use it, but those powers are not bound to individual bodies[131]. (This is given as the view of the stricter Platonists, as for instance Plotinus.)

He allows that the body can cause the soul to err[132].

ix. **Divine providence appears clearly in the order of**

[128] Cf. Sen. *N. Q. praef.* § 12, *homo hoc habet argumentum diuinitatis suae, quod illum diuina delectant*, Lactant. *Inst. diu.* II. 8. 68, *ut Hermes ait, mortale immortali, temporale perpetuo, corruptibile incorrupto propinquare non potest*, and G. P. Wetter, ΦΩΣ 87, Dieterich, *Mithrasliturgie*³, 55 f., with O. Weinreich's note, 232.

[129] Cf. *C. H.* XIII. 22, *νοερῶς ἔγνως σεαυτὸν καὶ τὸν πατέρα τὸν ἡμέτερον*, Onatas *ap.* Stob. I. I. 39, p. 48, *ὁ μὲν ὢν θεὸς αὐτὸς οὔτε ὁρατὸς οὔτε αἰσθητός, ἀλλὰ λόγῳ μόνον καὶ νόῳ θεωρατός*: Julian, p. 130 B, *ὅσσα...τοῦ εἶναι καὶ λογικῆς ψυχῆς καὶ νοῦ μετείληφεν* (and G. Mau, *Die Religionsphilosophie Kaisers Julians*, 6 ff.): Reitzenstein, *Poimandres*, 241.

[130] *Enn.* I. I.

[131] *ap.* Stob. I. 49. 41, p. 382. For view (2) cf. *C. H.* X. 13, Kroll, *de orac. Ch.* 47. The description of the body as an *ὄργανον* is common, cf. Max. Tyr. XI. 7 (=XVII. Dübn.), where *νοῦς* and *αἰσθήσεις* are alike *ὄργανα* at the disposal of *ψυχή*.

[132] *De myst.* I. 7, p. 21. 15. For the analogy cf. [Hippocr.] *De arte* 8 (VI., p. 14 Littré=II., p. 204 Jones), Max. Tyr. XLI. 4, for its application *C. H.* XVIII. I ff., p. 355 R.

the universe and on a smaller scale in the human body. It is further demonstrated by oracles and miraculous cures.

This kind of argument for Providence is as old as Xen. *Mem.* I. 4. 6, and very common[133]. Sallustius reinforces it by a reference to contemporary oracles and cures[134]. The decay of belief in the former, lamented by Plutarch, was succeeded by a genuine revival of faith, notably in the prophecies given at Claros[135]. The consultation of oracles had been forbidden in 357 A.D.: Julian removed the ban[136]. Scepticism on this subject was old[137]. As for marvellous cures, the Epidaurian

[133] Cf. H. A. Koch, *Quellenuntersuchungen zu Nemesios von Emesa*, 47: for the rhetorical argument from the ordered heavens cf. Cic. *De harusp. resp.* § 19, *Pro Milone*, § 83 f. Pronoia was worshipped (Höfer, *Roscher*, III. 3121 f.) and Julian speaks warmly of her (cf. *ep.* 13, p. 16. 23, 30, p. 37. 24; *nb.* 11, p. 14. 10, τῇ τοῦ πάντα ἐφορῶντος Σωτῆρος προνοίᾳ).

[134] I say contemporary, because he says γιγνόμεναι, not γενόμεναι. The two are closely connected, as the article is not repeated before θεραπεῖαι. This corresponds to facts: miraculous cures were often ascribed to the performance of the commands of an oracle, so at Colophon, Aristid. XXV. i., p. 491 Dindorf, at Delphi, *inscr.*, *Klio* XV., p. 46 (Pomtow). The Amphiaraeum at Oropus was strictly speaking an oracle. Philostr. *V. Apoll.* III. 44 mentions ἰατρικὴ as one of the gifts of the mantic art; Iambl. *De myst.* III. 3, p. 108 speaks of cures due to obedience to dreams.

[135] Cf. Dessau, 3230, 3230*a*, 3230*b* (dedications made *secundum interpretationem oraculi Clarii Apollinis* in England, Dalmatia and North Africa), Keil-von Premerstein, I., p. 8.

[136] Cf. Picard, *Éphèse et Claros*, p. 125 f., and for the survival of the *sortes Antiates*, Macr. *Sat.* I. 23. 13.

[137] Philodemus mentions ineffectual prophecies in Περὶ θεῶν α', col. XXV. 10; *ib.* col. iv. he explains the inspired state (of such people as the Pythia) as due to physical causes. On wrong prophecies cf. Cic. *De diu.* II. 47. 99; the Cynic Oenomaus treated them at length in his Γοήτων φωρά: a typical Christian attack is to be found in *Mart. S. S. Carpi et soc.* § 17, p. 14. 23 Gebhardt. An interesting document of the second-century revival is a fragmentary papyrus containing a dialogue on oracles: the freethinker's doubts were perhaps settled by a coup de théâtre (W. Schubart, *Hermes*, LV., p. 188 ff.). For the continued celebrity of Delphi and its increase of prosperity under Hadrian cf. H. von Gärtringen, *P. W.* IV. 2578 ff.; L. Weber, *Philol.* LXIX. 228 has drawn attention to alliance coins of Side and Delphi, also of Perga and Delphi, dating from the latter half of the third century (but his view that they illustrate Hellenic national consciousness in its struggle with native cults is hazardous: Perga had Pythian games, cf. G. F. Hill, *B. M. C. Lycia*, lxxix., and Apollo had long been at home in Side, where he had perhaps a non-Greek element, cf. C. T. Seltman, *A hoard from Side* (*Numismatic Notes and Monographs*, 22, 1924), 10 f. A *rapprochement* with Delphi is therefore not remarkable, and we must be slow to infer much from it). At the same time many minor oracular shrines had become insignificant in the first century of our era (Plut. *De def. orac.* V., p. 411 E), and the oracle of

inscriptions show that their evidential value was realised to the full; we hear of unbelievers who were converted or solemnly warned[138].

This providence costs the gods no effort; they exercise it in virtue of a function, as the sun warms and illuminates. That dismisses the Epicurean objection, that we make the gods drudges. Providence, then, is the incorporeal care of the gods for our souls and bodies.

That God's care for the world costs him no labour is argued by Theon in a *θέσις θεωρητική* on the subject 'Do the gods take thought for the universe?'[139]. That He acts in virtue of a function, *δυνάμει*, is stated in the popular work *Περὶ κόσμου* wrongly ascribed to Aristotle[140].

Sallustius clearly alludes to the first of the *κύριαι δόξαι* of Epicurus[141]. Epicureanism continued to exist in the fourth century; Lactantius answers at length its case against the

Zeus Ammon declined in Hellenistic and Imperial times (A. B. Cook, *Zeus*, I. 353).

138 Cf. Ditt. *Syll.*³ 1168. 23 ff., 35 ff., with O. Weinreich's notes, also *Suppl. epig. gr.* II. 58 (4th cent. B.C.; confession of sin before multitude at Epidaurus by man who had failed to pay his vow to Asklepios). In the third century Philostratus mentions the fame of the temple of Asklepios at Lebena (*V. Apoll.* IV. 34, cf. A. Walton, *The Cult of Asklepios* [*Cornell Studies*, III. 1894], 114: we may note the frequency with which Asklepios appears on the provincial coinage of Crete under Trajan and Hadrian, cf. Svoronos, *Numismatique de la Crète*, 347 n. 79 f., pl. XXXIV. 17, and 350 ff. n. 101 f., 107 f., 113, pl. XXXV. 15, 23). In 384 A.D. Libanius in his speech on behalf of the temples speaks of people going to Cilicia (that is, to Aegae: though there were other Cilician cults of Asklepios, cf. A. Walton, *op. cit.* 116) and returning disappointed because the shrine had been destroyed (XXX. 39, iii. 108 Förster. The destruction is commonly ascribed to Constantine, cf. the note of Gothofredus *ap.* Reiske, II. 187, n. 78).

139 *Progymn.* 12, I., p. 250 Walz (he adds that God can have the help of daemones and heroes, and other deities). Such considerations could not be foreign to the rhetorical schools, where the prosecution of Epicurus for impiety formed a subject of *suasoriae* (cf. Himer. *Ecl.* III., *Proleg. in stas.* VII., p. 43. 21 ff. Walz, R. Kohl, *Rhet. Stud.* IV., p. 87 f.).

140 P. 397 *b* 22: God is the creator and preserver of all things, *οὐ μὴν αὐτουργοῦ καὶ ἐπιπόνου ζῴου κάματον ὑπομένων, ἀλλὰ δυνάμει χρώμενος ἀτρύτῳ, δι' ἧς καὶ τῶν πόρρω δοκούντων εἶναι περιγίνεται* (for *ἐπιπόνου* cf. Menand. *Ἐπιτρ.* 657 Sudhaus = 551 Körte²); p. 400 *b* 10, his task of ruling is *ἄλυπον ἄπονόν τε καὶ πάσης κεχωρισμένον σωματικῆς ἀσθενείας* (cf. Aesch. *Suppl.* 106, and W. Headlam's note *ad loc.* in his translation).

141 *τὸ μακάριον καὶ ἄφθαρτον οὔτε αὐτὸ πράγματα ἔχει οὔτε ἄλλῳ παρέχει, ὥστε οὔτε ὀργαῖς οὔτε χάρισι συνέχεται· ἐν ἀσθενεῖ γὰρ πᾶν τὸ τοιοῦτον*, p. 71 Usener = p. 51 Von der Mühll.

belief in Providence[142]. But there is no need to suppose that Sallustius had any first-hand acquaintance with Epicurean texts; he is here well within the bounds of the commonplace.

Fate is the ordinance of the celestial bodies, controlling human affairs and in particular our bodily nature. Fate does not compel us to sin; we cannot escape our moral responsibility. The most that can be admitted is that human weakness or bad education may turn Fate's blessings to evil; so sunshine is good for all, but may be prejudicial to the fevered.

Fate, *Εἱμαρμένη*, as a fixed conception owes its importance chiefly to the rise of Stoicism and to the spread of astral ideas in the Greek world[143]. The general idea that bodily health is dependent on celestial phenomena is older[144].

The definition given by Sallustius is in harmony with the idea which we find in the *Poimandres*, that Fate is the rule of the seven lords of the planets; man is subject thereunto in respect of the mortal element in him (as contrasted with the divine). In another Hermetic text we read that the 36 decans (each being lord of a third of ten degrees of the zodiac) are responsible for the overthrow of kingdoms, revolts (or de-

[142] *Inst. diu.* III. 17, cf. Zeller, III. i. 390_2. Yet Julian (p. 301 C=p. 141. 23 Bidez-Cumont) states that the gods have very properly destroyed most of their treatises, also most of the writings of the Pyrrhonic school. Zingerle, *Sitz. Ber. Ak. Wien*, CVIII. (1885), 969, has drawn attention to the definite polemic against Epicurean ideas of S. Hilary of Poitiers, and to the fact that its tone is that of polemic directed against views actually held by contemporaries.

[143] Cf. Gundel, *P. W.* VII. 2623 ff., Cumont, *Astrology and Religion among the Greeks and Romans*. The Stoics did not thus distinguish Πρόνοια and Εἱμαρμένη.

[144] Cf. [Hippocr.] Περὶ ἑβδομάδων xxiii., Riess, *P. W.* I. 38. For *θεῖα σώματα* (p. 18. 5) of the stars cf. Bonitz, *Index Aristotelicus*, 324 *a*, 4 f., Diels, *Vorsokratiker*[4], I. p. 306. 12. The moon is credited with creative powers by Julian, *Ep.* 111 (=51 H.), p. 171. 18 Bidez-Cumont, *τὴν δὲ ἐξ αὐτοῦ* (sc. *τοῦ ἡλίου*) *καὶ παρ' αὐτοῦ δημιουργὸν τῶν ὅλων Σελήνην οὖσαν οὐκ αἰσθάνεσθε πόσων ἀγαθῶν αἰτία τῇ πόλει γίνεται*; cf. [Apul.] *Ascl.* 3, *corporum quorum augmenta detrimentaque Sol et Luna sortiti sunt*, Plut. *Is. et Os.* 41, p. 367 D, *τὴν μὲν γὰρ σελήνην γόνιμον τὸ φῶς καὶ ὑγροποιὸν ἔχουσαν εὐμενῆ καὶ γοναῖς ζῴων καὶ φυτῶν εἶναι βλαστήμασι*; with causing childlessness and bereavement by Serv. Dan. *ad Aen.* III. 139 (cf. an epitaph at Cesi in Umbria, *Notizie* 1913, 361, l. 10 f., *duodeuiginti natales ni numerarem, | surripuit menses tres mihi Luna suos*); we find in Sext. Empiric. *Adu. math.* IX. 79 and elsewhere the theory that various creatures of land and sea wax and wane with the moon; in Dracont. *Romul.* X. 540 Medea, after slaying her children, says *accipe, Sol radians, animas, tu corpora, Luna, | nutrimenta animae.*

structions? *ἐπαναστάσεις* is ambiguous) of cities, famines, pestilences, overflowings of the sea and earthquakes, and their servants, the Hypoleitourgoi, cause destruction of animals in this or in that land, and swarms of creatures which damage the crops; in yet another we are told that Fate determines the assignment of souls to bodies, in a fourth that the soul chooses that mode of life which is in accordance with Fate, in a fifth that the heavenly bodies are responsible for the proportions in which the hot and cold are mixed in the body, and therefore for our development[145]. Iamblichus asserts that freedom from Fate comes thanks to the divine part of the soul, and speaks of human freewill[146]. In him we find, as here, the argument that our deficiencies may turn Fate's good gifts to evil, and the same simile to illustrate it[147]. The express connection of *εἱμαρμένη*, Fate, with *εἱρμός*, chain, occurs elsewhere[148].

[145] For view (1) cf. *C. H.* I. 9, 15, Gundel, *l.c.*, 2636 (according to Herm. *ap.* Stob. II. 8. 31, p. 160 W. = p. 446. 7 S., souls, that choose evil rather than good pass under the ban of Fate); for view (2) cf. Herm. *ap.* Stob. I. 21. 9, p. 191 W. = p. 414. 7 S. (and on decans cf. A. E. Housman, *Manilius IV*, vi. ff.); for view (3) cf. Herm. *ap.* Stob. I. 41. 7, p. 290 W. = p. 440. 5 S.; for view (4) cf. Herm. *ap.* Stob. I. 49. 4, p. 321 W. = p. 442 S. (*ἑλομένη βίον τὸν καθ' εἱμαρμένην* ingeniously combines freewill, as in the Platonic *αἰτία ἑλομένου*, with determinism); for view (5) cf. Herm. *ap.* Stob. I. 49. 3, p. 321 W. = p. 452. 6 S. We may further note the statement of Herm. *ap.* Stob. I. 5. 20, p. 82 W. = p. 434 S., *τῇ δὲ εἱμαρμένῃ ὑπηρετοῦσιν οἱ ἀστέρες· οὔτε γὰρ εἱμαρμένην φυγεῖν τις δύναται οὔτε φυλάξαι ἑαυτὸν ἀπὸ τῆς τούτων δεινότητος. ὅπλον γὰρ εἱμαρμένης οἱ ἀστέρες· κατὰ γὰρ ταύτην πάντα ἀποτελοῦσι τῇ φύσει καὶ τοῖς ἀνθρώποις.*

[146] *De myst.* VIII. 6, p. 269. 9, *ap.* Stob. II. 8. 43, p. 173; *τὸ αὐτεξούσιον τῆς ψυχῆς*, *ap.* Stob. I. 1. 35, p. 43, due, he says, to the correction of Fate by the gods. Of this dispensation by the gods he speaks also, *De myst.* VIII. 7, p. 269. 18, *θεοῖς...οὓς ὡς λυτῆρας τῆς εἱμαρμένης ἔν τε ἱεροῖς καὶ ξοάνοις θεραπεύομεν*; this is a belief which we find in Apuleius, who makes Isis say (*Met.* XI. 6) *scies ultra statuta fato tuo spatia uitam quoque tibi prorogare mihi tantum licere* (cf. *J. H. S.* XLV. 97). Sallustius says nothing of this.

[147] *De myst.* I. 18, p. 55. 12, *ἔτι τοίνυν ἡ ἀσθένεια τῶν ἐνύλων καὶ περιγείων [τόπων] τὴν ἀκραιφνῆ δύναμιν καὶ καθαρωτάτην ζωὴν τῶν αἰθερίων μὴ χωροῦσα τὸ ἑαυτῆς πάθημα μεταφέρει ἐπὶ τὰ πρῶτα αἴτια, οἷον εἴ τις κάμνων τῷ σώματι καὶ μὴ δυνάμενος φέρειν τὴν ἡλίου ζωοποιὸν θερμότητα ἐτόλμα ψευδόμενος ἀπὸ τῶν οἰκείων παθῶν εἰπεῖν, ὡς οὐ λυσιτελής ἐστιν ὁ ἥλιος πρὸς ὑγίειαν ἢ ζωήν* (*τόπων* seems an obvious gloss); cf. Nemes. *De natura hominis*, xli., p. 330. 10 Matthaei, *οὐχ ἡ φύσις αἰτία τῶν κακῶν ἀλλὰ τὸ κακῶς ἦχθαι.* For the idea that what happens is good for the universe as a whole cf. Iambl. *De myst.* IV. 8, p. 192. 3, E. Schröder, *Plotins Abhandlung* Πόθεν τὰ κακά, 1916.

[148] As [Aristot.] *De mundo*, p. 401 *b* 9, Philo, *De aeternitate mundi*, XV. § 75

The view here rejected, that the stars are responsible for man's entire life and conduct and can compel him to sin, was that common in astrology[149]. There were however dissentients[150], and a regular polemical literature in defence of free-will[151]. Some of the traditional arguments against astral fatalism follow.

If Fate rules all, why do whole nations practise queer customs? ⟨Their members cannot all have the same horoscopes.⟩

This commonplace is so briefly expressed as to be unintelligible unless so expanded. The instances quoted are usual. The eating of fathers by the Massagetae is mentioned by Philo (who calls them Scythians), Jewish circumcision by Philo, Bardesanes, Origen, Procopius, and *Anonymus in Job*, Persian incest by Bardesanes, Gregory of Nyssa, and the *Anonymus* (Philo ascribes this custom to the Scythians)[152]. Firmicus Maternus quotes the argument as applying to all national characteristics, physical and moral[153].

(cf. XXI. § 112), G. Rudberg, *Forschungen zu Posidonios* (*Skr. Hum. Vetensk. Samf. i Uppsala*, XX. 3, 1918), 104.

[149] We read of a particular conjuncture, *Pap. Soc. Ital.* 158. 28, ποιεῖ δὲ καὶ μοιχοὺς ἐπιψόγους, cf. Plut. *De aud. poet.* iv., p. 19 F, Toutain, *Cultes païens*, II. 195 ff., also *C. H.* XVI. 11, p. 352. 12 R., τὰ δὲ ἄλλα τὰ ὑπ' ἀνθρώπων τολμώμενα ἢ πλάνῃ ἢ τόλμῃ (?) ἢ ἀνάγκῃ ἣν καλοῦσιν εἱμαρμένην. Manil., IV. 117, declares *nec refert scelus unde cadat, scelus esse fatendum*; cf. Aul. Gell. VII. 2. On the view that determinism is dangerous to morality, cf. p. xlii, n. 10 *supra*, also Diog. Oen. fr. XXXIII. col. iii. 10, p. 41.

[150] Firmicus Maternus, *Math.* I. 8, mentions the view that the beginning and the end of life are fixed by fate, the interim being in our power; for the determination of birth and death cf. Claudian, *Cons. Stil.* II. 434 ff. Lucilius, *A. P.* XI. 159, would not allow astrology thus much.

[151] Well represented by Nemesios of Emesa, *De nat. hom.* ch. xli., who agrees almost to the word with Chalcidius, Basil, and Gellius (cf. Gercke, *Rh. Mus.* XLI., p. 266 ff., H. A. Koch, *op. cit.*, p. 37 ff.). Philo (*De prouidentia*), like Sallustius, first rejects Epicurean attacks, then turns against Stoic determinism.

[152] Much material on this topic will be found in Wendland, *Philos Schrift über die Vorsehung*, 1892, 24 ff. (tabular comparison, p. 30 ff.), F. Boll, *Fleck. Jahrb. Suppl.* XXI. 181 ff. As for circumcision, Philo mentions the custom also as practised in Egypt, Arabia, Ethiopia, Origen as in Arabia, and Bardesanes, Origen, and Procopius refer to the self-mutilation of the Amazons (Philo and Bardesanes (?) mention also Egyptian animal-worship). The allusion in Sallustius to Persian incest was correctly interpreted by K. Praechter, *B. ph. W.* 1893, 617. Julian, *In Galil.*, p. 217. 2, treats circumcision, presumably that he may taunt the Christians (p. 228. 21) for their failure to practise it.

[153] *Math.* I. 2.

Why do astrologers call Saturn and Mars malignant, and then represent them as good, attributing philosophy and kingship, military commands and treasures to them? If they talk of trines and squares, it is strange that human virtue should remain the same everywhere, but the gods change with their positions.

These inconsistent views on Saturn and Mars are well attested[154]. The second point criticised is the belief that the planets exercised different influences when separated by 90° and when separated by 120° from the Eastern horizon; this theory was earlier attacked by Plotinus[155]. Sallustius em-

[154] Saturn and Mars are proverbially evil, cf. Serv. *ad Aen.* IV. 610, Herm. *ap.* Stob. I. 5. 14, p. 77 W. (=p. 530. 13 S.: στυγνὸς Κρόνος), Mayer, *Roscher*, II. 1475. But for φιλοσοφία cf. Firmicus, *Math.* III. 2. 18, p. 101. 26, *in nono loco Saturnus ab horoscopo constitutus magos famosos facit uel philosophos opinatos...et frequenter facit philosophos capillatos* (*ib.* III. 7. 1, p. 155. 23, Mercury produces philosophers, *ib.* III. 12. 6, p. 183. 6, Mars and Venus), for βασιλεία cf. Vettius Valens, II. 16, p. 71. 9 (Mars and the Sun), also II. 11, p. 66. 16 (Mars in a certain position: γίνονται γὰρ ἢ στρατηγοὶ ἢ τύραννοι), I. 22, p. 45. 27 (Ζεὺς Ἄρης Ἑρμῆς...ἀποτελοῦσιν...ἢ βασιλικὰ ἢ πολιτικὰ πράσσοντας), Firmic. *Math.* III. 2. 10, p. 99. 19, *Saturnus...reges faciet ac duces et maxima largitur insignia potestatis*, *Pap. S. I.* 158. 54 (Mercury and Saturn in a certain position cause men managing great affairs to become famous): for στρατηγία cf. also Firmic. *Math.* IV. 21. 2, p. 260. 28, (*Mars*) *dat arma ducatus ac gloriam...aut certe claras artes* (cf. Manetho, *Apot.* III. 61 ff.), III. 4. 2, p. 114. 13, *facit bellorum duces sed* (=yes, and) *quibus omnis committatur exercitus*, § 26, p. 122. 25, § 28, p. 123. 22, § 29, p. 123. 29, *potentes duces ac totius orbis dominos efficiet*, § 30, p. 124. 8, *erunt quidem reges imperatores*, VIII. 31. 9. ii., p. 358. 25 (Jupiter and Saturn: cf. Boll, *Mem. R. Acc. Bologna*, II. v.—vii. (1923), 114); for θησαυρούς Prof. Housman has kindly indicated to me *C. C. A. G.* II. 161. 10 (Saturn is θησαυριστικός), Paulus Alexandrinus, fol. L. 4 (when Saturn is in the nether ὑπόγειον, the fourth of the temples beneath the earth, he is εὑρημάτων δοτήρ): cf. also Firmicus, *Math.* III. 2. 10, p. 99. 32, (*Saturnus*) *dabit substantiam et hereditates*, § 14, p. 100. 28, § 20, p. 102. 25, III. 4. 12, p. 117. 17, § 13, p. 117. 29, § 33, p. 124. 27.

In *C. C. A. G.* II., p. 200 (=O. Kern, *Orphica*, 289) we find the general statement ὁ Ἄρης εἰς Κρόνον, ὅσα ὁ Κρόνος εἴωθε βλάπτειν, σῴζει οὗτος ταῦτα (cf. another quotation, *Orphica*, 292). Iambl. *De myst.* I. 18, p. 55, refers to Saturn and Mars, but more shortly: this coincidence with Sallustius occurs shortly before that noted p. lxxi *supra*. Plot., *Enn.* II. 3. 6, attacked the view that Mars and Venus produce adulterers. (It should also be remembered that Kronos, the god of the planet Saturn, was in Syria and elsewhere sometimes identified with the Sun-god, cf. Boll, *A. R. W.* XIX. 342 ff., Reitzenstein, *Das iranische Erlösungsmysterium*, 177 ff.)

[155] *Enn.* II. 3. 3 f. For the theory cf. *P. S. I.* 158. 2 (τοὺς πλάνητας) μὴ μένοντας ἐπὶ μιᾶς πράξεως ἀλλὰ μετατιθεμένους, *C. C. A. G.* II. 204 ff., Sext. Emp. *In mathem.* V. 39, p. 734. 27 Bekker.

ploys against it a commonplace familiar to us from Horace's line

Caelum, non animum mutant qui trans mare currunt[156].

Finally, to cast in a horoscope good birth or bad birth of ancestors shows that some things are merely indicated by the stars, and not all things are caused by them: the position of the stars at the moment of birth cannot be the cause of prior events.

This again is a commonplace[157]. Sallustius seems however to make a compromise between the determinist view and that of Porphyry, who like Plotinus would not have allowed that the stars control events[158]; in this he may be following Iamblichus. The popular view was no doubt that which assigned absolute power to the stars[159].

Providence and Fate are concerned with peoples, with cities, and with individuals. So is Fortune, that function of the gods which orders for good diverse and unexpected happenings; accordingly cities, as being composed of diverse elements, ought to pay special honour to Fortune. Her power is limited to the sublunar region.

A place had to be found for Tyche, not in the aspect she presents in the Greek novel as a capricious mistress of events, full of spite and malice[160], but rather as she appears in an invocation by a lyric poet, 'O Fortune, beginning and end of mortals, thou sittest on a throne of wisdom and givest honour to the works of man. The good thou givest is greater than the evil, and grace shines around thy golden wing. That which is assigned by thy balance is most blest; thou seest an escape from helplessness in our distress and bringest a

[156] Cf. Eurip. *fr.* 1047 N²., Ou. *Fasti*, I. 493, Sen. *Dial.* XII. 8.

[157] Cf. Origen *ap.* Euseb. *Pr. eu.* VI. 22. 54 ff., Procop. Gaz. *In Genesim*, lxxxvii. 96 Migne (possibly based on a lost work of Origen's): cf. also Fauorin. *ap.* Aul. Gell. XIV. I. 20.

[158] Cf. Boll, *l.c.* 116. Cf. Zeller, III. ii. 622, and note Plot. *Enn.* II. iii. 7, *ἔστω τοίνυν ὥσπερ γράμματα ἐν οὐρανῷ γραφόμενα ἀεὶ ἢ γεγραμμένα καὶ κινούμενα*....

[159] Cf. *J. H. S.* XLV. 97 f., *C. L. E.* 470. 2, 963. 3, 984. 3, 1092. 3, 1536. 4, also W. Ensslin, *Klio*, *Beih.* XVI. (1923), 82.

[160] Cf. Achilles Tatius, *passim*, as IV. 9, *παιζέτω πάλιν ἡ Τύχη*, V. 7, *φιλημάτων ἐφθόνησεν ἡ Τύχη*, VII. 5. Herm. *ap.* Stob. I. 41. 1, p. 277 W.=p. 432. 13 S., describes Tyche as *φορὰ ἄτακτος, ἐνεργείας εἴδωλον*. Liban., VI. 1, speaks of reviling of Tyche as common. (Plutarch regarded her as helpful, but not to be trusted, cf. Geigenmüller, *Neue Jahrb.* 1921, 258.)

bright light in darkness, O most excellent of the deities,' and elsewhere in earlier Greek literature, as guiding men. Sallustius may also have had in mind the common cult of Agathe Tyche, Good Fortune[161]. He argues that cities should honour Tyche; so in fact they did, as late as the fourth century of our era[162]. The limitation of Fortune's power to the sublunar region is in accordance with a widespread idea that there is no change above the moon[163].

If bad men prosper and good men suffer poverty, it is not surprising; the good make no exertion to obtain wealth, the evil make every exertion. Prosperity will not free the bad from their vice, and the good will be content with virtue alone.

To this objection to belief in a beneficent divine order Sallustius replies as Philo had done. Hellenistic philosophy tended to assert with much emphasis that the good man is independent of external circumstances; this belief crystallised in the term *αὐτάρκεια*, self-sufficiency, which we meet as early as Democritus, and later find as almost a technical term among the Stoics[164].

[161] *Ap.* Stob. I. 6. 13, p. 86 (=*Anth. Lyr.* II. 158, n. 4 Diehl). Cf. A. C. Pearson, *Fragments of Sophocles*, I. 239 (*ad* Ἰχν. 73), L. Ruhl, *Roscher*, V. 1310 ff., and *Anth. Lyr.* II. 313 f. Diehl, also a gem engraved with the words Τροφίμου Σελήνη Τύχη γυβερνοῦσα (*C. I. G.* 7304: τύχην ed., but Σ. and T. may be identified. Is γυβερνοῦσα a Latinism, due to *guberno?*). For the cult of Agathe Tyche cf. Ruhl, *l.c.*; 1318, 1328 f.

[162] For ἐκ διαφόρων πραγμάτων συνίσταται (p. 20. 5) cf. xi., where the constituent elements of the state are discussed. For fourth-century worship of city Τύχαι cf. Sozomen, *Hist. Eccl.* V. 4. 2 (τύχαιον of Caesarea), Julian, *Apophthegm.* 176, p. 223 Bidez-Cumont (τύχαιον of Antioch); on its desirability cf. Nicol. *Progymn.* 8. i., p. 408 Walz=[Liban.] *Prog.* 25, viii. 529 Förster.

[163] The denial that evil exists there is attributed to Heraclitus and to Empedocles by Hippolytus, *Refutatio*, I. 4. 3, p. 9. 22 ff. Wendland (quoted by Diels, *Vorsokratiker*⁴, i. 210. 29). For the limitation of the power of Fortune to sublunar parts cf. *Vita Pyth.* ap. Phot. *Bibl.* 249, p. 439 *b* 36 ff.

[164] For this objection to belief in Providence cf. Enn. *Telamon*, i., l. 269 ff. Ribbeck³, *ego deum genus esse semper dixi et dicam caelitum, | sed eos non curare opinor quid agat humanum genus; | nam, si curent, bene bonis sit, male malis, quod nunc abest.* For the reply given by Philo, *De prouidentia*, I. 56 cf. Wendland, *op. cit.* 17, W. Capelle, *De Cynicorum epistulis*, 23. Democritus uses the word αὐτάρκεια, B 246 Diels, ii. p. 109. 19. Cf. also *Gnomol. Vatic.* 53, p. 66. 9 Von der Mühll, πονηροὶ δέ, ὅσῳ ἂν μᾶλλον εὐτυχῶσι, τοσούτῳ μᾶλλον αὐτοῖς καταλυμαίνονται, Zosimus Panopolitanus, III. 49. 3, p. 229. 16 ff. Berthelot (=Scott, *Hermetica*, I. 540), ὁ δὲ Ἑρμῆς καὶ ὁ Ζωροάστρης τὸ φιλοσόφων γένος ἀνωτέρω τῆς

x. Our discussion of virtue and vice requires a further treatment of the soul. The unreasonable element, when it enters the body, creates spirit and desire; the reasonable supervenes and produces a threefold soul consisting of reason, spirit, and desire. Their virtues are wisdom, courage, and moderation. The virtue of the whole soul is justice, in the full sense of the word. To attain this, reason must make the necessary judgment, spirit must obey reason and despise seeming dangers, desire must pursue not what appears pleasant but what is so in a reasonable way.

This chapter is connected directly with the preceding consideration of the sufficiency of virtue. It is based on the traditional Platonism of which something has been said earlier[165]. The four 'Socratic' virtues were familiar to rhetoricians[166].

Accordingly in men of education you can see all virtues, in the uneducated some but not others, though virtues in such circumstances do not deserve that name. The vices are the opposite qualities: the vice of the reason is foolishness, that of the spirit is cowardice, that of the desire is license, that of the whole soul is injustice. Virtues are produced by a good polity and good training, vices by their contraries.

εἱμαρμένης εἶπον τῷ μήτε τῇ εὐδαιμονίᾳ αὐτῆς χαίρειν (*ἡδονῶν γὰρ κρατοῦσι*) *μήτε τοῖς κακοῖς αὐτῆς βάλλεσθαι πάντοτε ἐν ἀϋλίᾳ* (*ἐναυλίαν* Berth.) *ἄγοντας* (so Scott for *ἄγονται*), *ib.* p. 230. 1 (the wise man will not use magic, but will let Fate do what it will with the clay that is its property), and further in defence of Providence, Himer. *Ecl.* III. 17. A gnomic *ostrakon* of the second century A.D. (*J. Eg. Arch.* VIII. 157) says, l. 6, [*ζήσεις ἐν ὄλβῳ*] *χρημάτων καταφρονῶν*. For the commonplace that riches do not give happiness cf. *Gnomol. Vat.* 81, p. 69 M., Varro, *Menipp.* fr. 36 Buecheler.

[165] P. xxxvii *supra*, cf. K. M. Westaway, *The Educational Theory of Plutarch*, p. 41 ff.: for the adjective *τριμερής* cf. Arist. *Top.*, p. 133 *a* 31, [Plut.] *De plac. phil.* IV. 4, p. 898 E (*ib.* I. 1, p. 874 E, of philosophy), Hippol. *Ref.* V. 47, p. 81. 6 Wendland, [Arist.] *De uirt. et uit.*, p. 1249 *a* 30 (this last popular work has a parallel to *δεῖ γὰρ τὸν λόγον κρῖναι τὰ δέοντα*: p. 1250 *a* 30, *τῆς δὲ φρονήσεως ἐστὶ τὸ βουλεύσασθαι, τὸ κρῖναι τὰ ἀγαθὰ καὶ τὰ κακά*. The classification of virtues and vices is there followed by the remark, p. 1251 *b* 29, *διὸ καὶ δοκεῖ παράδειγμα πολιτείας ἀγαθῆς εἶναι ψυχῆς σπουδαία διάθεσις*). A similar account of virtues and vices is given by the Pythagorean Theages *ap.* Stob. III. I. 117, p. 77. 3 ff.

[166] Cf. Menander, *περὶ ἐπιδεικτικῶν*, II., ix. p. 222, Aphthon., i. p. 109 Walz, Nicolaus, pp. 415, 417, for the rejected sense of *δικαιοσύνη* cf. Liban. IX. 17.

That the educated man has all virtues, and that good qualities are produced by living in a city with a good constitution, are again commonplaces[167].

xi. Constitutions also correspond to the triple nature of the soul; the king will be reason, and his rule monarchy; the soldiers will be spirit, and their rule aristocracy, the commoners will be desires, and their rule timocracy. The opposites of these constitutions are tyranny, oligarchy, and democracy.

Plato asserts clearly that the same elements exist in the individual soul as in the state. His psychology fits his ideal social structure; it is indeed possible that Mr F. M. Cornford is right in urging that the former is based on the latter, and the latter derived from a primitive Greek social structure with three age-grades such as we see at Sparta[168]. The classification of three true constitutions and three corrupt is due to Aristotle, and became a commonplace[169]. As local administration still existed in the fourth century, this chapter is not mere verbiage. Neoplatonism was not inconsistent with an interest in the political wellbeing of mankind[170], and the author of our treatise, if the identification later adopted is correct, played an active part in public life[171].

167 For the former cf. Aristid. Εἰς βασιλέα I. p. 102 Dind., and further Herm. *ap.* Stob. I. 49. 4, p. 322 W.=p. 444 S., ὅταν δὲ ἀμφότερα (sc. θυμός and ἐπιθυμία) ὁμονοήσῃ καὶ ἴσην ἕξιν ποιήσῃ, καὶ ἔχηται ἀμφότερα τοῦ τῆς ψυχῆς λογισμοῦ, γίνεται δικαιοσύνη· ἡ γὰρ ἴση ἕξις αὐτῶν ἀφαιρεῖ μὲν τὴν ὑπερβολὴν τοῦ θυμοῦ, ἐπανισοῖ δὲ τὸ ἐνδέον τῆς ἐπιθυμίας. Prof. Pearson reminds me of the Stoic doctrine that the ideal wise man has all virtues; we may remark that Philodem. *De ira* xxviii. 21 ff., p. 59 Wilke, lays down that no one can be just πάθεσιν ὀργίλοις συνεχόμενος.

For the latter, Aphthon., i. p. 88, Theon, p. 230, Nicol., p. 338, Julian, p. 248 B, 268 C (conversely a good polity is the product of a good character: cf. v., p. 10. 8. Procl. *ad* Hes. *Op. et Di.* 111, p. 112. 23 Gaisford). We may note Porphyry's remark, *Ep. ad Marcellam* 9, ἀπαιδευσία μὲν τῶν παθῶν πάντων μήτηρ.

168 *C. Q.* VI. (1912), p. 246 ff.: (on Sparta cf. also M. P. Nilsson, *Klio*, XII. (1912), p. 308 ff.). But cf. R. Hackforth, *C. Q.* VII., p. 265 ff.

169 So in [Plut.] *De uita et poesi Homeri*, ch. 182, p. 1216 Wytt., Menand. Rh. Διαίρεσις τῶν ἐπιδεικτικῶν, III. i., ix. p. 194, Doxopater, *Prol.*, vi. p. 27, Anon. *Proleg. in Hermog. Rhet.*, iv. p. 16, Theophylact. *Inst. reg.* II. 6 (CXXVI. 269 A, B Migne). In these texts δημοκρατία is good, and is contrasted with ὀχλοκρατία or λαοκρατία.

170 Cf. G. Rudberg, *Symbolae arctoae* I. (1922), 1 ff.

171 Passamonti, *l.c.* 664, regards this as the reason why he prefers kingship. But is not this preference part of the traditional theory? Cf. Plut. *An seni res*

xii. Since the gods are good and create all things, how are there evils in the universe? They must be purely negative: no nature of evil can exist among gods or among intellects or among souls or among bodies. To suppose that evil spirits exist is impossible: the gods could not make evil spirits, and we cannot limit their creative activity. Accordingly positive evil does not exist; evil is merely something that appears in connection with certain human activities. Men sin, not for the sin's sake, but to gain some object that seems good, such as pleasure or revenge. The soul errs because it is not of the first order of being; to guard it from error the gods have created many defences, arts, sciences, virtuous accomplishments, prayers, sacrifices, initiations, laws, polities and punishments; when it has left the body it is cleansed of its sins by divine spirits.

Here we come to a very controversial problem, treated by Julian in a special treatise now lost[172]; for its early history Dr E. Schröder's excellent monograph may be consulted[173]. Iamblichus denied that matter was positively evil, and said that it was better to confess ignorance than to accept any lying statement to the discredit of the gods, yet he admitted the existence of evil daemones (as did Julian) and had much to say of their activities[174]. In Proclus, however, we find a view in agreement with that here maintained. Here then our

publica xi., p. 790 A, ἥ τε βασιλεία τελειοτάτη πασῶν οὖσα καὶ μεγίστη τῶν πολιτειῶν..., *De unius in re publica dominatione*, iv., p. 827 B, constitutions having been likened to ὄργανα, εἰ δ' αἵρεσις αὐτῷ δοθείη, καθάπερ ὀργάνων, τῶν πολιτειῶν, οὐκ ἂν ἄλλην ἕλοιτο πλὴν τὴν μοναρχίαν, Πλάτωνι πειθόμενος, τὴν μόνην δυναμένην τὸν ἐντελῆ καὶ ὄρθιον ἐκεῖνον ὡς ἀληθῶς τῆς ἀρετῆς τόνον ἀνασχέσθαι..., Cic. *De re publica*, I. 54, 69, with the observations of E. Meyer, *Caesars Monarchie*[3], 179 f.

[172] πόθεν τὰ κακά, mentioned by Suidas s.v. Ἰουλιανός, I. ii., p. 1010. 10 Bernhardy; cf. R. Asmus, *Byz. Zeit.* III. 142[2]. In *Ep.* 89 *b*, p. 141 Bidez-Cumont (=p. 301 A Spanheim), Julian says that the gods do no evil to man or to one another, in *Orat.* II., p. 90 A, B, that evil is banished from heaven and exists around earth.

[173] *Plotins Abhandlung* πόθεν τὰ κακά (Borna-Leipzig, 1916). He remarks well, p. 194, that the scope of the discussion of this problem by Plotinus is outside the interests of Sallustius.

[174] *De comm. math. sci.* iv., p. 15. 12 Festa, *De myst.* III. 13, p. 130, 31, p. 177, IV. 7, p. 190 f., 13, p. 198. A belief in evil daemones was traditional; thus Chrysippus, fr. 1104 Arnim, admitted their existence, and in *C. H.* XVI. 13, p. 352. 23 R., we read that some daemones have good and evil commingled in them.

author seems to part company with Iamblichus, possibly following the lead of some disciple of his[175]. It is not impossible that some contemporary Neoplatonists asserted and some denied the existence of evil daemones[176]; and it is even possible that Iamblichus may in some lost work have put forward the view given by Sallustius. It is thinkable that the innovation was in part intended to strengthen the defence of paganism against Christianity[177].

[175] Procl. *De mal. subst.*, p. 214. 12 ff. Cousin, Schröder, p. 194_2, 195; for Julian's opinions cf. v., p. 173 B, we need a fresh rite when the sun is waning, *ἵνα μηδὲν ὑπὸ τῆς ἀθέου καὶ σκοτεινῆς δυσχερὲς πάθωμεν ἐπικρατούσης δυνάμεως*, *Ep.* 89 *b*, p. 128. 5 Bidez-Cumont = p. 288 A Spanh., *τὸ τῶν πονηρῶν δαιμόνων τεταγμένον φῦλον*. It is of interest that Julian of Laodicea, writing *circa* 500 A.D., denies that any stars are evil, cf. *C. C. A. G.* IV. 105. 28 (for which reference I am indebted to Prof. Cumont).

[176] Iamblich. *ap.* Stob. I. 49. 32, p. 365. 16, § 37, p. 372. 11, remarks on the different opinions held at different times by Amelius, Porphyry, and Plotinus. Geffcken, *Ausgang*, 283, draws attention to divergences of opinion within the *De mysteriis*.

[177] The Christians regarded the pagan deities as evil spirits (cf. *Acta Maximi*, I. i., p. 121. 5 Gebh., *Mart. S. Crispi*, I. 6, p. 13. 16, *Passio S. Symphorosae*, p. 20 R., Marc. Diac. *Vita Porph.* 59, Lebas-Waddington 2498) and attributed to such the phenomena of oracular inspiration. Sallustius could say: is their existence consistent with the perfection of God? (He could also discredit the effective evidential value of Christian exorcism, for which cf. *Mart. S. Pionii*, XIII. 6, p. 107. 10 Gebh. and Abgar's letter, several times reproduced in inscriptions, C. M. Kaufmann, *Handb. altchr. Epigr.*, p. 413, Picard, *B. C. H.* XLIV. (1920), 41–69 (Philippi).)

Further, this denial of positive evil in the universe would tend to counter Christian otherworldliness (cf. S. Aug. *Ciu. D.* I. 9, *qui in hoc mundo peregrinantur et spem supernae patriae prae se gerunt*, and hagiographical texts *passim*, as *Acta S. Maximi*, I., p. 122. 7 Gebh., *propterea enim me manifestaui ut tandem carens miserabili et temporali uita aeternam reciperem*, *Acta S. Epipodii*, p. 65 R. (the magistrate exhorting the saint), *ut cum oblectatione et cum gaudio quasi iuuenis austeritatem refugiens mundi huius beatitudine perfruaris*: Pionius however admitted that life was good, *Mart.* 5, p. 101. 6 Gebh.). The spread of such ideas may well have been helped by the pessimism indicated by popular gnomic poetry (cf. G. A. Gerhard, *Phoinix von Kolophon*, 265) and apparent even in the early Empire (cf. S. Dill, *Roman Society from Nero to Marcus Aurelius*, 292). Plutarch might say that the soul 'despises those who bewail and revile life as a place of evils' (*De tranq. an.* 19, p. 477 C) but they existed, and had since the beginnings of the Orphic movement. There was further a conviction that degeneration had set in (cf. Lucr. II. 1157 ff., W. Schmid, *P. W.* V. 859. 45 ff.). The courtly style continued to delight in such circumlocutions as *aureis temporibus* (*Dess.* 5520: 379—383 A.D.), *aureo saeculo* (*Dess.* 5555: c. 370 A.D.), *clementissimis temporibus* (*Ann. Épigr.* 1920. 15: Diocletian etc.), *τῆς εὐδαίμονος ταύτης βασιλείας* (*P. Oxy.* 71. i. 4: A.D. 303), *ἐν τοῖς μακαριωτάτοις ὑμῶν καιροῖς*

To turn to points of detail, the view that vengeance is a good thing was normal[178], the statement that soul errs because it is not 'first being' agrees with the teaching of Iamblichus[179], and the theory that punishment is curative goes back to the *Gorgias*[180]. Of the purgation of the soul we hear more elsewhere[181]. On Hellenistic views of sin the valuable observations of Dr K. Latte (*Archiv für Religionswissenschaft*, XX. 295 ff.) should be read.

xiii. **This is a sufficient treatment of the gods of the universe, and of human affairs for those who are neither capable of being taught the whole of philosophy nor yet incurable in soul[182].**

(Ditt. *O. G. I.* 519. 9: the Philips), and the coinage presented such happy legends as Ο ΚΟΣΜΟΣ ΕΥΤΥΧΕΙ, ΕΥΤΥΧΕΙΣ ΚΑΙΡΟΙ, FELICITAS SAECVLI, FELICITAS PVBLICA, FELICITAS ORBIS, FELICITAS TEMPORIS, HILARITAS TEMPORVM, SECVRITAS SAECVLI, LAETITIA, but of genuine joy in life there was none too much. Libanius remarks that if all the year were like the Kalends of January οὐκ ἂν ἦσαν ἐν ὥσπερ νῦν λόγῳ παρὰ τοῖς ἀνθρώποις αἱ μακάρων νῆσοι (IX. 10, i. p. 395. 15 ff. Förster): this seems to indicate the same desire of escape from the present as we see in Horace, *Ep.* 16. The prophecy in the *Asclepius* 25 says *tunc taedio hominum non admirandus uidebitur mundus nec adorandus.*

[178] Cf. Ditt. *Syll.*³ 1268 ('Delphic precepts'), Julian, p. 272 C (ἀνθρώποις ἅπασι κοινὸς Ἕλλησιν ἅμα καὶ βαρβάροις νόμος): the Socratic view is expressed in *P. Oxy.* 1795, col. ii., μηδ' ἀδικῖν ζήτει μηδ' ἂν ἀδικῇ προσερίσῃς.

[179] Cf. xviii. p. 32. 30, Iambl. *De myst.* x. 4, p. 290, ἐν μέσαις αὐτῶν (*sc.* τῶν ψυχῶν) ταῖς οὐσίαις, and *ap.* Stob. I. 49. 43, p. 385 (Hermes, *ap.* Stob. I. 49. 3, p. 321. 13 W. = p. 450 S., makes it fallible): of πρώτη οὐσία are made the eternal bodies as contrasted with man, according to Herm. *ap.* Stob. I. 41. 8, § 2, p. 291 W. = p. 408. 12 S.; but *ap.* Stob. I. 49. 4, p. 321 W. = p. 442 S., we are told on the same authority that the soul is οὐσία αὐτοτελής.

[180] Cf. Julian, *Ep.* 89 *b*, p. 129. 6 Bidez-Cumont = p. 289 B Spanheim, for this view: commonly punishment is regarded merely as a deterrent, yet [Aristid.] i., p. 105 Dind., hopes that it may educate; cf. *Schol. Monac.* in Hes. *Op. et Di.* 242 (*ap.* Usener, *Kl. Schr.* I. 126) for the common theory.

[181] Cf. Dieterich, *Nekyia* 200 ff., Norden, *Aen.* VI.² 29 ff., W. Kroll, *De oraculis Chaldaicis*, 47. Iamblich. *ap.* Stob. I. 49. 65, p. 454. 25, states that in the view of most Platonists and Pythagoreans disembodied spirits are purified by αὐταὶ αἱ μερισταὶ ψυχαί, in the view of οἱ ἀκριβέστεροι by more perfect souls and the one general Soul (the World-Soul, cf. lxv, n. 118 *supra*) and by the order of the universe, and by Nous and the general arrangement of things, in the view of οἱ ἀρχαιότεροι by the visible gods, and in particular by the Sun (cf. the invocation of the Sun in Dracontius, *Romulea*, x. 540, quoted p. lxx, n. 144 *supra*, to receive the souls of Medea's children), and by the unseen creative causes, and the better orders of beings, heroes, daemones, angels and gods. Sallustius approximates to the last view. In an instance noted p. xciv, n. 223 *infra* Sallustius clearly agrees with a view described by Iamblichus as that of the older thinkers.

[182] Cf. p. xxviii, n. 69 *supra*.

Here commence the appendices.

I have mentioned that second things are made by first things: this is not inconsistent with my denial of creation in time. What is made by technical skill or by nature is subsequent to its creator; what is made in virtue of a function is brought into existence at the same time as its creator, since the function is inseparable (so are the sun's light, fire's heat, snow's cold). Now the universe is not made by technical skill: that would account for its form only and not for its matter. Nor is it made by nature: that would necessitate that its creators should give of themselves, incorporeal though they are. As then creation must be in virtue of a function, the universe is coeval with the gods and cannot perish unless they lose their functional power. So those who speak of an end of the world deny the existence or the power of the gods.

Creation *κατὰ δύναμιν*, as we have seen earlier, involves no toil for the gods. The problem treated in vii. is here further considered, in the same traditional style[183].

The original Creator must have made not only men and animals, but also divine beings of various orders to fill the gap between Him and us: such intermediate stages are necessary.

The place of these intermediaries in the world-order occurs in Maximus Tyrius, but this emphasis on the divine hierarchy is probably due to the teaching of Iamblichus[184].

xiv. **Again, how is belief in the changelessness and impassivity of the gods to be reconciled with the idea**

[183] On creation in virtue of a function cf. p. lxix, n. 140, also Philol. *ap.* Stob. I. 20. 2, p. 173. 12 (*διὸ καὶ καλῶς ἔχει λέγεν κόσμον εἶμεν ἐνέργειαν ἀΐδιον θεῶ τε καὶ γενέσιος κατὰ συνακολουθίαν τῆς μεταβλατικᾶς φύσιος*: this fragment is condemned by Diels, *Vors.* I. 318, 32 B 21). On the tradition cf. p. xxxviii, n. 123, p. lxii f. *supra*. Orelli notes in this connection the distinction between two kinds of *ἀϊδιότης* by Proclus, *Inst. Theol.* 55, one static, the other dynamic.

[184] Max. Tyr. XI. 12: Iambl. *passim*, as *De myst.* I. 5, p. 16. 6 ff., VIII. 8, p. 271. 10 ff. Praechter, *Genethliakon Robert*, 105 ff., has urged that Iamblichus was concerned with the metaphysical problem of bridging the gap between First Being and matter. This point is important, but we must allow that he was also eager to find a place for much contemporary belief in his system (cf. J. Bidez, *Rev. ét. gr.* 1919, p. 36 ff.; H. Bogner, *Philol.* LXXIX., p. 262). In Nemesios we find the notion that man is the bridge between the world of sense and the world of intellect (W. W. Jaeger, *Nemesios von Emesa*, 100 ff.).

that they take joy in the virtuous and shun the bad, are angry with sinners and are appeased by worship? The gods do not feel joy (else they would be liable to feel pain[185]) or anger (that is an emotion), nor are they won by gifts (that would mean that they were under the dominion of pleasure[186]). Human conduct cannot affect the divine nature for good or for evil. The gods are always good and help us; they never harm us. We, when we are good, are by our likeness given union with them; if we become bad, we are separated from them. Our sins prevent the divine brightness from shining on us and subject us to chastising spirits: it is as false to say that the gods shun the evil as to say that the sun hides himself from the blind. If by prayers and sacrifices we find release from our sins, the explanation is that by our acts and by our turning to the divine we cure our evil and enjoy the goodness of the gods again; we do not effect any change in them.

Here Sallustius averts the shafts of Christian polemic[187]. His view of human relations with the gods agrees closely with that of Iamblichus, its probable source[188].

[185] Cf. *contra*, Herm. *ap.* Stob. I. 41. 1 (*b*) § 13, p. 275 W. (=p. 428. 8 S.), *πᾶν τὸ λυπούμενον καὶ ἥδεται [ζῷον θνητόν]· οὐ πᾶν τὸ ἡδόμενον λυπεῖται [ζῷον ἀΐδιον].*

[186] Here Sallustius (as Plato, *Rep.* 364 D ff.) rejects the older Greek view, *δῶρα θεοὺς πείθει.* An Epicurean criticism of belief that the gods can be propitiated is made by Philodem., Περὶ *θεῶν α′* xvii. 9, *ἀλλὰ εἰκὸς τῷ μὲν ὑποστησαμένῳ τοὺς θεοὺς ἐν τῷ ζῆν μόνον ἱλαστοὺς ἀργαλεωτέραν εἶναι τὴν περὶ τοῦ θανάτου ταραχὴν ὡς ἂν αἰωνίους ἐφ' αὑτῷ συμφορὰς προβάλλοντι.*

[187] Celsus carried the war into the enemy's camp, by criticising the way in which the Old Testament speaks of God's wrath (*ap.* Orig. *Contra Cels.* IV. 71 ff., VI. 53, 58). Anger is allowed to *terreni dii atque mundani* in *Ascl.* 37.

[188] Cf. *De myst.* I. 11, with an interesting quotation from Heraclitus (p. 40. 11), 12, p. 41. 4, *ἀφθόνως οἱ θεοὶ τὸ φῶς ἐπιλάμπουσιν εὐμενεῖς ὄντες καὶ ἵλεῳ τοῖς θεουργοῖς, τάς τε ψυχὰς αὐτῶν εἰς ἑαυτοὺς ἀνακαλούμενοι καὶ τὴν ἕνωσιν αὐταῖς τὴν πρὸς ἑαυτοὺς χορηγοῦντες ἐθίζοντές τε αὐτὰς καὶ ἔτι ἐν σώματι οὔσας ἀφίστασθαι τῶν σωμάτων ἐπί τε τὴν ἀΐδιον καὶ νοητὴν ἑαυτῶν ἀρχὴν περιάγεσθαι…*; (l. 15), *εἰ δὴ κάθαρσιν παθῶν καὶ ἀπαλλαγὴν γενέσεως ἕνωσίν τε πρὸς τὴν θείαν ἀρχὴν ἡ διὰ τῶν κλήσεων ἄνοδος παρέχει τοῖς ἱερεῦσι, τί δήποτε πάθη* (*-ῶν* Parthey, *male*) *τις αὐτῇ προσάπτει; οὐ γὰρ τοὺς ἀπαθεῖς καὶ καθαροὺς εἰς τὸ παθητὸν καὶ ἀκάθαρτον ἡ τοιαύτη κλῆσις κατασπᾷ. τοὐναντίον δὲ τοὺς ἐμπαθεῖς γενομένους ἡμᾶς διὰ τὴν γένεσιν καθαροὺς καὶ ἀτρέπτους ἀπεργάζεται*: cp. VIII. 8, p. 272. 9. Iamblichus gives the same explanation of their supposed anger (I. 13, p. 43. 2): *αὕτη* (*sc. ἡ μῆνις τῶν θεῶν*) *τοίνυν οὐχ, ὡς δοκεῖ τισι, παλαιά τίς ἐστι καὶ ἔμμονος ὀργὴ ἀλλὰ τῆς ἀγαθουργοῦ*

xv. These considerations decide the problem of sacrifice. The gods need nothing; the honours[189] we pay them are for our own benefit. Their providence extends everywhere, and all who are fit may enjoy it. Fitness is obtained by imitation, and imitation is the basis of all cult: the shrines correspond to the sky[190], the altars to the earth, the images to life (that is why they are made in the likeness of living beings), prayers to the intellectual element, the magic vowels to the unspeakable powers of the sky, plants and stones to matter, and the animals sacrificed to the unreasonable life in us. From all this the gods receive no benefit, but we gain union with them.

Animal sacrifice, essential as it was to paganism, appeared repugnant to some of the best minds in non-Christian circles[191]. Christian polemic attacked it with vigour[192]. For the Julianic

κηδεμονίας περὶ (*malim* τῶν) θεῶν ἀποστροφή, ἣν αὐτοὶ ἑαυτοὺς ἀποστρέψαντες, ὥσπερ ἐν μεσημβρίᾳ φωτὸς κατακαλυψάμενοι, σκότος ἑαυτοῖς ἐπηγάγομεν καὶ ἀπεστερήσαμεν ἑαυτοὺς τῆς τῶν θεῶν ἀγαθῆς δόσεως. δύναται οὖν ἡ ἐξίλασις ἡμᾶς ἐπιστρέψαι πρὸς τὴν κρείττονα μετουσίαν.... Cf. Julian, p. 171 B: (ἡ μήτηρ τῶν θεῶν) ἀγανακτεῖ μὲν οὐκέτι [*leg.* οὔποτε]. For λύσις, release, cf. *De myst.* III. 3, p. 108. 12, III. 10, p. 121. 11: it is an Orphic term, cf. Pind. *fr.* 131. 1 Schröder, Plat. *Rep.* 364 E, Orpheus *ap.* Olympiodor. *in Phaed.* B. ια′, p. 87. 13 Norvin (=O. Kern, *Orphica*, n. 232, p. 245, cf. *ib.*, p. 82), Plut., *Cur Pythia nunc non...*, 20, p. 404 A.

189 For τιμῶν p. 28. 8 cf. Porph. *De abst.* II. 5, Liban. XXIV. 36, XXX. 36, 41, Julian, *Ep.* 89 *b*, p. 134. 6. Bidez-Cumont (=p. 294 A Spanheim) says in very similar fashion οὐδὲ γάρ, εἰ μηδενὸς ὁ θεὸς δεῖται, διὰ τοῦτο οὐδὲν αὐτῷ προσοιστέον. οὐδὲ γὰρ τῆς διὰ λόγων εὐφημίας δεῖται. τί οὖν; εὔλογον αὐτὸν ἀποστερῆσαι καὶ ταύτης; οὐδαμῶς. οὐκ ἄρα οὐδὲ τῆς διὰ τῶν ἔργων εἰς αὐτὸν γιγνομένης τιμῆς, ἣς ἐνομοθέτησαν οὐκ ἐνιαυτοὶ τρεῖς οὐδὲ τρισχίλιοι, πᾶς δὲ ὁ προλαβὼν αἰὼν ἐν πᾶσι τοῖς τῆς γῆς ἔθνεσι.

190 Cf. Philo, *Spec. leg.* I. 66, p. 222 M., τὸ μὲν ἀνωτάτω καὶ πρὸς ἀλήθειαν ἱερὸν θεοῦ νομίζειν τὸν σύμπαντα χρὴ κόσμον εἶναι, νεὼ μὲν ἔχοντα τὸ ἁγιώτατον τῆς τῶν ὄντων οὐσίας μέρος, οὐρανόν..., also R. Eisler, *Weltenmantel und Himmelszelt*, 606 f. (the code of Hammurabi prescribes the building of the temple of Sippar on the model of the heavenly temple). According to *Ascl.* 24 *b Aegyptus imago sit caeli*: in *Alchimistes grecs*, II. 18 Berthelot, an egg is τὸ τοῦ κόσμου μίμημα.

191 Porphyry in his *De abstinentia* reproduced the arguments of Theophrastus and the imaginings of Dicaearchus against it: the *Corpus Hermeticum* extols λογικαὶ θυσίαι (as XIII. 21). The wise Ammianus Marcellinus disapproved of Julian's hecatombs (cf. XXII. 12. 6, XXV. 4. 17, Ensslin, *Klio*, *Beih.* XVI. 54 ff.).

192 It had earlier Epicurean material ready to hand (cf. Philodem. Περὶ θεῶν α′ I., *col.* xvii. 9, quoted in n. 186, [Lucian] *De sacrificiis* 1 : and for God's freedom from needs Eurip. *H. F.* 1345, Philo, *passim* [cf. Zeller, III. ii., 402 8]: Proclus, like Sallustius, accepted this belief, cf. *ad* Hes. *Op. et Di.* 291, p. 200. 19 Gaisf.,

reaction a philosophic defence was requisite, and it was afforded by the theory of Iamblichus: he saw a natural symbolism in all the apparatus of worship and magic[193]. To this conception of *συναφή*, union with the gods, we shall return later[194]: of the acquirement of fitness by imitation we have heard in iii. and iv.

xvi. **I had better say a little more concerning sacrifice. Since all that we have is given to us by the gods, it is reasonable that we should offer appropriate first fruits; further, prayers without sacrifice are mere words, whereas, if sacrifice is added, the words gain life, the word giving power to the life and the life animating the word. Moreover, the happiness of anything is in its appropriate perfection, and its perfection is found in union with its origin. So we pray for union with the gods. As then the life of the gods is the first order of life, and we too have life of a sort, our life desires union with theirs; for this it needs an intermediary, and between life and life the intermediary is life. For this reason in former times all sacrificed, and the truly blessed sacrifice now, and that with minute accuracy of ritual.**

The question of sacrifice was, says Iamblichus, 'the one

ad Tim. 18 B, I. 44 Diehl). But though Proclus starts from the same basis, his explanation of our offerings differs markedly from that of Sallustius.)

[193] Cf. *De myst.* V. 23, p. 233. 10, *ταῦτα τοίνυν κατιδοῦσα ἡ θεουργικὴ τέχνη κοινῶς τε οὑτωσὶ κατ' οἰκειότητα ἑκάστῳ τῶν θεῶν τὰς προσφόρους ὑποδοχὰς ἀνευρίσκουσα, συμπλέκει πολλάκις λίθους βοτάνας ζῷα ἀρώματα ἄλλα τε τοιαῦτα ἱερὰ καὶ τέλεια καὶ θεοειδῆ κἄπειτα ἀπὸ πάντων τούτων ὑποδοχὴν ὁλοτελῆ καὶ καθαρὰν ἀπεργάζεται.* We have in Sallustius these material means and the characteristic word *ὑποδοχή*: for *λίθους βοτάνας* cf. *De myst.* III. 27, p. 166. 15, IV. 13, p. 197. 13. *χαρακτῆρες* are magic symbols, as for instance the vowels ΑΕΗΙΟΥΩ, commonly connected with the planets (cf. Th. Hopfner, *P. W.*, *Suppl.* IV., 1183 ff., Dornseiff, *Das Alphabet in Mystik und Magie*, 35 ff.): Julian mentions them, p. 216 C, *ὅπερ [δὲ] δὴ τῶν χαρακτήρων ἡ ἀπόρρητος φύσις ὠφελεῖν πέφυκε καὶ ἀγνοουμένη· θεραπεύει γοῦν οὐ ψυχὰς μόνον ἀλλὰ καὶ σώματα καὶ θεῶν ποιεῖ παρουσίας* (the bracketing of δὲ is due to Mr E. Harrison), which should be rendered, 'And this benefit the unspeakable nature of magical letters naturally gives, even though not understood; it certainly heals not only souls but bodies also, and causes the gods to appear' (the Loeb edition mistranslates). What Sallustius says about images tacitly rejects the constant suggestion that the pagans worshipped them as gods (for this cf. Geffcken, *Apol.*, 325, s.v. *Götterbilder*; for its justification in fact *J. T. S.* XXVI. 175 f.).

[194] p. xcviii *infra*. On the kind of communion involved in a sacrificial meal cf. Nilsson, *History of Greek Religion*, 95 f.

question considered alike by those concerned with learning and by those less versed in dialectics[195].' The first explanation here given, that sacrifice is of the nature of an *ἀπαρχή* or offering of first fruits, is not regarded as adequate by Iamblichus[196]. Sallustius puts it forward, perhaps because he wishes to strengthen his case with every available argument,

'One sure, if another fails.'

His main thesis is that urged by Iamblichus, that sacrifice is a bond of union between creator and creature, a *σχέσις συνδετικὴ τῶν δημιουργούντων πρὸς τὰ δημιουργούμενα*[197]; in Iamblichus we find also the view that the mediation between life and life must be by life. Sallustius then sides with Iamblichus against Porphyry, who rejected animal sacrifice; he is with Iamblichus also in the importance which he attaches to prayer[198]. It need hardly be said that this view that the gods need nothing from a man is foreign to early Greek thought, as is also the passionless state ascribed to them[199].

[195] *De myst.* v. 1, p. 199. 5.

[196] *ib.* v. 5, p. 206. 7.

[197] *ib.* v. 9, p. 209. 10; cf. v. 10, p. 211. 3, *τὰ μέντοι τελειότατα καὶ ἡγεμονικώτατα τῶν αἰτίων τῆς ἐν ταῖς θυσίαις ποιήσεως συνάπτεσθαι λέγομεν ταῖς δημιουργικαῖς καὶ τελειοτάταις δυνάμεσιν.*

[198] *ib.* VI. 3, p. 243. 15, *οὐδεμία γὰρ γίνεται κοινωνία τῷ καθαρῷ πρὸς τὸ ἐναντίον, διὰ δὲ τῆς ψυχῆς τῶν ζῴων συνάπτεσθαι αὐτοὺς* (*sc.* *τοὺς δαίμονας*; *αὐτὴν* Parthey *male*) *ἀνθρώποις ἔχει τινὰ λόγον. αὕτη* (*αὐτὴ* Parthey) *γὰρ ἔχει τινὰ οἰκειότητα πρὸς ἀνθρώπους μὲν διὰ τὸ ὁμογενὲς τῆς ζωῆς, πρὸς δαίμονας δὲ διότι σωμάτων ἀπολυθεῖσα χωριστή πως ὑπάρχει· μέση δὲ οὖσα ἀμφοτέρων ὑπηρετεῖ μὲν τῷ ἐφεστηκότι, ἐξαγγέλλει δὲ τοῖς ἔτι κατεχομένοις ἐν σώματι ἅπερ ὁ ἐπιβεβηκὼς προστάττει, κοινὸν δὲ σύνδεσμον ἀμφοτέροις τούτοις πρὸς ἀλλήλους δίδωσι.* For *οἰκεία τελειότης* (p. 28. 27) cf. *De myst.* III. 20, p. 149. 9, III. 27, p. 165. 14, Iambl. *ap.* Stob. II. 31. 122, p. 234 (*πρόεισιν ἐπὶ τὴν οἰκείαν τελειότητα τεταγμένως ἐφ' ἥνπερ αὐτὴν προχωρεῖν ἄξιον*); for *εὐδαιμονία* (p. 28. 27) cf. the definition of *εὐδαιμονία*, *De myst.* X. 5, p. 290. 17, as lying in the knowledge of the Good. For the views of prayer held by Plotinus, Porphyry, and Iamblichus cf. H. Schmidt, *R. G. V. V.* IV. i. 44 ff., esp. 50 f. (analysis of *De myst.* v. 26, in which note p. 238. 14, *ἔργον δὲ οὐδὲν ἱερατικὸν ἄνευ τῶν ἐν ταῖς εὐχαῖς ἱκετειῶν γίνεται.* Plotinus regarded prayer as effective, not in itself, but by reason of the sympathy of all parts of the universe). In general on the development of prayer cf. some excellent remarks in Schrader, *Reallexikon indog. Alt.*², II. 139 f.; Pliny, *N. H.* XXVIII. 10, says that it was an essential part of all ancient Roman sacrifices.

[199] Here Sallustius is again in agreement with Iamblichus, who says *De myst.* v. 10, p. 214. 1, *εἰ δὲ ἀδύνατον ἡμᾶς ἀρχηγοὺς εἶναι τῶν δαιμόνων, τῷ αὐτῷ λόγῳ καὶ τῆς τροφῆς αὐτῶν ἐσμεν αἴτιοι* (*leg.* *ἀναίτιοι*). As for Porphyry's contention (which employed an idea of Dicaearchus) that primitive sacrifice was bloodless, it may be

The statement that all who are truly happy (*εὐδαίμονες*) now do sacrifice suits a supporter of Julian very well[200].

xvii. **We have stated that the gods will not destroy the universe. It must be added that its nature is indestructible. It might be supposed to be destroyed**

by itself:

by something else which exists, corporeal or incorporeal; a rectilinear movent (*i.e.* an element) clashing against an orbital movent (*i.e.* a planet), or *vice versa*;

by something else not in the sum of things existent.

But in none of these ways is its destruction possible.

Destruction must be in form: but this does not affect matter, since new products arise,

or in matter. But matter either perishes and is not replaced (if so, why has it lasted so long?)

or perishes and is replaced (if so, either

(*a*) *from things existing:* but if the supply lasts for ever, so will the universe. If it does not, all things existing perish.

or (*β*) *from things not existing:* This is impossible: still, were it true, while non-existents are the universe will continue to be. Surely non-existents do not also perish).

If matter survives but will lose all form, why do we not see this happening to parts of the whole? In any case, on this hypothesis it is the beauty, not the existence, of things, that will perish.

remarked that the facts seem to be opposed to it, cf. Schrader, *op. cit.* II. 138; the tradition that Pythagoras prohibited all animal sacrifices is perhaps due to Timaeus, cf. A. Delatte, *Vie de Pythagore de Diogène Laërce* (*Mém. Ac. Roy. Belg.* XVII. ii., 1922), 175 ff., 192 f.

[200] Cf. Julian, p. 186 D, *πόλει παραβάλλοντες εὐδαίμονι, πολλῶν μὲν ἱερῶν, πολλῶν δὲ ἀπορρήτων τελετῶν πλήρει*, and the somewhat later Orphic *Lithica*, 100, p. 112 Abel, *θυσίαι δ' ἱεροπρεπέες τελέθουσιν, | ἃς ἀγαθοὶ ῥέζουσι βροτοί.* For the statement that in the past all men used to sacrifice cf. a quotation from Julian p. lxxxiii, n. 189 *supra*, also Gaius, *Inst.* II. 55, *uoluerunt ueteres maturius hereditates adiri, ut essent qui sacra facerent, quorum illis temporibus summa obseruatio fuit, et ut creditores haberent a quo suum consequerentur.*

Further, what perishes must

(α) *be resolved into its components:* then something else results.

or (β) *vanish.* If so, surely God would vanish. If His power prevents that, it cannot be limited to self-preservation.

Again, if the universe perishes, it must perish

(α) *according to nature.* But this would imply that it came into being contrary to nature; and what can so perish we can destroy; on the contrary we can change elements, but we cannot destroy them.

(β) *contrary to nature:* this would require the existence of another nature changing the nature of the universe. But this is unproved.

Whatever perishes is subject to old age; and yet the universe is unchanged after the immense lapse of time. This should prove sufficient for those who require stronger proofs. May the universe be propitious to me.

This excursus again continues ch. vii., and its subject-matter has been discussed earlier: the emphasis here is on the fact that the universe is in its nature indestructible[201]. We may note as of interest the confident assertion that the universe shows no signs of age: some thought otherwise[202].

[201] p. lx ff. *supra*: λέγουσι, p. 32. 3, is another indication of the presence of the tradition. It is stated p. 30. 12 that things incorporeal, as φύσις and ψυχή, preserve things incorporeal. φύσις must be explained (as by Orelli) by a reference to Iamblich. *ap.* Stob. I. 5. 18, p. 81. 9, φύσιν δὲ λέγω τὴν ἀχώριστον αἰτίαν τοῦ κόσμου καὶ ἀχωρίστως περιέχουσαν τὰς ὅλας αἰτίας τῆς γενέσεως, ὅσα χωριστῶς αἱ κρείττονες οὐσίαι καὶ διακοσμήσεις συνειλήφασιν ἐν ἑαυτοῖς.

Praechter, *Woch. klass. Phil.* 1900, 184, has noted the emphasis of τὴν φύσιν, p. 30. 7; this chapter is not a mere repetition of what has been said in vii.

[202] As Aul. Gell. III. 10. 11, *et nunc quasi iam mundo senescente rerum atque hominum decrementa sunt*, cf. *Passio S. Symphoriani*, v. p. 70 R., *cum aeternam mundi uertiginem rapax tempus obducit*, [Apul.] *Ascl.* 26, *haec et talis senectus ueniet mundi*, also references given by R. Hirzel *ap.* Gardthausen, *Augustus und seine Zeit*, II. 882 f. The author of the *Acta S. Dasii* regarded the end of the world as near (so ch. iii., οὔτε γὰρ λήγοντος τοῦ κόσμου τὸ ἔθος τὸ κακὸν τέλος λαμβάνει: cf. Cumont, *Revue de Philologie*, XXI. (1897), 152). Assertions of the agelessness of the universe meet us in Theocr. XVI. 71, [Arist.] *De mundo*, p. 397 *a* 16, (ὁ κόσμος) δυνάμει δὲ ἀγήρως τε καὶ ἄφθαρτος, Philo, *De aeternitate mundi*,

As for the final prayer, the universe is often credited with divinity[203].

xviii. **Again, the fact that unbelief has arisen in certain parts of the earth and will often arise hereafter should not disturb men of sense. Such unbelief does not affect the gods, any more than can our worship; the human soul, moreover, being of a middle nature, cannot always judge aright. Further, all parts of the universe cannot enjoy the providence of the gods equally at all times, any more than the whole body can possess all five senses. That is why the founders of religious feasts established also days on which there should be no worship: it was a concession to human weakness. Contempt of the gods or deification of kings in a former life may bring as its punishment deprivation of knowledge of the gods in this.**

ἀθεΐαι here must refer primarily to Christianity[204]. Sallustius in effect replies to the Christian argument from their success[205]. There is a quiet irony in *περί τινας τόπους τῆς γῆς γενέσθαι*[206]. For the argument that all parts cannot

§ 61 (of the elements), Galen, Ὅτι ὁ ἄριστος ἰατρός, 2. (II), p. 3 Müller = I. 56 K., Aristid. Πρὸς Δία, I., p. 5 Dindorf, οὐδὲ γῆρας εἴσεισιν εἰς αὐτό. In *Kore Kosmou* § 42 (*ap.* Stob. I. 49. 44, p. 399 W. = p. 480. 16 Scott) we read that the nature of the gods ages and recovers its youth.

[203] As Manil. I. 523, *deus est qui non mutatur in aeuo*, Plin. *N. H.* II. 1 (Bickel, *Philol.* LXXIX., p. 360, traces the conception to a Pythagorean source), *C. H.* XII. 15, and *passim*.

[204] Cf. Julian, *Ep.* 89 *b*, p. 146. 15 Bidez-Cumont (= p. 305 D Spanh.) for ἀθεότης of Christianity, as also p. 357 D, and p. 346 B for ἄθεοι ἄνδρες of Christians: so in Iambl. *De myst.* III. 31, p. 179. 12 οἱ ἄθεοι must mean Christians; cf. the inscription of Arycanda, τῆς τῶν ἀθέων ἀπεχθοῦς ἐπιτηδεύσεως (Mommsen, *Ges. Schr.* VI., 555 ff., Diehl, *Inscr. lat. chr.* I. 1 *b* 15, p. 1), and numerous texts collected by A. Harnack, *Texte und Untersuchungen*, *N. F.* XIII. iv. 8 ff.: Libanius uses ἀθέων, *Ep.* 695 F. = 608 W., δυσσεβεῖς, *Or.* XIII. 11 (cf. in general Förster-Münscher, *P. W.* XII. 2538 ff., for his attitude to Christians). The Christians argued that the words should be applied to atheist philosophers like Diagoras [cf. Athenag. *Leg.* 4] or to renegades [*Mart. S. Apollonii*, § 4, p. 45. 13 Gebh.].

[205] Cf. Tertullian, *Apol.* xxxvii., *hesterni sumus et uestra omnia impleuimus*, S. Aug., *Ciu. D.* XXII. 5, *ecce iam credit mundus terrenum sublatum Christi corpus in caelum, resurrectionem carnis et ascensionem in supernas sedes, paucissimis remanentibus atque stupentibus uel doctis uel indoctis, iam crediderunt et docti et indocti*, and again *Mart. S. Pionii*, xiii., p. 107. 7 Gebh.

[206] It makes an effective contrast to Firmicus Maternus, *De err.* 20, *licet adhuc in quibusdam regionibus idololatriae morientia palpitent membra*: cf. Anthimus, Περὶ τῆς ἁγίας ἐκκλησίας 1 (ed. Mercati, *Studi e testi*, V., p. 95. 22), (αἱ αἱρέσεις) οὔτε πάλιν πανταχοῦ εἰσιν ἀλλ' εἰς τόπους σφόδρα βραχεῖς περιγεγραμμένας.

equally enjoy Providence it is difficult to quote a parallel[207]. The explanation of ἡμέραι ἀποφράδες[208] seems to be peculiar to Sallustius, but may well come from Iamblichus.

The view of the deification of kings as a sin of the first magnitude is of considerable interest, whether we accept or reject Prof. G. Kaerst's view that the deification of Alexander and of the Diadochi promoted Euhemerist rationalism[209]. These remarks would not have offended Julian[210]. The *know-*

[207] But cf. Iambl. *De myst.*, III. 12, p. 128. 9 (oracular power), *οὐ δύναται τὰ πανταχοῦ καὶ ἀεὶ προγινώσκειν ὡσαύτως...*, p. 129. 7, *οὐδέν τε ἄμοιρον ἑαυτῆς οὔτε τῶν ζῴων οὔτε τῶν ἀπὸ (? ὑπὸ) φύσεως διοικουμένων ἀπολείπει, ἀλλὰ τοῖς μὲν μᾶλλον τοῖς δὲ ἧττον ἀφ' ἑαυτῆς δίδωσί τινα μοῖραν προγνώσεως.*

[208] On which cf. schol. in Luc. *Tim.* 43, p. 117. 14 ff. Rabe, Marin., *Vita Procli* 19, p. 16 Boiss. (Proclus kept the *ἀποφράδες* of the Egyptians more carefully than they did themselves). At Rome the temples were closed during the nine *dies parentales* (Wissowa, *Religion und Kultus*², 232).

[209] *Hist. Zeitschr.* LXXIV., p. 226: but the importance of Euhemerus has been exaggerated, cf. F. Jacoby, *P. W.* VI., 970. 47 ff.

[210] Eunapius remarks, *fr.* 23 (*F. H. G.* IV., p. 23), *καὶ βασιλείας τε ἔτυχεν οὐχ ὅτι ἤρα βασιλείας ἀλλ' ὅτι τὸ ἀνθρωπεῖον ἑώρα δεομένους* (*leg.* -*ον*) *βασιλεύεσθαι.* Apotheosis after death is to be the fate of all righteous souls, according to xxi., and therefore the cult of dead kings or emperors hardly comes under this condemnation. The *Conuiuium* shows that Julian would not suspect *lèse-majesté* here: there is no reason to suppose that he approved worship of kings as gods in their lifetime (*Script. orig. Const.* p. 53 Preger = p. 215. 32 Bidez-Cumont, *Διὸς εἴδωλον καὶ Ἀφροδίτης ἐν τῷ τόπῳ ἀνατεθεικὼς καὶ ἑαυτόν* is not very weighty testimony, while *Orat.* I., p. 8 A *καθάπερ θεὸν διατελοῦσι σεβόμενοι* occurs in an encomium, and implies no more than the Homeric *θεὸς ὡς τίετο δήμῳ*, *Odyss.* XIV. 205). In Virgil's Inferno Salmoneus, who claimed such cult, is placed with Phlegyas who says (*Aen.* VI. 620)

discite iustitiam moniti et non temnere diuos:

so we may have two traditional types of sin here. (The suggestion that these words *καὶ τοὺς...ἐκπεσεῖν* can be regarded as a Christian interpolation is very improbable.)

For the difference between worship of living and worship of dead kings cf. Herm. *ap.* Stob. I. 49. 45, p. 408 W. (= p. 496. 12 S.), *ὁ μὲν βασιλεὺς τῶν μὲν ἄλλων θεῶν ἐστιν ἔσχατος, πρῶτος δὲ ἀνθρώπων· καὶ μέχρις ὅτου ἐπὶ γῆς ἐστι, τῆς μὲν ἀληθοῦς θειότητος* (*θεότητος* Scott *bene*) *ἀπήλλακται, ἔχει δὲ ἐξαίρετόν τι παρ' ἀνθρώπους ὃ ὅμοιόν ἐστι τῷ θεῷ.* A criticism of honours to living kings is probably to be seen in Rhian. *ap.* Stob. III. 4. 33, p. 227 Hense (= Meineke, *Anal. Alex.* 199 f.: Klinger, *Eos*, XXVI. 79 ff., summarised *Phil. Woch.* 1924, 1304, well explains l. 14, *μνᾶται δ' εὔπηχυν Ἀθήνην*, as a reference to the housing of Demetrius Poliorcetes in the opisthodomos of the Parthenon). In *P. Lond.* 1912 (published by H. I. Bell, *Jews and Christians in Egypt*, 24) Claudius deprecates the appointment of a high priest to himself and the erection of temples in his honour; at the same time, as N. H. Baynes remarks, *J. H. S.* XLIV. 311, the prefect, in the edict ordering the publication of the letter, calls on the Alexandrians to admire *τὴν μεγαλειότητα τοῦ θεοῦ ἡμῶν Καίσαρος.* *P. Oxy.* 1612 contains an interesting criti-

ledge of the gods which man may lose for his sins in a previous incarnation is γνῶσις in the heightened sense, a mystical knowledge conveying a definite illumination[211].

cism of Caesar-worship, with, as its general drift, 'let the men of Nicaea perform their rites in honour of Caesar as the Athenians perform their rites at Eleusis; we need not imitate them': probably this is aimed at some new development (cf. edd. *ad loc.*, also L. Deubner, *Sitz. Ber. Akad. Heidelb.*, 1919, XVII. 8 ff., who suggests that some innovation not much prior to the date of writing, that is, the third century of our era, is meant, and that the city concerned is Alexandria).

[211] Cf. *C. H.* XVIII. 13, p. 359 R., ἡ γνῶσις τοῦ παντός, ἥπερ ζωὴν πᾶσι πρυτανεύει, Iambl. *De myst.* III. 3, p. 107. 14, ἐὰν δὲ (*sc.* ἡ ψυχὴ) τοὺς λόγους τῶν γιγνομένων ἀνάγῃ πρὸς τοὺς αἰτίους αὐτῶν θεούς, δύναμιν ἀπ' αὐτῶν προσλαμβάνει καὶ γνῶσιν ἀναλογιζομένην ὅσα τε ἦν καὶ ὅσα ἔσται..., VI. 7, p. 247. 4, τίνα ἔχει τὴν δύναμιν διὰ τὴν πρὸς θεοὺς ἕνωσιν ἣν παρέσχεν αὐτῷ τῶν ἀπορρήτων συμβόλων ἡ γνῶσις, Julian V., p. 180 A, δίδου πᾶσι μὲν ἀνθρώποις εὐδαιμονίαν ἧς τὸ κεφάλαιον ἡ τῶν θεῶν γνῶσίς ἐστι, cf. 336 C, and E. Norden, *Agnostos Theos*, 87 ff.

γνῶσις can also mean no more than the knowledge of the name of the deity whose activities are observed. This sense should, I think, alone be used to explain ἀγνώστῳ θεῷ in Acts xvii. 23 (on which cf. Wikenhauser's full treatment, *Neutestamentl. Abh.* VIII. 3–5, 369 ff.), and οὐκ ἄγνωστος θεός in *P. Giss.* I. 3 (cf. O. Weinreich, *A. R. W.* XVIII., 34 ff.). The dedication was probably made because the spot was observed to be the seat of manifestations of divinity: so we read in *Aen.* VIII. 351 (cf. Norden, 62)

hoc nemus, hunc, inquit, frondoso uertice collem
quis deus incertum est, habitat deus.

Such uncertainty commonly attached to heroes (cf. Rohde, *Psyche*[3], I. 174), and to deities of healing. Marinus, in his *Life of Proclus*, relates (ch. 22, p. 25 Boissonade) that there was at Adrotta a shrine of a god thought by some to be Asclepius, because he had a sacred table, and at times gave oracles directing people to the recovery of their health or to deliverance from the greatest dangers. Others, because of a vision of two young men hurrying thither on horseback, regarded the shrine as belonging to the Dioscuri (they were at Byzantium credited with giving λύσις τῶν παθῶν, Hesych. Miles. VI. 15 [*F. H. G.* IV., p. 149]). Proclus for his piety was vouchsafed the truth: the god referred to Iamblichus as an authority for the correct names, Machaon and Podalirius, and was most complimentary. Another vague figure was the female daemon of Menouthi, whose activities were superseded by SS. Cyrus and Joannes (cf. L. Deubner, *De incubatione*, 90). The sanctity of holy places is older and more lasting than that of deities: cf. for illustrations in Greece M. P. Nilsson, *History of Greek Religion*, 23 f., 299, A. M. Woodward, *J. H. S.*, XLIV. 255 f. (on Hymettos), 264 (Delphi), 273 (Naxos), in Asia Minor W. M. Ramsay, *Pauline and other Studies*, 172 ff., in Italy A. Della Seta, *Museo di Villa Giulia*, I. 279 ff. (cult at Satricum on site of temple of Mater Matuta before temple was built): S. Hilary of Poitiers inveighs against the continued cult of high places (cf. Zingerle, *Sitz. Ber. Ak. Wien*, CVIII. (1885), 968). So also ritual is sometimes older than the deity to whom it is addressed, cf. L. Deubner, *A. R. W.* XIII. 490 f., *Neue Jahrb.* 1911, 321 ff. for Roman examples, Nilsson, *op. cit.* 86 (Thargelia), 91 (Thesmophoria), 93 (Eiresione), 98 and *Arch. Jahrb.* XXXI. (1916), 317 ff. for Greek examples.

ἐπεγέγραπτο in *Acts* does not imply that the inscription was original. In any

xix. Nor is it surprising that punishment for this and for other offences does not follow directly on their commission. In a measure the soul punishes itself: moreover it is immortal and must not pay the full penalty in a short time. Further, it is necessary that there should be human virtue, and immediate punishment would make men act righteously from fear alone. Souls are chastised on leaving their body; while bearing their punishment they have with them the unreasonable element, in whose company they sinned: hence arise the spectral forms seen on tombs, especially of malefactors.

A speaker in Plutarch complains that the slow action of Divine justice destroys faith in Providence, and Proclus discusses this question in his treatise *On ten reasons for doubting Providence*[212]: hence the importance of the question to Sallustius.

That the guilty soul punishes itself is a rhetorical commonplace[213]. That merit lies in honest action uninspired by fear

case the ethnographical parallels collected by Sir James Frazer (*Pausanias*, II. 35) suggest that we need not refer the phenomenon to any highly developed religious speculation. It is, further, improbable that the desire to include all deities for completeness' sake is here. For that cf. the Byzantine exorcisms mentioning 72½ diseases or 365½ reptiles and wild beasts (F. Pradel, *R. G. V. V.* III. iii. 73, Perdrizet, *Negotium perambulans in tenebris*, 19, 17); it may be observed in the dedications to *ἄγνωστοι θεοί* at Olympia (Pausan. v. 14. 8), at Pergamon (Hepding, *Ath. Mitth.* XXXV. (1910), 455 f., Weinreich, *l.c.*, 29 ff.), and in a *πάνθεος περιβωμισμός* (Weinreich, *D. L. Z.* 1913, 2959). (The *di incerti* of Varro are merely part of his classification: cf. E. Bickel, *Der altrömische Gottesbegriff* (1921), 13 ff.) It may be added that, whereas Sallustius uses *γιγνώσκειν* in the usual Hellenistic way, *εἰδέναι* has earlier a nuance of mysticism, as [Eur.] *Rhes.* 973, *σεμνὸς τοῖσιν εἰδόσιν θεός* (cf. Pind. fr. 137, *οἶδε μὲν βίου τελευτάν, οἶδεν δὲ διόσδοτον ἀρχάν*): this use is clearly parodied by Aristoph. *Nub.* 1241, *καὶ Ζεὺς γελοῖος ὀμνύμενος τοῖς εἰδόσιν* (the teaching of Strepsiades involved an initiation-scene: cf. Dieterich, *Rh. M.* XLVIII., 275 ff. (=*Kleine Schriften*, 117 ff.). It should be noted that the conception of philosophical teaching as an initiation and the application thereto of terminology taken from the mysteries continued in use after Plato, cf. E. Bréhier, *Idées philosophiques et religieuses de Philon*, 242 ff., Porph. *Ad Marc.* 8).

[212] *De sera numinis uindicta*, 3, p. 549 B; viii. p. 153 Cousin. Iamblichus, *De myst.* IV. 5, p. 187. 4 refers to punishment for sins in a previous life as explaining sufferings. (In *C. H.* XVI. 10 ff., p. 352 Reitz. *ἀσέβεια* is the supreme offence, visited with storm, earthquake, famine and war: these punishments are enforced by *δαίμονες*: in *Ascl.* 28 sins which escape punishment in this life receive special punishment in the next.)

[213] Cf. Cic. *Rosc. Am.* 67, *Pis.* 46 f., *Harusp. Resp.* 39, Liban. XXX. 37 (III. p. 107. 4 Förster), Theon, I., p. 223 Walz, Plut. *De sera...*, 11, p. 556 D, Julian,

we find in Himerius[214]: punishment by extremes of heat and cold is mentioned by Plutarch[215], punishment by racking winds in the *Asclepius*[216]. The 'shadowy apparition at the tomb' (σκιοειδὲς σῶμα) comes from *Phaedo* 81 B, and rests on a popular Greek belief, rejected by Plotinus, but accepted by Porphyry and Iamblichus[217].

XX. **As for transmigration, if the soul passes to a reasonable creature, it becomes its soul, if to an unreasonable, it accompanies it externally, as our guardian spirits accompany us: a reasonable soul can never be-**

VII., p. 215 A. Plato speaks of punishment of the individual by his δαίμων, *Phaed.* 107 D; in *C. H.* XIII. 7 our sins are themselves our torturers, cf. X. 21.

For punishment by δαίμονες, p. 34. 15, cf. K. Latte, *A. R. W.* XX. 295, for εἴς τινας τόπους τῆς γῆς θερμοὺς ἢ ψυχρούς cf. Plato, *Phaed.* 111 C τόπους δ' ἐν αὐτῇ (*sc.* τῇ γῇ) εἶναι κατὰ τὰ ἔγκοιλα αὐτῆς κύκλῳ περὶ ὅλην πολλούς..., 113 D ἐπειδὰν ἀφίκωνται οἱ τετελευτηκότες εἰς τὸν τόπον οἷ ὁ δαίμων ἕκαστον κομίζει..., 114 B οἱ δὲ δὴ ἂν δόξωσι διαφερόντως πρὸς τὸ ὁσίως βιῶναι, οὗτοί εἰσιν οἱ τῶνδε μὲν τῶν τόπων τῶν ἐν τῇ γῇ ἐλευθερούμενοί τε καὶ ἀπαλλαττόμενοι ὥσπερ δεσμωτηρίων.... There is probably here a reminiscence, direct or indirect, of the *Phaedo.*

[214] *Orat.* VII. 15, ἔστω γνώμῃ δικαίᾳ (? -ος) μὴ φόβῳ τῶν νόμων τοῦ λήμματος (? *del.* τ. λ.). Cf. Hor. *Epp.* I. 16. 52, *oderunt peccare boni uirtutis amore,* | *tu nihil admittes in te formidine poenae.*

[215] *De sera...*, 22, p. 567 C: for heat *Apoc. Pet.* 23, for cold *Apoc. Pauli*, 42 (M. R. James, *Apocrypha*, 547), and for Orphic elaboration of punishment hereafter, Rohde, II³., p. 368.

[216] 28, *inter caelum et terram mundanis fluctibus in diuersa semper aeternis poenis agitata rapiatur.*

[217] Cf. Pausan. VI. 6. 7, F. Cumont, *Rev. ét. gr.* 1919, 115, H. A. Koch, *op. cit.* 20. Malefactors executed for their crimes were commonly supposed, as βιαιοθάνατοι, to have a peculiar destiny hereafter, as in *Aen.* VI. 426 ff. They had not reached the τέλος θανάτοιο, cf. *Ascl.* 29, *uitam uiolenter amittunt ut non naturae animam debitam sed poenam pro meritis reddidisse uideantur*, and in general Norden, *Aen.* VI². 11 ff., 41 ff., Rohde, *Psyche*², II. 411 ff. In *P. Par.* 1885 a bone from the head of a βίαιος, probably equivalent to βιαιοθάνατος, is used in a love-charm, as were commonly parts of ἄωροι, cf. R. Wünsch, *Aus einem griechischen Zauberpapyrus*, 17 *ad* l. 2577. In a Cyprian *defixio* published by L. Macdonald, *Proc. Soc. Bibl. Arch.*, Feb. 1891, the βιαιοθάνατοι, ἄωροι and ἄποροι ταφῆς are invoked with the powers of the underworld (I. 31: cf. *P. Par.* 2730, τὰν Ἑκάταν σὲ καλῶ σὺν ἀποφθιμένοις ἀώροις | κεἴ τινες ἡρώων θάνον ἀγναῖοι (ἀγύν- pap.) καὶ (τε pap.) ἄπαιδες): perhaps we may explain as a survival of some such belief the traditional veneration of executed criminals at Palermo (discussed by E. S. Hartland, *Folklore*, XXI. (1910), 168 ff.).

It may further be recalled that a spear was carried in the funeral procession in honour of a man slain by violence, and then planted on his grave, which was watched for three days, no doubt because his spirit was feared and protection against it desired (Eitrem, *Opferritus*, 290_2). It was of course a very common belief that the dead man dwelt in his tomb, cf. P. Gardner, *J. H. S.*, V. 127 ff.

come the soul of an unreasonable being. Belief in a number of incarnations is forced on us by the sight of congenital diseases of body or of soul, also by the difficulty of supposing that the soul, on leaving the body, remains idle for ever, or that there are innumerable souls: an infinite number of souls is impossible in a world whose order is finite: so also is the birth of new souls, as that would be incompatible with the perfection of the universe.

This belief was widespread in antiquity. Sallustius, like Iamblichus, denied that the soul entered animals[218]. Plotinus explained misfortunes as the appropriate results of sins in a previous incarnation[219]. The argument that there cannot be an unlimited number of souls suggests the primitive belief in 'a fixed number of souls which preserve the tribe by their continual reincarnation[220].' Here it is explained from Limit and the Unlimited, two of the oldest conceptions of Greek philosophy.

xxi. **Souls that have lived virtuously are freed from the unreasonable element and purified from all body: so they have union with the gods and govern the whole universe with them. Still, if they attained none of these rewards, virtue itself and the glory it gives, and the life free from pain and from all other tyranny would suffice**

[218] Cf. Orelli *ad loc.*: for the teaching of Iamblichus cf. *De myst.* I. 8, p. 24. 2, ἔτι οὐδὲ ἔνεστι τοῖς σώμασι τὰ γένη τῶν κρειττόνων, ἀλλ' ἔξωθεν αὐτῶν ἡγεμονεύει, and Nemesios of Emesa, *De nat. hom.* II., p. 111 Matthaei, *C. H.* x. 19. On the other hand, Plotin., *Enn.* III. 4. 2, teaches plain transmigration into animals and plants for those who have deserved it (cf. *Kore Kosmou*, § 39 *ap.* Stob. I. 49. 44, p. 397 W. = p. 478. 15 S., for the former). According to S. Augustine, *Ciu. D.* X. 30, Porphyry rejected this view. For the history of the word μετεμψύχωσις cf. L. and S., *ed. nou.*, ix., for the phrase οἱ εἰληχότες ἡμᾶς δαίμονες cf. Hierocl. *ap.* Phot. *Bibl.* 251, p. 466 *b* 7, τοῦ τὴν ζωὴν ἡμῶν εἰληχότος δαίμονος.

[219] *Enn.* III. ii. 13. Hierocl. *ap.* Phot. *Bibl.* 251, p. 463 *a* 19 ff. makes this liability to bear punishment a distinction between man and beast.

[220] E. E. Sikes, *The Anthropology of the Greeks*, 36: cf. E. S. Hartland, *Primitive Paternity*, I. 157 ff. (196 ff. on the son as inheriting his father's soul, *à propos* of which cf. J. G. Frazer, *G. B.*[3] IV. 188 ff., and H. J. Rose's convincing explanation, *C. Q.* XVII 59 f., of the *genius* as the life-spirit of the family (cf. also now W. F. Otto, *Die Manen* [1923], 59 ff.); *ib.* 193 he discusses ritual illustrating the idea that a newborn child has the soul of an ancestor). E. S. Hartland (247) finds such belief 'practically universal.'

to render happy those who had chosen to live virtuously and had attained their aim.

Freedom from the body and from unreasonable soul is the prize of virtue[221]. The eschatological hope here held out meets us early in Orphic texts, but became very common[222]: in its present form it is what Iamblichus calls the older view as contrasted with the strict Platonic view, according to which the liberated souls contemplated the celestial order instead of sharing its government[223].

The sad and noble words with which the book ends express finely the Cynic aim[224] which was the goal of Hellenistic philo-

[221] With καθαραί cf. Iambl. *Protr.* xiii. p. 65. 2, οὕτω μὲν καθαροὶ ἀπαλλαττόμενοι τῆς τοῦ σώματος ἀφροσύνης, *C. H.* x. 16, Herm. *ap.* Stob. I. 49. 6, p. 324 W. (=p. 446. 22 S.), *Ascl.* 11, Nicol. *Prog.* xii., I. 391. 2 Walz.

[222] Cf. p. liv, n. 70 *supra*, Menand. Rh., Περὶ ἐπιδεικτικῶν xi., IX. 294 Walz (as a commonplace for an ἐπιτάφιος), πολιτεύεται μετὰ τῶν θεῶν ἢ τὸ Ἠλύσιον ἔχει πεδίον. For instances of deification in Greek epitaphs cf. Rohde, *Psyche*², II. 384 ff. (the term ἀποθέωσις is used of the death of a private person, Lebas-Waddington 1636, at Aphrodisias in Caria, ἀποθεοῦσθαι in Lydia, Keil-von Premerstein I., n. 183, p. 85, III., n. 57, p. 48. But we must not attach too much significance to the term, which became conventional: thus ἐκθέωσον is used as a simple euphemism for 'kill' in *P. Paris.* 2455, and ἀποθῶσον for ἀποθέωσον in *P. Parthey*, I. 5): for deification on a Greek monument from South Russia cf. E. H. Minns, *Scythians and Greeks*, 304, as held in Lycia W. Arkwright, *J. H. S.* XXXI. 270₈, on Roman grave altars W. Altmann, *Die römischen Grabaltäre der Kaiserzeit*, 281 ff. (this is quite distinct from the older Roman belief in collective *di manes*, for which cf. W. F. Otto, *op. cit.*, 55 ff.).

[223] *De anima*, *ap.* Stob. I. 49. 67, p. 458. 17 (αἱ ψυχαὶ) ἀπολυθεῖσαι δὲ τῆς γενέσεως κατὰ μὲν τοὺς παλαιοὺς συνδιοικοῦσι τοῖς θεοῖς τὰ ὅλα, κατὰ δὲ τοὺς Πλατωνικοὺς θεωροῦσιν αὐτῶν τὴν τάξιν. The so-called view of earlier thinkers is affirmed by Hierocl., *In carmen aureum*, I., p. 482 Mullach, Julian, *Orat.* VII., p. 234 C, Procl. *in Tim.* 41 D, iii., p. 271. 17 Diehl (the Creator's wish for the soul). Earlier Iamblichus contrasts οἱ πρεσβύτεροι with Numenius, *ap.* Stob. p. 458. 6, and οἱ ἀρχαιότεροι with Porphyry, p. 457. 13, and reckons οἱ παλαιότεροι as allies of Plutarch (doubtless the Neoplatonist) and Porphyry in one matter against Plotinus.

[224] Cf. Juvenal, XIII. 19 ff., *magna quidem sacris quae dat praecepta libellis | fortunae uictrix sapientia*, Πρὸς Ἱππόμαχον (Cramer, *Anecd. Par.* I., 166. 14), I. 7, τὸ δὲ δὴ μέγιστον ἄλυπος βίος καὶ ἐλεύθερος, Vell. Paterc. II. 35. 2, Seneca, *Ep.* 64. 3, [Diog.] *Ep.* 7, Max. Tyr. XXXVI., Iambl. *Protr.* IX., p. 53. 7, *Ep. ad Maced. ap.* Stob. II. 8. 44, p. 173. 20, Julian, p. 195 C, 207 D, 208 D, Procl. ad Hes. *Op. et Di.* 288, p. 199. 10 Gaisf.: for virtue as its own reward cf. Cic. *Phil.* I. 9, II. 114, *De rep.* VI. 8, and Virg. *Aen.* IX. 254. For the conjunction of happiness here and happiness hereafter cf. an anonymous epigram, *A. P.* IX. 208:

ὅς κεν Ἐπικτήτοιο σοφὴν τελέσειε μενοινήν,
μειδιάει, βιότοιο γαληνιόων ἐνὶ πόντῳ,
καὶ μετὰ ναυτιλίην βιοτήσιον εἰσαφικάνει
οὐρανίην ἀψῖδα καὶ ἀστερίην περιωπήν.

sophy. Such should be the fortune of those who had chosen virtue and attained her[225].

Plotinus closes his Enneads with significant words (VI. 9. 11) *καὶ οὕτω θεῶν καὶ ἀνθρώπων θείων καὶ εὐδαιμόνων βίος ἀπαλλαγὴ τῶν ἄλλων τῶν τῇδε, φυγὴ μόνου πρὸς μόνον*: on the basis of this attitude in Egyptian religion cf. Cumont, *Monuments Piot*, XXV. 77 ff. and in particular *ib.* 83, 87, on the phrase *μόνου πρὸς μόνον*, of solitary communing with the divine). *ἀδέσποτος* means 'free from the tyranny of passions': cf. Porph. *Ep. ad Marcellam*, 34.

[225] *γνῶσις*, *δύναμις*, and *προαίρεσις* are the three *ἀρχαί* of virtue according to Theages *ap.* Stob. III. I. 117, p. 76. 11 ff.

CHAPTER III

SOURCES AND AUTHORSHIP

§ I

The results of this analysis of the treatise may be tabulated thus:

i.	Qualifications of learner.	In all introductory treatises.
	He must know κοιναὶ ἔννοιαι:	κ. ἔ. used by various schools.
	gods perfect, etc.	Platonic commonplace[1].
ii.	functions of First Cause.	View common in fourth century A.D.
iii.	Myths make the mind work and mystically show forth nature, which likes concealment.	Hellenistic commonplace, so used by Origen. So Julian.
	Their strangeness is useful.	So Julian.
iv.	Classification of myths.	In rhetorical fashion. (The allegorisation is a Stoic commonplace.)
	Story of Kronos.	(Much criticised myth.)
	No Egyptian materialism.	(Attacked by Christian writers.)
	Story of Paris.	(Much criticised myth.)
	Story of Attis.	Taken from Julian.
v.	Summary.	
	Nature of First Cause.	Platonic.
vi.	Divine hierarchy.	Probably from Iamblichus[2].
vii.	Universe uncreated and immortal, etc.	Commonplace, as in Philo.
viii.	*Nous* perfects our souls.	Iamblichus.
	Some souls are mortal, some immortal.	Iamblichus.
	Rational element conflicts with irrational.	Commonplace.
ix.	Providence seen in the order of the universe, and in that of the human body.	Commonplace.

[1] Found in Iambl. Περὶ θεῶν (cf. *Protr.* xxi., p. 120. 17, where read θεῶν for θεοῦ).

[2] Perhaps ultimately from the lost Περὶ θεῶν, cf. *De myst.* VIII. 8, p. 271. 12: this treatise was very likely used by Macrobius, as Wissowa suggested: cf. p. lv, n. 75 *supra*.

	Its workings are effortless.	Commonplace.
	Fate not omnipotent.	Antiastrological commonplace.
	Chance sublunar in effect.	Uses commonplace.
	Poverty, etc. of good <no argument against providence>.	Commonplace.
x.	Parts of soul, virtues and vices.	As in Platonic epitomes.
xi.	Corresponding constitutions.	Plato, with modification from Aristotle.
xii.	No objective evil in universe.	? Neoplatonic source later than Iamblichus.
xiii.	The mention of creation does not imply that universe, etc. ever came into being in time.	(Continues problem of vii.)
	Intermediary stages between god and man.	Platonic tradition developed by Iamblichus.
xiv.	The gods passionless. Evil deeds separate us from them: sacrifice and the like do not affect them, but heal our wickedness and give us union with them again.	Iamblichus.
xv., xvi.	Sacrifice and offering: a theory.	Iamblichus.
xvii.	Universe by nature immortal.	(Continues commonplace of vii.)
xviii.	Godlessness.	
	All universe cannot equally enjoy divine goodness.	(Nearest parallel in Iamblichus)
	A punishment for sins in previous life.	
xix.	Why sins are not punished at once.	(Common cause of doubt of Providence)
	Soul punishes itself,	Rhetorical commonplace.
	is punished hereafter,	Orphic.
	and that with the body, hence spectres are seen.	Plato.
xx.	Transmigration.	Plotinus, Iamblichus accept this belief.
xxi.	The reward of virtue hereafter.	Orphic, etc.
	The reward of virtue here.	Cynic: commonplace of Hellenistic philosophy.

The conclusions to be drawn from these facts are fairly clear. Our author is an adherent of Neoplatonism in the form which Iamblichus gave to it. In his treatise ideas and (as we shall see) language taken thence are combined with traditional elements which had become common property. We can hardly hope to determine with precision the exact sources employed, except for the Attis-myth in iv. Whether Sallustius used Iamblichus directly or in some epitome, whether his knowledge is due mainly to written sources or to oral instruction, cannot now be said. It should be remarked that even in his following of Julian he shows originality.

The following points of verbal contact with Iamblichus may be noted[3]:

ii., p. 2. 14, *οὐδὲ τόπῳ περιέχονται.*	*περιέχ.* in *De myst.* I. 8, p. 27. 14, p. 28. 17, I. 17, p. 50. 16, III. 17, p. 143. 3.
iv., p. 6. 7, *βοτάνας καὶ λίθους καὶ ζῷα.*	*De myst.* V. 23, p. 233. 12, *λ. β. ζ. ἀρώματα.*
p. 8. 13, *δυνάμεις γονίμους.*	*De myst.* II. 1, p. 67. 15.
viii., p. 14. 20, *τελειοῦσα τὴν ψυχήν.*	(for *τελειῶ* cf. p. li., n. 59 *supra*.)
p. 14. 23, *ἐκ τῶν δευτέρων παράγονται θεῶν.*	for *παράγω* cf. *De myst.* II. 1, p. 67. 6, III. 18, p. 144. 18, III. 22, p. 152. 15, p. 153. 15, III. 28, p. 168. 4, V. 20, p. 227. 8, VIII. 3, p. 265. 5 (and restore *παράγουσι* in place of *προσάγουσι*, V. 24, p. 235. 4).
xix., p. 34. 20, *τοῦ σώματος ἐξελθοῦσαι.*	*ap.* Stob. I. 49. 67, p. 457. 9, *ἐπειδὰν ἐξέλθωσι τοῦ σώματος.*

The term *συναφή*, of union between god and man, is used repeatedly by Sallustius[4]. Iamblichus is not the first to use it so, but he uses it with marked frequency, as also its synonym *ἕνωσις*[5]. Again, Sallustius pictures divine power as light in xiv., p. 26. 26, *τῶν ἁμαρτημάτων θεοὺς μὲν ἡμῖν οὐκ ἐώντων ἐλλάμπειν, δαίμοσι δὲ κολαστικοῖς συναπτόντων.* In the *De mysteriis* *ἐλλάμπειν* is almost a technical term. The divine light is treated as an objective illumination vouchsafed in visions[6];

[3] There is no reason to refuse the treatise *De mysteriis* to Iamblichus: K. Rasche, *De Iamblicho libri qui inscribitur de mysteriis auctore* (Diss. Münster, 1911) has made a convincing case for the attribution (cf. also W. Kroll, *P. W.* IX. 650, J. Geffcken, *Ausgang*, 283 f. in its defence).

[4] xv., p. 28. 19, xvi., p. 28. 28; *συνάπτω*, iv., p. 6. 26, xiv., 26. 23, xvi., 28. 29, xxi., 36. 13.

[5] *Protr.* xxi., p. 112. 5, *De myst.* I. 12, p. 42. 16 etc. (of the savour of sacrifice, V. 3, p. 201. 7, *συναπτομένη τε αὐτῇ πρὸς τὸ πᾶν*, of sacrifice, V. 22, p. 231. 8, of the parts of the universe by sacrifice, V. 26, p. 240. 12, of man with god by prayer, *ib.*, p. 237. 16, p. 239. 3). We find earlier in Porphyry, *De abstinentia*, II. 34, *δεῖ ἄρα συναφθέντας καὶ ὁμοιωθέντας αὐτῷ τὴν αὐτῶν ἀναγωγὴν θυσίαν ἱερὰν προσάγειν τῷ θεῷ*, in a spiritualised sense. For *ἕνωσις* cf. *C. H.* I. 6, 10, Plot. *Enn.* VI. 9. 9 (*ἑνωθῆναι*, of soul-union with God), Iambl. *De myst.* I. 12, p. 41. 6, X. 7, p. 293. 3 (by sacrifice, V. 20, p. 228. 6, by prayer, 26, p. 238. 3). *Coniunctio* in [Apul.] *Ascl.* 7 might be a rendering of *συναφή* or of *ἕνωσις*.

[6] *ἔλλαμψις*, *De myst.*, p. 40. 18: *ἔλλαμπω*, 71. 9 etc.: *ἐπιλάμπω*, p. 41. 5, 126. 16, 129. 5, 130. 13 etc.: *καταλάμπεσθαι*, p. 149. 4. *ἐλλάμπω* is used by Plotinus of something shining upon the soul, *Enn.* I. 1. 8, II. 9. 2, IV. 3. 17 (and in Christian texts, cf. Steph. *Thes.* III. 757 C), and earlier by Plut. *De genio Socratis* xx., p. 589 B. For divine light and fire cf. *De myst.* III. 6, p. 113. 7, *τοῦ τῶν θεῶν πυρὸς καὶ φωτός*, earlier *C. H.* I. 21, *φῶς καὶ ζωή ἐστιν ὁ θεὸς καὶ πατήρ*, cf. §§ 21, 32, Porph. *Ep. ad Marcellam* 20, *διὰ φωτὸς τοῦ θεοῦ τῆς ἀληθείας λαμπρυ-*

if the worshipper is fit[7], he can receive it (χωρεῖν) and is filled with it (πληροῦται[8]). Sallustius also speaks of this fitness in xv., p. 28. 10, ἡ μὲν πρόνοια τῶν θεῶν διατείνει πανταχοῦ, ἐπιτηδειότητος δὲ μόνον πρὸς ὑποδοχὴν δεῖται. Iamblichus also lays stress on such fitness, and on imitation of the gods[9]. This conception of divine light, no mere metaphor, is common in Gnostic and Hermetic texts and elsewhere[10]: still, its pre-

νόμενος καὶ ῥᾷον προχωρῶν, 26. The Stoics identified god and soul with fire, cf. A. C. Pearson, *Fragments of Zeno and Cleanthes*, 138, on n. 86, M. Adler, *Sto. uet. fragm.*, IV. 125. The Pythagorean Secundus, who flourished under Trajan, defines God (*Sent.* 3, in Mullach, *Fragmenta*, I. 512) as πολυώνυμος δύναμις, παγκρατὴς χείρ, φῶς, νοῦς, δύναμις (?). For the gift of divine light in visions cf. Iambl. *De myst.* III. 2, p. 104. 3, 8, p. 117. 2.

[7] Cf. *De myst.* III. 11, p. 125. 3.

[8] χωρεῖν, *De myst.*, p. 86. 5, 87. 6, 125. 6, 233. 9, 234. 12, *Acta Pauli et Theclae*, §6, p. 239. 17 Bonnet-Lipsius (so χώρα, *De myst.* III. 29, p. 173. 4): πληροῦσθαι, *De myst.*, p. 107. 2, 113. 9, etc., πλήρωσις *ap.* Stob. I. 49. 65, p. 454, cf. Plotin. *Enn.* VI. 9. 9, ὁρᾶν δή ἐστιν ἐνταῦθα κἀκεῖνον (*sc.* τὸν θεὸν) καὶ ἑαυτόν, ὡς ὁρᾶν θέμις, ἑαυτὸν μὲν ἠγλαϊσμένον, φωτὸς πλήρη νοητοῦ, μᾶλλον δὲ φῶς αὐτὸ καθαρόν, ἀβαρῆ, κοῦφον, θεὸν γενόμενον, μᾶλλον δὲ ὄντα, ἀναφθέντα μὲν τότε, εἰ δὲ πάλιν βαρύνοιτο, ὥσπερ μαραινόμενον. For divine power conceived as a fluid cf. F. Preisigke, *Vom göttlichen Fluidum nach ägyptischer Anschauung* (*Schr. Pap. Inst.* Heidelberg, I., 1920).

[9] Cf. *De myst.* I. 15, p. 48. 1, τὴν πρὸς αὐτὸ (*sc.* τὸ ἱκετευόμενον, the gods) ὁμοιότητα ἀπὸ τοῦ συνεχῶς αὐτῷ προσομιλεῖν κτώμεθα, τελειότητά τε θείαν ἠρέμα προσλαμβάνομεν ἀπὸ τοῦ ἀτελοῦς, also I. 11, p. 37. 11, III. 9, p. 119. 6, ὥστε μετέχειν αὐτῶν (*sc.* τῶν θεῶν) τὸ τὴν τυχοῦσαν ἔχον (*sc.* μέλος) πρὸς αὐτοὺς ὁμοιότητα. Iamblichus uses several times the phrase ἐπιτήδειος πρὸς ὑποδοχήν as III. 2, p. 105. 1, 11, p. 127. 8, V. 23, p. 232. 18, τὴν τελειότητα, ἑαυτῆς ἐπιτηδείαν κέκτηται πρὸς θεῶν ὑποδοχήν; ὑποδοχὴ τοῦ θεοῦ occurs also III. 11, p. 125. 17, τῶν θεῶν V. 26, p. 238. 16, ἐπιτήδειος and ἐπιτηδειότης in this sense repeatedly in the *De mysteriis*. Earlier, in Porphyry, *Ep. ad Marcellam*, 19, we find παρασκευαστέον δὲ αὐτὸν (*sc.* τὸν νοῦν) καὶ κοσμητέον εἰς καταδοχὴν τοῦ θεοῦ ἐπιτήδειον.

[10] Metaphors from light are common among Neoplatonists (Wendland, *Berl. Phil. Woch.*, 1899, 1411), and we have one in vii., p. 14. 3. But the use here discussed does not rest on metaphor alone; its basis is a definite belief, cf. G. P. Wetter, ΦΩΣ (*Skrifter utgifna af K. Humanistiska Vetenskaps-Samfundet i Uppsala*, XVII. i., 1915), *passim*. His view that the origin of the idea is to be sought in Oriental precursors of Manichaeism has been made very improbable by M. P. Nilsson, *G. G. A.* 1916, 41 ff. For the idea as exemplified by Plotinus and in Egyptian thought cf. Cumont, *Monuments Piot*, XXV. 89 ff. Light and life are commonly connected in ritual, cf. Dieterich, *Nekyia*, 241, L. R. Farnell, *Cults*, II. 614 (symbolism of Eileithyia lifting torch), S. Eitrem, *Opferritus*, 155 ff. Light played a prominent part in the mysteries of Eleusis, cf. Plut. (?) *ap.* Stob. IV. 52 *b*, 49, p. 1089. 14. ΔΙΟΣ ΦΩΣ, the title of a torch-bearing Dionysus on a black-figured amphora illustrated by A. B. Cook, *Zeus*, II. 273, fig. 177, may mean 'light of Zeus' and not 'man of Zeus': in Eurip. *Bacch.* 1082 f. the god manifests himself by a pillar of light and fire, cf. l. 597, and in [Arist.] *Mir. ausc.* 122, p. 842 a,

sence, as also the emphasis laid on *συναφή*, in Sallustius are most easily explained on the hypothesis that the latter was a follower of Iamblichus. Naturally, many ideas which may be traced to Iamblichus occur in Plotinus or in Porphyry; though Iamblichus modified Neoplatonism, he did not create it. Yet when we consider the views in which Sallustius agrees with Iamblichus against his Neoplatonic predecessors[11], and the linguistic points of contact, we shall probably be correct in assuming that Sallustius used one or more handbooks of commonplace philosophy and some work or works by Iamblichus or by a disciple of his[12]. The explanation of the myth

20 he is said to display a blaze of fire in a sanctuary of his among the Bisaltae, when the harvest will be good. Such theophanies in or with fire are recorded of the Mother (Schol. Pind. *Pyth.* III. 137 *b*), of Gennaios of Heliopolis (Damasc. *Vit. Isid. ap.* Phot. *Bibl.* 242, p. 348 *a*, 37 ff., cf. G. F. Hill, *J. H. S.* XXXI. 59), and of other deities (F. Pfister, *P. W. Suppl.* IV. 315); for a similar trait in Christian legends cf. M. R. James, *The Apocrypha of the New Testament*, 33, 46, 79.

[11] His explanation of the myth of Attis we have seen to be based on Julian, who used ideas of Iamblichus; it is quite different from that of Porphyry, recorded by Euseb. *Pr. euang.* III. 11. 12, and Julian says, p. 161 C, *ἀκούω μὲν ἔγωγε καὶ Πορφυρίῳ τινὰ πεφιλοσοφῆσθαι περὶ αὐτῶν, οὐ μὴν οἶδά γε, οὐ γὰρ ἐνέτυχον, εἰ καὶ συνενεχθῆναί που συμβαίη τῷ λόγῳ.* Sallustius agrees with Iamblichus against Plotinus and Porphyry in his view of Heimarmene (p. lxx. ff. *supra*), and against Porphyry in his view of sacrifice.

[12] R. Asmus, *Sitz. Ber. Ak. Heidelb.*, 1917, iii., *Philol.* LXXVI. 266 ff., LXXVII. 109 ff., regards a lost commentary by Iamblichus on the *First Alcibiades* as the basis of most of Julian's thought, and as influencing this treatise also (p. 86). Such a theory cannot well be proved, cf. Richtsteig, *Byz. neugr. Jahrb.* I. 413 ff. We have noted (p. xcvi. n. 1, 2) possible points of contact with the Περὶ θεῶν of Iamblichus, an extensive work, it would appear, of the type to which Sallustius refers when he says, vi. p. 10. 31 ἐν τοῖς περὶ τούτων λόγοις. The commonplace element in our treatise may of course be due in part to oral teaching. It should here be recalled that we have twice seen Sallustius taking what Iamblichus calls the view of the older authorities (p. lxxx., n. 181, xciv., n. 223). On the other hand, in his denial of the existence of objective evil and of evil daemones he seems to be in advance of Iamblichus, and perhaps follows some pupil of his (p. lxxviii. f. *supra*): E. Schröder, *Plotins Abhandlung*, 194, places him philosophically between Iamblichus and Proclus. Zeller's rejection of the view that he is of the school of Proclus (III. ii. 793_1) has not been questioned. E. R. Dodds, *ap.* G. G. A. Murray, *Five Stages of Greek Religion*, 219, writes 'Many of his sections come straight from Plotinus: xiv. and xv. perhaps from Porphyry's *Letter to Marcella*, an invaluable document for the religious side of Neo-Platonism. A few things (prayer to the souls of the dead in iv., to the Cosmos in xvii., the doctrine of *τύχη* in ix.) are definitely un-Plotinian: probably concessions to popular opinion.' In the light of what has been said it will, I hope, be clear that in all probability Sallustius made no direct use of either Plotinus or Porphyry.

of Attis he clearly took from Julian. It would be unsafe to assume that our author had read widely in philosophy; he may not have been familiar with the more esoteric writings of Iamblichus, and there is no reason to suppose that he had any acquaintance with the works of earlier Neoplatonists.

§ 2

In the Ambrosian manuscript the summary prefixed to the text is headed *Σαλουστίου φιλοσόφου κεφάλαια τοῦ βιβλίου.* Various Sal(l)ustii are known to us: among them is a fifth-century philosopher[13]. He, however, was a Cynic, not a Neoplatonist, and Zeller was no doubt right in rejecting the idea that he is the author of our treatise. Zeller urged that the treatise should be attributed to Julian's intimate friend, to whom he dedicated Oration IV, and on whose departure he wrote himself a consolation (VIII). This Salustius was a pagan of high education, who by wearing a beard acquired some right to the title of philosopher; Julian speaks of him as 'perfect in rhetoric and not unversed in philosophy,' and suggests that they should join in venerating Iamblichus the beloved of heaven[14].

This hypothesis gained greatly in probability when Professor Cumont drew attention to the fact that the Attis-myth in iv. was directly copied from Julian's Fifth Oration. He

[13] Cf. for him K. Praechter, *P. W.* I A, 1967 ff.

[14] VIII., p. 252 B, IV., p. 157 D: from p. 157 C it would appear that Julian's friend had not read Iamblichus Περὶ θεῶν. The identity of this friend has been disputed. Seeck, *Die Briefe des Libanius* (*Texte und Untersuchungen*, XXX.), 263 ff., *P. W.* I A, 2072. 42, makes him Saturninus Secundus Salutius (called Σαλούστιος in our Greek texts), who held office in Aquitania and in Africa before being Julian's assistant (*quaestor*, says Seeck) in Gaul, was made *praefectus praetorio Orientis* in 361, an office he held for some time under the new régime, refusing an offer of the Empire made to him after Julian's death, and died probably before 377, and not Flavius Sallustius, made *praefectus praetorio Galliarum* in 361 and consul in 363 (as Cumont, *Revue de philologie*, XVI. 52). Seeck's conclusions are probably right, but I am not competent to criticise them; the identification of our author is accepted in Lübker, *Reallexikon des klassischen Altertums*[8], 906 *a* (8). The character of the treatise itself points to its writer not being a professed philosopher; E. Passamonti, *Rend. Acc. Lincei*, 1892, 727, seems greatly to exaggerate its philosophical importance. I retain the spelling Sallustius as being conventional.

argued further that the treatise was composed *circa* 363, in the service of Julian's reaction[15]. This date is probable, as is also the identification of the author with the Emperor's intimate friend. The tone of the work suggests that paganism has waned, but still possesses a not inconsiderable following; in the next chapter it will be urged that considerations of prose-rhythm certainly point to a date between 300 and 430 A.D.

Moreover, this statement of faith is so made as to parry the usual onslaughts of Christian polemic. As Julian strove to meet Christian care for the poor and for the dead by similar care, so Sallustius met theology with theology[16]. He asserted divine perfection as the Christians did (i.); like them he separated deity from matter (v.) and would not identify the gods with the planets and with the elements. Unedifying myths he handled with circumspection, not only pointing

[15] *Rev. phil.*, *l.c.* But we can hardly accept his conjecture that τῶν γραψάντων αἱ ψυχαί, iv. p. 10. 3, refers to the dead Julian (cf. p. lv., n. 77 *supra*: such language would indeed be appropriate, cf. Liban. *Ep.* 1220 F. = 1186 W., κἀκείνῳ, περὶ οὗ σὺ καλῶς δοξάζεις τοῦ τῶν θεῶν αὐτὸν γραφόμενος χοροῦ, *Orat.* XXX. 40, μέγας δέ ἐστιν ὅμως καὶ τεθνεώς, but the supposed allusion is quite unnecessary), or his suggestion that the words ἐφ' οἷς ἱλαρεῖαι καὶ στέφανοι, referring to the Hilaria, could have been written under Julian or under Eugenius (392–4), but not at any other time after the official triumph of Christianity (but the festival may have been celebrated in a private way even when it was forbidden), or his contention that the statement in xviii., p. 32. 27, that ἀθεΐαι have arisen in certain parts of the world points to 363 rather than a later date. Strange as the remark that unbelief (meaning Christianity) has arisen in some places on the earth would seem to us in a writer of the fourth century, it is not impossible; Marinus in his *Life of Proclus* makes only casual allusions to its predominance (ch. 30, p. 24 Boissonade, ch. 29, p. 23, ch. 15, p. 12). A partisan can rise above facts and statistics. Cumont's date is, however, probably right.

It may perhaps be here suggested that much of the treatise had been written before the author read Julian's Fifth Oration, which Asmus dated March 27th, 362. In that case we might more easily understand the curious insertion in iv. of the Attis-myth derived thence; it has been remarked that this insertion is in the nature of an afterthought (p. li., n. 56 *supra*).

[16] The *locus classicus* is *Ep.* 84 *a* (= 49 H.). Cf. Cumont, *l.c.* 54; more recently, *Studia Pontica*, III. 41 f., n. 27, he remarks on the construction of separate baths for men and for women at Phazemonitis σαοφροσύνης ἕνεκα σφῆς (l. 7) by one Jovinus, and suggests that he was the *magister equitum* of Julian, who certainly disapproved of public baths (cf. VI., p. 186 D, τὰ περιττὰ καὶ βδελυρὰ καὶ φαῦλα...λουτρὰ δημόσια καὶ χαμαιτυπεῖα καὶ καπηλεῖα). H. Grégoire, *Studia Pontica*, III. 88 f. n. 68 *a*, draws attention to a charitable foundation at Neoclaudiopolis, possibly belonging to this movement.

to their possible meaning, but justifying their existence and rejecting dangerous materialistic interpretations (iii., iv.). On the question of Fate he took up a position which was secure from the polemic waged against astral determinism (ix.). Sacrifice he defended by an ingenious theory, image-worship he rejected by implication (xv.). His account of the origin of atheism is perhaps an answer to the Christian argument from facts[17], and his proof that those who believe in an end of the world are atheists (xiii.) has an obvious controversial value.

This quiet implicit rejection of hostile views would suit the wise administrator who curbed Julian's fiery activity and whose calm acceptance of sorrow won the praise of Libanius[18]. It may be conjectured that this treatise was written before Julian's death and, when it was clear that his reaction could not survive its author, was not published, or, if published, had only a very small circulation: certainly it cannot have been regarded as in any sense an official manifesto[19]. No allusion

[17] It would be hazardous to see in the closing words an implied criticism of the Christian promise of Heaven and threat of Hell (for such criticism cf. Geffcken, *Apol.*, 96).

[18] Seeck, *ll.cc.*, gives full references. In *Ep.* 1224 F. (= 1143 Wolf) Libanius, who could show a similar spirit of moderation (as *Ep.* 819 F. = 730 W.), praises the πεπαιδευμένη ψυχή of Salu(s)tius. Whether this Salustius was the author of prose arguments to the plays of Sophocles (mentioned before one to *O. C.*, where Σαλουστίου ὑπόθεσις Πυθαγόρου may be an error for Σ. ὑ. Πυθαγορείου, and before one to *Ant.*) we cannot say: cf. A. C. Pearson, *Fragments of Sophocles*, I. xxxiii., K. Praechter, *P. W.* I A, 1964. Eminent pagans later showed a tendency to edit the Latin classics. Yet cf. against the identification A. Gudeman, *P. W.* II A, 661 f.

[19] Had it been such, it would probably have perished with the anti-Christian polemic of Celsus, Porphyry, and Julian: it would at least have provoked some reply. The eloquent *Relatio pro ara Victoriae* of Symmachus called forth two rejoinders: yet Symmachus merely asked for toleration of the survivals of a dead faith, while Julian sought to make a serious revival, as is illustrated by certain inscriptions in his honour, as one in Numidia (Dessau 752), *restitutori libertatis et Ro[manae] religionis*, which is comparable with Julian's words, *Ep.* 61 [= 42 H.], p. 72. 20, Bidez-Cumont, ἕως μὲν οὖν τούτου πολλὰ ἦν τὰ αἴτια τοῦ μὴ φοιτᾶν εἰς τὰ ἱερά, καὶ ὁ πανταχόθεν ἐπικρεμάμενος φόβος ἐδίδου συγγνώμην ἀποκρύπτεσθαι τὰς ἀληθεστάτας ὑπὲρ τῶν θεῶν δόξας, ἐπειδὴ δὲ ἡμῖν οἱ θεοὶ τὴν ἐλευθερίαν ἔδοσαν..., another at Beyrouth (Jalabert, *Mélanges de la faculté orientale..., Beyrouth*, II. 265, n. 62), *re]creatori [sacrorum et] exstincto[ri superstitionis]*, and yet another at Mursa in lower Pannonia (Dessau 8946 = Diehl, *Inscr. lat. christ.* 11), *bono r(ei) p(ublicae) nato d(omino) n(ostro) Fl. Cl. Iuliano [princip]um max(imo) trium-f(atori) semp(er) Aug(usto) ob deleta uitia temporum preteri[torum*, and again by

to it has been detected in contemporary literature; though much has been lost, we have a great body of writing by Libanius, by S. Basil, and by the Gregories.

the remark of Libanius, XXIV. 36 (ii. 530 Förster), *οὗτος ὁ πολλῶν ἐξελάσας ἀχλὺν καὶ πάντων δ' ἄν, εἰ μὴ προαπῆλθε.* It is tempting to see an anticipation of this plan in the legend *FEL(icium) TEMP(orum) REPARATIO* on the inverse of an *aureus* struck by Julian when Caesar and not yet Emperor; a specimen of the coin in the British Museum is reproduced on the cover of this book (another will be found illustrated in *Collection R. Jameson*, III. 176, n. 485, pl. XXIII.: the coin type is Cohen, no. 8, the seated figures Rome and Constantinople). Nevertheless, the legend was employed earlier by Constantine and Constans (to which fact Mr Mattingly kindly drew my attention), and Julian may well have attached no special meaning to it.

CHAPTER IV

STYLE AND FORM

§ 1. *Vocabulary and Grammar.*

In this connection the question we must ask about an author of the later Empire is: is he an Atticist? The term means little more than 'classicist,' and is used with reference to the past: Athens in the fourth century was the home of the modern style in oratory, Antioch of the ancient. Be this as it may, Atticism in words, word-forms and syntax is common in the so-called modern styles: the ornate Gregory Nazianzen is as fond of them as are the Attic Julian and Libanius[1]. We find in Sallustius a number of Atticisms signalised as such by the grammarians[2]:

The use of the Infinitive with the article as a substantive, p. 2. 20, τό γε ζητεῖν and 22 other examples: for this in Julian cf. Boulenger, *Syntaxe de Jul.*, 194.

The Accusative of Respect, p. 2. 2, τὴν φύσιν ἀγαθούς, p. 36. 11, τά τε ἄλλα εὐδαιμονοῦσαι, cf. Boulenger, 48.

The Absolute Infinitive, p. 10. 11, ὡς δὲ ἐν βραχέσιν εἰπεῖν, cf. Boulenger, 120.

Also other Atticisms which are clearly such though not mentioned in our ancient authorities:

The use of the article and a neuter adjective as a substantive, p. 20. 20, μὴ τὸ φαινόμενον ἡδὺ ἀλλὰ τὸ μετὰ λόγου, p. 24. 27, τὸ φύσει ποιοῦν, cf. Boulenger, 193.

The use of ὅσος for ὅς, p. 2. 5 ὅσας, cf. Schmid, IV. 611.

The use of the singular verb with a neuter plural: so more than 30 times (the MS. gives *contra*, p. 2. 11, γίνονται—εἰσίν, which in view of the context may clearly be removed by emendation, as may 26. 3 δύνανται). Cf. Boulenger, 37 f. (exceptions in Julian very doubtful).

[1] Cf. Norden, *Kunstprosa*, 349: Przychocki, 274 ff.: cf. for Athenagoras Geffcken, *Apol.*, 163, for Synesius Christ-Stählin, II. 1400_{12}. Galen, on the other hand, does not claim to be an Atticist (Christ-Schmid, II. 913 f.).

[2] Their *testimonia* are conveniently summarised by Schmid, IV. 633 ff., Przychocki, 276 ff.

ἐχρῆν, not χρῆν, p. 2. 26, 30. 2.

ἐθέλω not θέλω, p. 10. 26, cf. Deferrari, *Lucian's Atticism: the Morphology of the Verb* (1916, Princeton), 10 f.

Some marks of the *koine* in Sallustius are not avoided even by the most scrupulous Atticists of the Empire: such are

The imperative plural middle in -έσθωσαν: p. 2. 10, γινέσθωσαν (this is the only form in Aelian; even Lucian relegates -σθων to the stiff Greek of a mock law[3]).

Ἀπόλλωνα for Ἀπόλλω: cf. Schmid, IV. 581, for its use in Atticists (though Cobet, *V. L.*², 263, regards such instances as in general due to copyists). It occurs p. 12. 19.

-ονα for -ω in the accusative of comparatives in -ων: -ω is much commoner in Atticists: p. 12. 25, κρείττονα (cf. Iambl. *De myst.* I. 13, p. 43, κρείττονα, III. 15, p. 136. 8, πλείονα).

ἠδυνήθη for ἐδυνήθη, p. 30. 19. This form like ἠβουλόμην is common from 300 B.C. onwards. Lucian usually has ἐδ-, ἐβ-.

A problem arises in connection with p. 30. 6, ἂν φθεροῦσιν. ἄν with the future indicative, participle, or infinitive is probably impossible in Attic: H. Richards, *Notes on Xenophon and others*, 277 ff., points out that in a number of cases not easily emended otherwise δή can be substituted for ἄν. There is evidence for ἄν with future infinitive and future participle in Lucian (Schmid, I. 245), with the former in Philostratus (Schmid, IV. 76, 90), with future indicative in Galen (J. Marquardt, *praef. ad* Galen. *Op. min.* I. xlv. f.). The MSS. appear to give ἂν ἐσομένης in Julian, V., p. 170 B (in defence of ἄν and the future participle, cf. A. B. Keith, *C. Q.* VI. 121 ff.). On the whole we may regard the ἄν in Sallustius, who writes in general with correctness, as probably intrusive. Richards, *op. cit.*, 282, has drawn attention to wanton insertions of ἄν in passages of other kinds in which it clearly cannot have stood in the original. Another point which may conveniently be discussed here occurs at p. 34. 28, where the MS. offers us οὐ γὰρ μήποτε λογικὴ ἀλόγου ψυχὴ γένοιτο. Attic use requires γένηται, as Prof. Muccio proposed to read. Of the optative, Stephanus, *Thesaurus* (ed. Paris.), V. 2346 D, gives examples. One of these comes from Synesius, three from Plotinus (though in one the subjunctive has some manuscript authority), and one from Libanius, which disappears when the passage is correctly punctuated (*Ep.* 1158 F. = 1115 W., ...ὡς σέ τι

[3] R. J. Deferrari, *op. cit.* 20, correcting Schmid, IV. 589, 597.

λελυπηκὼς ἄκων, οὐ γὰρ δὴ ἑκών γε· μήποτε οὕτως ἀτυχήσαιμι, as Förster reads). It will also be observed that οὐ μή is correctly used with the subjunctive in papyri (cf. Moulton and Milligan, *Vocabulary of the Greek Testament*, 464 *a*) and in inscriptions of the Empire (as Ditt. *Syll.*³, 1042. 16 [second or third century A.D.], 1236, both texts written by unlearned men). If the idiom could survive in such circles, though the feeling for the exact use of moods was no doubt waning, as we see for instance in the use of subjunctive for optative in a wish, διαμείνῃ τὸ γένος τῶν Ῥωμαίων, Ditt. *O. G. I.* 653 [Amida in Armenia, third century A.D.], it is very likely that Sallustius, who had no doubt read some Plato and other Attic texts at school, would use it correctly, and we may therefore accept the emendation γένηται. (Mullach's proposal to read ἂν for μή postulates a less probable corruption.)

Questions of orthography are in later Greek far from easy:

Sallustius has -ττ- not -σσ-: p. 2. 9, κρεῖττον, 12. 25, κρείττονα, 14. 17, τάττει, 14. 31, ἡττηθεῖσα, 16. 13, τάττον, 4. 26, αἰνίττεται, 22. 4, πράττεται, 34. 22, ταραττόμεναι.

-σσ- occurs in Attic inscriptions of the fourth century B.C., but Lucian always has -ττ- except in verbs not so spelt in Attic[4].

He also has συν-, not ξυν- in compounds without exception. συν- is invariably used by S. Gregory in his letters (Przychocki, 295₀): Julian has συν- commonly (Boulenger, 52).

A decision on γιν-, γιγν- is difficult. The Ambrosianus gives us

γινέσθωσαν (1).	
γίνομαι, etc. (7).	γίγνομαι, etc. (6).
γινόμενος, etc. (11).	γιγνόμενος (1).
γίνεσθαι (1).	
γινώσκω (1).	

The γιν- forms are popular: from 277 B.C. they alone are used in Ptolemaic papyri[5]. If we may trust the manuscripts, Aristides and Philostratus prefer γιγν-, Herodes Atticus and Aelian γιν-. (The pronunciation might be the same in either case.) It is natural to suppose that γιν- is a vulgarisation, and that accordingly, when our MS. tradition gives γιγν- in *some* cases, that form should be restored in *all*. It has however been observed that, though Lucian's text gives 116 examples of γίγνομαι and 63 of γίνομαι, 73 of the former examples occur in eight dialogues: this creates the impression that these latter have passed through an Atticising recension. Even so, there are 45 cases of γινώσκω to 13 of γιγνώσκω. It is therefore quite likely in Lucian, and, we may add, in Sallustius, that

[4] Deferrari, 1 ff.

[5] Mayer, *Grammatik der griechischen Papyri aus der Ptolemäerzeit* (1906), 164 ff.

the γιν- forms are very often correct, and the γιγν- forms due to alterations[6]: in the present edition the MS. is followed in each case, since it is impossible to determine whether the author's practice was consistent. Their spelling σώζω has also been accepted: it is epigraphically attested for the first century B.C.[7]. The Attic forms πλέον (p. 28. 17) and οἶμαι (p. 28. 20) are used.

One more grammatical difficulty may for convenience be discussed here. In ix., p. 18. 24, we read τὸ δὲ καὶ πατέρων εὐγένειαν ἢ δυσγένειαν προλέγειν ὡς οὐ πάντα ποιούντων, τινὰ δὲ σημαινόντων μόνον τῶν ἄστρων διδάσκει (so Mullach for διδάσκειν). The sense required would be more clearly given by omitting διδάσκει and inserting ἐστί after ποιούντων. At the same time, the text as it stands is defensible, as an instance of the practice of using ὡς with a genitive participle followed by a verb which should naturally have the participle as its object. Examples which may be quoted are Soph. *Aj.* 281, ὡς ὧδ' ἐχόντων τῶνδ' ἐπίστασθαί σε χρή, Aesch. *P. V.* 760, ὡς τοίνυν ὄντων τῶνδέ σοι μαθεῖν πάρα, Plato, *Meno*, 95 E, ἐν τούτοις μὲν ὡς διδακτοῦ οὔσης τῆς ἀρετῆς λέγει (cf. for further illustration of the point Goodwin, *Moods and Tenses* (1897), § 917 f., p. 365 f., Kühner-Gerth, II. 93 f.).

§ 2. *Particles and sentence-construction.*

The most frequent particle is δέ: this couples sentence after sentence in a mechanical way. An antithetic μὲν...δέ is used repeatedly: we find also καὶ...δέ ('yes, and'), p. 4. 8, 12. 16, 16. 20[8]; καὶ μέντοι καί[9], p. 6. 11. οὐδὲ...οὐδέ occurs p. 2. 11/13/14 15/16, 16. 31: it seems to be indistinguishable from οὔτε... οὔτε, having lost its proper sense, *ne...quidem...neque.* Here Julian's practice sometimes agrees[10]. It may indeed be that our author wrote οὔτε...οὔτε, and that his text was vulgarised: at the same time it will be observed that μηδὲ...μηδέ occur in an acrostic epigram in a papyrus of the first century of our

[6] I take these facts from R. J. Deferrari, *op. cit.* 36, with whose conclusions I agree. Such an introduction of old forms is not unparalleled. Our Renaissance Latin MSS., as the Datanus of Catullus, are full of old spellings or spellings thought to be such which have been deliberately introduced into the text.

[7] Cf. Meisterhans, *Gramm. att. Inschriften*³, 179₁₄₈₄.

[8] Classical (cf. Kühner-Gerth, II. 253) and very dear to Aelian (Schmid, III. 339).

[9] Also in Dio of Prusa (Schmid, I. 186), Lucian (*ib.* 427), Aristides (II. 307), Aelian (III. 340: a favourite of his).

[10] Cf. Boulenger, 138.

era (*P. Oxy.* 1795, col. ii., 1, μηδ' ἀδικῖν [= -εῖν] ζήτει μηδ' ἂν ἀδικῇ προσερίσης [= -ῃς]). Further, as Prof. Schmid has remarked, the correct use of particles declined under the Empire[11]. The forms οὐδὲ...οὐδέ have therefore been left in the text.

Sallustius writes in balanced clauses, which are not however isosyllabic or isotonic, as p. 2. 1 ff.,

> δεῖ μὲν ἐκ παίδων εὖ ἦχθαι καὶ μὴ ἀνοήτοις συντρέφεσθαι δόξαις
> δεῖ δὲ καὶ τὴν φύσιν ἀγαθοὺς εἶναι καὶ ἔμφρονας
> δεῖ δὲ αὐτοὺς καὶ τὰς κοινὰς ἐννοίας εἰδέναι.

He is fond of short balanced cola as (p. 2. 13 f.): οὐδὲ ἐκ σωμάτων εἰσι ∼ οὐδὲ τόπῳ περιέχονται. But he is capable of more sustained sentences.

§ 3. *Rhythm.*

It was observed by Wendland that there are traces in the less technical chapters of Sallustius of an observance of the law of the accentual clausula as formulated by Prof. U. von Wilamowitz-Moellendorff for Himerius[12]. The law states that a period tends to close thus:

∼ ∼ ∼́ ∼ ∼,

less often ∼ ∼́ ∼ ∼.

Prof. Norden rightly regards this as a preliminary stage of what we know as Wilhelm Meyer's law, which with some modifications is the norm of Byzantine fine writing[13]. It is

[11] I., p. 179 f.

[12] *Berl. Phil. Woch.* 1899, 1414; *Hermes*, XXXIV. 215 ff. Wilamowitz notes the use of this clausula also in the edict of Ampelius, Ditt. *Syll.*³ 905 [= *Syll.*² 423] and in Menander Rhetor, who is less regular in its use than Himerius. D. Serruys, *Philologie et Linguistique, Mélanges offerts à Louis Havet* (1909), 475 ff., on the basis of a minute study of Himerius, formulates a further law (p. 489): 'Devant un proparoxyton final le proparoxyton pénultième est exclus, à moins que le mot final ne porte l'accent sur le syllabe initiale' and finds (p. 492) that the last word is generally proparoxytone. (B. Keil *ap.* Reitzenstein, *Poimandres*, p. 371 ff. finds accentual rhythm in *C. H.* XVIII., Norden, *Agnostos Theos*, 66, in the *Kore Kosmou.*)

[13] Meyer's law (stated in *Der akzentuierte Satzschluss*, 1891 = *Gesammelte Abhandlungen*, II. 202 ff. and modified by P. Maas) is that between the last two accented syllables of a sentence there must be *two* or *four* unaccented syllables. This law is observed by Themistius (Christ-Schmid, II. 1013), S. Gregory of Nyssa, Synesius (P. Maas, *B. ph. W.* 1906, 776 f.: Syn. uses it, allowing 6 as well as 2 and 4, more regularly in his treatises than in his letters, except such

characteristic of Himerius, the modern (as opposed to Libanius the ancient), that he should substitute accent for quantity as the basis of the clausula[14].

In Sallustius we have these specimens of ~́ ~ ~ ~́ ~ ~: *μύθοις ἐχρήσαντο, θεῶν ἀγαθότητα, μύθοις εἰρήκασιν, γεννήσασι μένουσιν, λέγεται ῥίπτεσθαι, οἷον ἐπάνοδος, ἵλεῳ γένοιντο, κόσμον ἀφίκετο, οὐσίαν ἐνόμισαν, κινδυνεύειν ἐθέλωσι, ὁρωμένοις οὐ κρύπτεται, εἴρηνταί τε καὶ ὕμνηνται, ἤδη προείρηται, ἕπεται πάθεσιν, τοῖς μηχανήμασι* (as emended by Wendland, p. 16. 7), *ἐνεργεῖν οὐκ ἂν δύναιντο, ἕνεκα γίνεσθαι, τρίβειν τὰ σίτια, ἐκείνους ἀνάγοντες, τετράγωνα λέξουσιν, γενέσεως γένοιτο, τύχῃ νομίζεται, πραγμάτων συνίσταται, τύχης ἂν γένοιτο, γίνεται δίκαιος, ἡμάρτανον ἄνθρωποι, ἁμαρτημάτων καθαίρουσιν, εἴπομεν γίνεσθαι, δύναμιν γίγνεται, ἀσωμάτων ἡ δύναμις, ποιοῦσιν ἀδύνατον, ἵλεῳ γίνονται, ὄψεων κρύπτεσθαι, λέλυται ζήτησις, ἕνεκα γίνονται, ὁμοιότητι γίνεται, διδομένων ἀπάρχεσθαι, θυσιῶν ἀπαρχόμεθα, λέγειν ἀκόλουθον, σώζει τὰ σώματα, σώζοντος φθείρεται, φθείρεσθαι δύναται, ὁρῶμεν γινόμενα, λέγουσι φθείρεσθαι, ὄντα ἀπόλλυται, γίνεται ἕτερα, ὅπερ οὐ φαίνεται, φθείρειν δυνάμεθα, οὔτε μετέβαλε, ταράττειν τοὺς ἔμφρονας, σῶμα αἰσθάνεται, ἀφοσιούμενοι φύσεως, γνώσεως στέρεσθαι, ἁμαρτήσασιν ἕπονται, ἐνταῦθα πλανώμεναι, ἥσπερ καὶ ἥμαρτον, ἔχοντες τίκτονται, σώματα φέροιντο* (57 instances): ~́ ~ ~ ~́ with one or no unaccented syllable following occurs in more than 30 other cases. ~́ ~ ~ ~ ~ ~́ ~ ~ or ~́ ~ ~ ~ ~́ ~ or ~́ ~ ~ ~ ~ ~́ occurs 13 times, ~́ ~ ~ ~ ~ ~ ~ ~́ ~ once. On the other hand an interval of *three* unaccented syllables occurs 21 times, an

as are really speeches, as *Ep.* 57 Hercher: it will be remembered that Cicero in his letter to Lentulus, *Ad fam.* I. 9, has oratorical clausulae), S. Gregory Nazianzen (in his letters: Przychocki, 340 ff.), the writer of the letters to Phalaris (Wilamowitz, *Textgeschichte d. gr. Lyr.* 35[2], *Abh. Ges. Wiss. Gött*ing., N. F. IV. 3, 1900), Procopius of Gaza (he has usually 2 or 4 unaccented syllables in the gap, seldom 3, but he does not eschew the juxtaposition of accented syllables [P. Maas, *Byz. Zeit.* XXI. 52 f.]: he is less rigorous in a technical work, as in his Commentary on *Genesis* [Würthle, *Rhet. Stud.* VI. 94]), Nestorius (P. Maas, *Byz. Zeit.* XXI. 52 f.), Agathias (who however often allows 5; Franke, *Bresl. phil. Abh.* XLVII. 67 ff.), and, to give a late example, by Konstantinos Manasses (P. Maas, *Byz. Zeit.* XI. 505 ff.).

[14] Cf. Norden, p. 428, Wilamowitz, *Hermes*, *l.c.* Libanius does not observe Meyer's law (Christ-Schmid, II. 999): he uses quantitative rhythm (cf. Münscher, *Bursian*, 170 (1915), 147 ff., for a summary of Heilmann's dissertation on this subject, and of other recent studies).

interval of *one* 14 times, an interval of *five* twice, of *seven* once, of *nine* once; no interval 8 times[15].

On a rough calculation accentual clausulae conforming to the type occur three times in four. It must not however be supposed that accent superseded quantity completely and at once[16]. The poet Nonnus took into account both accent and quantity: in prose Archbishop Proclus serves as a type of the transition[17]. The chief rhythms of post-Demosthenic prose are according to Norden

(1) – ⏑ – – ⏓,
(2) – ⏑ – ⏕ ⏖ –,
(3) – ⏑ – ⏑,

with various other resolutions[18]. The prevalent types may be labelled cretic and trochee, double cretic, ditrochaeus. In the first eight chapters of Sallustius we have as examples of – ⏑ – – ⏓ or its resolutions: *μύθοις ἐχρήσαντο, θεῶν θεωροῦντες, ἐναντία ψυχῇ, σωμάτων εἰσι, δρωμένων καιρός, ἐστὶν ἀνθρώπων, ἀναγομέναις ψυχαῖς, ἔστι τῶν ψυχῶν* (*Χάριτας δ' ἐν Ἀφροδίτῃ*, p. 12. 16 if *δέ* is elided, which is doubtful: the MS. gives hiatus), *τὴν γένεσιν εἶναι, ἤδη προείρηται, ἀθάνατον οἶδεν* (11 clear cases); of – ⏑ – – ⏖ ⏓: *τοιοίδε γινέσθωσαν, οὐδέποτε γίνεται, δυναμένοις εἰδέναι, αἰνίττεται τοῦ θεοῦ, μῆλον εἶναί φησι, λοιποῦ μεθ' αὐτῆς ἔχειν, συνάπτεται τοῖς θεοῖς,*

[15] These statistics make no claim to an exactitude which could only be illusory, for several reasons. Firstly, it is extremely hard to determine the fourth-century accentuation of a word, and these calculations are based on the accents in ordinary use. Secondly, uncertainty must exist as to the nature of the break in sense at which a clausula may be expected. Thirdly, we do not know exactly where elision was practised: H. B. Dewing's valuable article, *A. J. P.* XXXII. (1911), 188 ff., esp. 201, shows that hiatus was often allowed where, in earlier times, elision would have been normal. Still, they indicate clearly the tendency of the prose writing of Sallustius.

[16] S. Aug., *De doctr. chr.* IV. 10 (XXXIV. 99 Migne), quoted by G. Reynolds, *The Clausulae in the De ciuitate dei of S. Augustine*, p. 6, bears witness to the decline of sensitiveness thereto in Latin.

[17] Norden, *Kunstprosa*, 922 f.

[18] *Kunstprosa*, 924: for their later use cf. A. Boulanger, *Aelius Aristide* (1923), 434. For this purpose it is of no importance whether – ⏑ – ⏑ ⏑ ⏑ – should be explained as cretic + paeonic rather than as a double cretic with resolution. It is certainly a traditional quantitative form.

Forms (1) and (3) are characteristic of Chariton, [Herod.] Περὶ πολιτείας (cf. Heibger, *De clausulis Charitoneis*, Diss. Münster, 1911; *ib.* 99, it is noted that [Herod.] has a preponderance of heavy endings), and Galen (Ritzenfeld, *B. ph. W.* 1907, 540 ff.).

ὥσπερ ἀναγεννωμένων, γίνεται τῆς νυκτός, εἰσιν ἐγκόσμιοι (10 cases); of – ⏑ – ⏑: *οὐδὲν πέφυκεν* (1 case). Even in these chapters such types as – ⏑ ⏑ – ⏑, – ⏑ – ⏑ –, – – – ⏑ ⏑ occur in addition to the orthodox clausulae, and there is a marked tendency to purely spondaic closes. After the end of vii. quantitative rhythm seems to disappear in the complexity of the argument: it appears fitfully, as in ix., *ἐπ' ἀγαθῷ γίνεται* (⏖ ⏑ – – ⏑ –), *ἕκαστον ἄνθρωπον*, in x., *ψυχῆς δέονται*, in xi., *πολιτεία καλεῖται*, xii., *πάντα ποιούντων, φαίνεται τὰ κακά* (– ⏑ – ⏖ ⏑), *ἁμαρτημάτων καθαίρουσι*, xiii., *ἀρκέσει ταῦτα, κατὰ δύναμιν γίγνεται*, xiv., *κολαστικοῖς συναπτόντων*, xv., *ὑποδοχὴν δεῖται* (⏖ ⏑ – – –), xvi., *-ων ἀπάρχεσθαι, -ων ἀπαρχόμεθα*, even in xvii., where the dialectic is fiercest, xviii., *γίνεται ταῦτα, τῶν θεῶν ἐκπεσεῖν*, xix., *οὐκ ἂν εἶχον*, xxi., *καὶ δυνηθεῖσιν*. Type (1) predominates.

In any case Sallustius is no observer of law in this matter: he ends with *ἔστιν ἰδεῖν* when *ἰδεῖν ἔστιν* would restore the cretic base[19]. But his instinct for quantity causes certain rhythms to recur.

Clearly he belongs to the transitional period. That he shows clear clausula-rhythm agrees with his express purpose of writing an exoteric work[20]: the clausula is in truth the touchstone of prose rhythm[21].

[19] p. 6. 11, *ἄλλ|οις ἰδεῖν ἔστιν* would give – ⏑́ – | – ⏑.

[20] Clausula-rhythm rests in the first instance on a preference for and natural tendency to use certain types of ending; this unconscious tendency is well exemplified by the fact, noted by Ritzenfeld, *B. ph. W.* 1907, 540 ff., that Galen has the same proportion of good *clausulae* in his popular *Protrepticus* and in his technical *Περὶ μυῶν ἀνατομῆς*: the only natural explanation of this is that the rhythm was natural to him. Still, it became an ornament deliberately used. S. Augustine says, *De doctrina Christiana*, IV. 20. 41 (XXXIV. 109 Migne), *sicut in meo eloquio, quantum modeste fieri arbitror, non praetermitto istos numeros clausularum* (cf. *ib.* 26. 56, p. 117 Migne): on one occasion he apologises for failing to add clausulae to a work, pleading shortness of time (G. Ammon, *Phil. Woch.* 1922, 1069 f.). We have MSS. of Plutarch in which the order of words has been changed to secure accentual closes (Pohlenz, *G. G. N.* 1913, 338 ff., De Groot, *Handbook of antique prose rhythm*, I. 139).

Such ornament would most naturally be omitted in an esoteric treatise, cf. p. cx., n. 13 *supra*: in Procl. *In Rep.* II., p. 1–4. 9 Kroll (a specimen taken at random) there is no clear trace of cretic-trochaic clausulae, and if we seek accentual closes we find intervals of 2 unaccented syllables 12 times, of 4, 7 times, but also of 1 syllable 3 times, of 3, 7 times, of 5 twice: the final word is 7 times proparoxytone (that is, half the clausulae are accentually irregular).

[21] The rhythm of the clausulae recurs in the rest of the sentence, but its existence therein is harder to seize and to define.

§ 4. *Hiatus.*

The literary movement conveniently called the Second Sophistic did not show an Isocratean zeal in the avoidance of hiatus. In the third century, however, Longinus forbad hiatus, and in the fourth century Themistius eschews it in his speeches, though not in his diatribes, while Libanius is fairly strict. S. Gregory Nazianzenus avoids hiatus in his funeral orations and also in his letters. Certain instances noted in the latter would not have been countenanced by the strictest authorities: such are those after -ᾱ -ει -η -ι -οι -ου -υ -ω (yet the MS. authority is in some cases uncertain). Later the school of Gaza was strict in avoiding hiatus[22].

Sallustius is no purist. Apart from minor examples, as ἀκοῦσαι ἐθέλοντας, κακύνεται εἰ[23], or such as are defended by a pause, as ἀσώματοι, οὐδέ, or again χαίρει, ἀνομοιότητα, we have also ὅτι ἀμετάβλητος, ἄνθρωποι ὀρθῶς, οὐσίαι οὐδέ, νοῦ αἱ, ζῴου αἱ, θεῖοι οἱ, ὅτι ὥσπερ, ποταμῷ ἐρασθῆναι, τροφὴ ὥσπερ in the first four chapters[24].

[22] Cf. for references Lübker, *Reallexikon*[8], 464 *b*, *s.v.* Hiat, also for Longinus Christ-Schmid, II. 891, for Themistius, *ib.* 1012, for Libanius, *ib.* 999, for S. Gregory, Przychocki, 297 f., and in general H. B. Dewing's paper, quoted p. cxi, n. 15 *supra*. A. Boulanger, *Aelius Aristide*, 428, notes that Aristides allows hiatus, but nevertheless employs certain traditional devices (as crasis, elision, choice of synonyms) to avoid it.

X. Hirth, *Diss. phil. Arg.* XII. i., 149 ff., and Przychocki, 299 ff. enumerate devices for the avoidance of hiatus, as the use of ἕνεκεν, μέχρι(ς) [-ι alone commended by Atticists], οὕτω(ς), ὅσπερ, ὅπερ for ὅς, ὅ.

[23] This -αι counts as short: cf. Przychocki, 306.

[24] Julian however, though he could bear μεθίεσθαι, ἅτε, p. 120 A, δὴ οὖν, p. 138 D, σοι ἄξιον, p. 223 C, is sensitive and avoids hiatus (for this purpose he uses ἕνεκεν for ἕνεκα); cf. Ammon's review of Klimek's study, *Phil. Woch.* 1920, 193 ff. Technical writers have no respect for these minutiae: cf. [Iambl.] *Theol. Arithm.* 43 ff., p. 58. 2, πρωτογόνου ἑνός, l. 20, μονάδι ἀσχίστῳ, p. 59. 1, συντυγχάνει ἐν, p. 60. 9, βραχὺ ὑποβεβηκώς, τρίτῃ ἔτι ἐλάσσων, l. 12, αὖ ἀπό, ὀγδόῃ ἴσως, l. 16, ἡ τρίτη ἑβδομάς, Iambl. *De myst.* II. 3, p. 71. 4, οὗτοι εἶναι οἱ, II. 2, p. 70. 2, δεῖ ἀμφισβητεῖν, 70. 6, δυνηθείη ἀψεύστως, Procl. *ad R. P.* II., p. 82. 27, ὕλῃ ὄν.

§ 5. *Figures of speech.*

Sallustius writes in a plain manner. He uses *antithesis* freely, *chiasmus* twice[25], rhetorical questions repeatedly[26]; he is fond of parentheses[27].

His style has the merit of being unostentatious: at the same time, its brevity makes it sometimes obscure, as for instance in ix.

§ 6. *Plan and form.*

The tractate falls into two clearly defined halves: the first is a general exposition of the subject (i.—xiii. *ἀρκέσει ταῦτα*), the second consists of a series of appendices on disputed questions[28]. Even so the arrangement is clumsy: vii., xiii., xvii. are concerned with the same subject, and the insertion of the Attis myth in iv. is awkward. From these indications and from the lack of an opening it may be conjectured that the work is unfinished[29]. Praechter argues from p. 24. 16, *περὶ δὲ τοῦ μὴ γένεσθαι ταῦτα μηδὲ ἀλλήλων χωρίζεσθαι λείπεται λέγειν, ἐπειδὴ καὶ ἡμεῖς ἐν τοῖς ⟨ ⟩ λόγοις ὑπὸ τῶν πρώτων τὰ δεύτερα εἴπομεν γενέσθαι*, from the inadequate reference to Nous (p. 14. 19), and from the phrase *ἐν τοῖς περὶ τούτων λόγοις* (p. 10. 31), that the author occupied himself with making excerpts from a larger treatise: the first passage he regards as due to the inadvertent copying of a cross reference in the original to something not reproduced in the shorter

[25] p. 14. 4, *τὰ μὲν νοῦν μιμεῖται καὶ κύκλῳ κινεῖται, τὰ δὲ ψυχὴν καὶ ἐπ' εὐθείας· καὶ τῶν μὲν ἐπ' εὐθείας...τῶν δὲ κύκλῳ...*: p. 20. 9, *τῶν μὲν κακῶν ἡ εὐτυχία οὐκ ἂν ἀφέλοι τὴν κακίαν, τοῖς δὲ ἀγαθοῖς ἡ ἀρετὴ μόνον ἀρκέσει. οἱ δὲ περὶ τῆς ἀρετῆς καὶ τῆς κακίας λόγοι πάλιν δέονται....*

[26] p. 4. 15 ff.; 16. 13 ff.; 18. 16 ff.; 22. 14; 36. 1 ff.

[27] p. 2. 11, 13, 14; 6. 21; 8. 10, 18, 21; 14. 13; 26. 17; 28. 17; 30. 12.

[28] So Praechter, referring to Norden, *Kunstprosa*, 90_2 for the excursus in antiquity: cf. the arrangement of Aristotle's treatment of friendship in *Eth. N.* VIII., IX. (first the general treatment, then *ἀπορίαι*) or the *Vita Hesiodi* (it ends with an *ἀπορία*: such *ἀπορίαι* could be collected independently, as in the work of Basil preserved in Cod. Patmiac. 31 [Krumbacher^2, 131]). With *λείπεται λέγειν*, 24. 17, cf. Nemes. *De nat. hom.* xli., p. 324 Matthaei, *ὑπόλοιπόν ἐστιν εἰπεῖν διὰ ποίαν αἰτίαν αὐτεξούσιοι γεγόναμεν.*

[29] It has been suggested (p. ciii *supra*) that it was never published.

work[30]. The actual phrase does not indeed occur earlier; but it is perhaps possible to regard it as referring to the creation of the *ἐγκόσμιοι θεοί* by the *ὑπερκόσμιοι* (in vi., p. 10. 30 f.). The gods are expressly included in creation (*ταῦτα* in l. 16 refers to *θεῶν καὶ κόσμου καὶ τῶν ἀνθρωπίνων πραγμάτων* in l. 13 f., and below, p. 26. 7, we read *μεγίστης δὲ δυνάμεως οὔσης οὐκ ἀνθρώπους ἔδει καὶ ζῷα μόνα ποιεῖν ἀλλὰ θεούς τε καὶ †ἀνθρώπους καὶ δαίμονας*), and by referring the phrase to them we understand *μηδὲ ἀλλήλων χωρίζεσθαι* (compare p. 2. 15 ff. *supra*, *αἱ τῶν θεῶν οὐσίαι...οὐδὲ τῆς πρώτης αἰτίας ἢ ἀλλήλων χωρίζονται*). As for *ἐν τοῖς περὶ τούτων λόγοις*, it is a plain reference to treatises such as the more elaborate works of Iamblichus (as the Περὶ θεῶν) or similar philosophers[31].

The literary form to which this work would appear to belong is the *isagoge*. This type of introductory treatise with its fixed features (dedicatory introduction to son or to other young man, demand of suitable preliminary qualifications in the learner, sketch of the history of the art, division of the body of the work into two parts, one concerned with the *ars*, one with the *artifex*) is known to us from a number of examples collected by Norden, who has put the *Ars Poetica* in this category[32]. Sallustius gives us the *artifex* in i., passes to the *ars* in ii. (cf. esp. p. 2. 9 f.); iii. gives the historical section. But the resemblance should not be pressed.

[30] *P. W.* I A, 1963.

[31] So in Hermetic treatises we read X. 1, *τῶν γενικῶν λόγων των πρὸς αὐτὸν ἐκλελαλημένων ἐστὶν ἐπιτομή...ἀλλαχοῦ δὲ...ἐδιδάξαμεν*, XII. 5, *λόγος ὃν ἔμπροσθέν μοι διεξελήλυθας* (so Scott reads), XIII. 1, *ἐν τοῖς γενικοῖς*, *Exc.* VI., p. 410. 14 Scott (*ap.* Stob. I. 21. 9, p. 189 W.), *ἐν τοῖς ἔμπροσθεν γενικοῖς λόγοις ὑπέσχου*, although the *Corpus* did not exist as a collected whole (cf. *J. Eg. Arch.* XI. 132). A close parallel to the phrase of Sallustius occurs in Julian IV. (dedicated to a S. who is probably our writer), p. 157 C, *τελειοτέροις δ' εἰ βούλει περὶ τῶν αὐτῶν καὶ μυστικωτέροις λόγοις ἐπιστῆσαι, ἐντυχὼν τοῖς παρὰ τοῦ θείου γενομένοις Ἰαμβλίχου περὶ τῶν αὐτῶν τούτων συγγράμμασι τὸ τέλος ἐκεῖσε τῆς ἀνθρωπίνης εὑρήσεις σοφίας.*

[32] *Hermes*, XL. (1905) 481 ff., cf. Barwick, *ib.* LVII. (1922) 1 ff. The isagoge of Albinus as we have it lacks the introductory section, just as does our treatise. It is possible that some remarks which originally stood at the beginning have been lost; it is tempting to suggest that Sallustius may have intended to dedicate the work to Julian, and on the latter's death did not write the dedication or suppressed it if he had written one.

CHAPTER V

THE TRANSMISSION OF THE TEXT

§ 1. *Manuscripts.*

Ambrosianus B 99 *sup.* (n. 121 in Martini-Bassi, *Cat. Codd. gr. Bibl. Ambr.* I. 130 f.) is a volume composed of three parts. The first (*folia* 1–6) contains the close of the *Homeric Allegories* of Heraclitus, then a table of contents for this text and the text itself, all in a hand attributed to the thirteenth century (though it is difficult to feel any confidence that it does not belong to the fourteenth), followed by some verses of Tzetzes written in a hand probably of the fourteenth century. The second includes Moschus Siculus, *Europa*, two notes beginning ἰστέον ὅτι ἐγκύκλιον παιδείαν, and the *Axe* of Simmias, the *Altar* of Dosiades, and the *Syrinx* of Theocritus with scholia, in various hands attributed to the thirteenth and fourteenth centuries. The third is a fourteenth century *Odyssey* with scholia.

Barberinianus I. 84 (now in the Vatican, written and possessed by Constantius Patricius, a humanist of the latter half of the sixteenth century) contains a number of philosophic opuscula in a small neat Renaissance hand: Sallustius occupies *folia* 41–54.

Ambrosianus O 123, of the sixteenth century, contains on *folia* 59–66 Sallustius in 38 chapters, commencing at ζῴου αἱ αἰσθήσεις (p. 2. 17), and thereafter Moschus *Europa*, the note ἰστέον ὅτι..., Simmias and Dosiades, just as the accident of binding has combined them in Ambrosianus B 99. This part of the manuscript was written by Manuel Morus of Crete (Martini-Bassi, *Catalogus Codicum*, II. 693: they number it as 598).

It can hardly be doubted that G. Muccio, who first drew attention to Ambrosianus B 99, and to whom is due further the credit of determining its reading in certain places where the writing has become very faint, was right in maintaining that it was the parent of the Barberini text: it cannot be asserted with confidence that the copying was direct. The text of Manuel Morus is obviously a copy of B 99: that it should contain the same combination of Sallustius and other writings can hardly be accidental, and a brief examination showed me that the copying was very close. Both Ambrosian MSS. belonged to Pinelli[1]. On Ambrosianus B 99 alone depends our knowledge of what Sallustius wrote: it may be added that its witness is honest if defective[2]: all its readings (apart, for instance, from its omissions of *iota subscriptum* and its spelling of ὑγίεια as ὑγεία) are given in the *apparatus*; some of them were published by Muccio: the record here given is based on a collation of the manuscript made by me in March 1923, and on a rotograph.

§ 2. *The tradition.*

In the Ambrosian MS. Sallustius was preceded by Heraclitus. The short fragment of the latter is older than any extant MS. of the earlier part of his work, and it has been shown that the book from which these six leaves were detached was the parent of all MSS. of Heraclitus except Vaticanus 305, which is descended from a kindred text, and the New College MS. (n. 298), which has peculiar readings: Vaticanus 871 ends in the middle of the page at the exact point at which Ambr. begins, and may very plausibly be regarded

[1] *Studi italiani*, III. 8 ff. The confusion of the title in the Barberini MS., its false expansions of compendia in Ambr., its reproduction of one which proved incomprehensible, are decisive. I give its readings in an Appendix for completeness, from my own collation corrected by the aid of one which Prof. Cumont kindly gave me. The lost *codex Saregicus*, known to us from De Rycke's description, had the same error as Barb. in its title, and similar contents (in part identical), and may have been an intermediary stage in the tradition. That O 123 is a copy of B 99 was seen by H. Schrader, *Hermes*, XXII. 339.

[2] Muccio's suspicions of widespread interpolation, expressed in *Studi italiani*, VII. 45 ff. (as that xiii., xvii. are later additions), were rightly rejected by P. Wendland, *B. ph. W.* 1899, 1409 ff.: xvii. was earlier suspected by Passamonti.

as descended from the other half of Ambrosianus B 99 after it had suffered injury[3].

Vaticanus 305 contains further Porphyry *Quaestiones Homericae* and *De antro nympharum*, and [Heraclitus] *De incredibilibus*. As there is other evidence for this connection of Porphyry and Heraclitus it is by no means improbable that the archetype of these MSS. contained some Porphyry, Heraclitus, Sallustius, and the pseudo-Heraclitea[4].

Such gatherings of kindred matter came into being when the parchment book superseded the papyrus roll, that is, in and after the fourth century of our era. Photius in the ninth century mentions a volume (*cod.* 186) containing Conon and Apollodorus, another (*cod.* 189) in which the paradoxographical works of Sotion and of Nicolaus preceded the local mythology of Acestorides, and various theological collections[5]. We have a geographical corpus containing Marcianus, Menippus (abridged), Scylax, Dionysius, Scymnus, excerpts from Heraclides Criticus and from Strabo, the *Mansiones Parthicae* of Isidore, and possibly four other peripli: this appears in varying degrees of completeness in a number of manuscripts[6]. A combination of Agathemerus and two Anonymi is preserved in eleven copies[7]. Cod. Heidelb. 398 contains a small collection of Paradoxographi side by side with geographical texts[8], and we have various rhetorical corpora[9].

Many of such productions may be due to that revival of learning which began in the ninth century in the East, at the

[3] Oelmann, *Proleg. ad Heraclit. Alleg. Hom. ed. Soc. Phil. Bonn.*, xi ff. A. Brinkmann, *Rh. M.* LXII. 614 ff., has since drawn attention to the mutilated Heraclitus in Monacensis gr. 487, a descendant and (he argues) a direct copy of *Ambr.* before its injury. Here, as in Vat. 871 and B. M. 16 C XVII., Harpocration comes before Heraclitus: in Vat. 871 Horapollon is placed between the two, in Escor. Σ–I–20 he follows Heraclitus. It is hard to see why Harpocration and Horapollon should have been conjoined with Heraclitus and Sallustius, but we must allow for chances of binding.

[4] Probably attached to the collection by the accident of name, as Reinhardt suggests, *P. W.* VIII. 510.

[5] Others of his codices contained a medley of theological matter.

[6] Cf. C. Müller, *Geographi graeci minores*, I. ix.

[7] Müller, *op. cit.* II. xli. ff.

[8] Cf. O. Keller, *Rerum naturalium scriptores Graeci minores*, I. viii.

[9] Cf. H. Rabe, *Rh. Mus.* LXVII. (1912) 321 ff. A Latin parallel is the corpus of herbal texts discussed in *Folklore*, XXXVI., 1925, 93 ff.

very time when the Carolingian renaissance began in the West. Among its activities was the compilation of convenient bodies of excerpts, such as those which pass under the name of Constantine Porphyrogennetos.

The additional evidence for the association of Heraclitus and Porphyry in the MS. tradition is afforded by the Scholia on the Iliad[10]. Those in Venetus A quote Porphyry seldom, and in an abridged form: those in Ven. B (and its brothers, Townleiensis, Escorialenses Ω and υ I. 1) quote Porphyry more frequently, and Heraclitus once (on V. 392). The second hand in B (thirteenth century) adds copiously from Porphyry and from Heraclitus[11]. It is likely that he used a longer form of the scholia copied in a shorter form by the first hand and by the scribes of the kindred texts: similar was the MS. which Eustathius must have used[12], and similar the source from which Leidensis Vossianus 64 (fifteenth century) drew Porphyriana and Heraclitea, in some cases fuller than those of B^2[13]. These facts support the idea that a combination of matter from Porphyry and Heraclitus had found its way into Scholia: it may fairly be regarded as more probable that the scribe of B^2 used other scholia to amplify his own than that he read Heraclitus. Naturally certainty in these matters is not to be attained. Now in the Leidensis two quotations from Heraclitus are given under the name of Porphyry[14]: so also the

[10] In their present form they represent the addition of notes from ὑπομνήματα to texts with brief marginal notes, like our papyri of Pindar's Paeans and of the *Ichneutae* (cf. J. W. White, *The Scholia on the Aves of Aristophanes*, liv. ff.: further examples are *P. Oxy.* 1234, 1360 [Alcaeus], 1361 [Bacchylides], 1790 [Ibycus]). For Homer we have good specimens of the ὑπόμνημα in *P. Oxy.* 221, 1086, and 1087.

[11] For this supposition of the existence of a longer form and of a shorter we may compare the Scholia of Aristophanes: the eleventh-century Ravennas follows the latter, the twelfth-century Venetus the former (J. W. White, *op. cit.*, p. lxxi. ff.). B and B^2 can hardly have used the *same* original, as A. Gudeman seems to suggest (*P. W.* II. A, 634. 49): the agreement of B and T points clearly to the existence of some lost common ancestor giving the shorter form. That the longer form and the shorter form belong to the same tradition is fairly clear: B^2 continues notes of B after a ~ to indicate the transition (Hiller, *Fleck. Jahrb.* XCVII. [1868], 802).

[12] Cf. Cohn, *P. W.* VI. 1460 ff.: it contained also critical information such as is given in Ven. A.

[13] Cf. Schrader, *Hermes*, XX. 380 ff.

[14] Oelmann, *op. cit.* xxiv.

Scholia on Od. XXII. 233 given in Cod. Vindob. phil. gr. 133 quotes three lines of Heraclitus as by Porphyry[15].

Porphyry and Heraclitus were then both used in Scholia prior to Eustathius (twelfth century) and to B², prior, also, if our conjecture is correct, to the parent of B τ Esc υ I. 1; as the last is dated 10th–11th century such Scholia could not well be later than *circa* 900. If the confusion of Porphyry and Heraclitus in Leidensis Vossianus also goes back to this source and is not purely accidental, it shows how closely the two were associated and would suit, though not prove, the theory that a small allegorical corpus containing them was formed in the ninth century. That Sallustius was even then associated with them is not unlikely: yet we can hardly look for extensive traces of his use, since he does not treat Homer's subject-matter apart from the Judgment of Paris, which is mentioned in passing in *Il.* XXIV. 29 f. However, when Eustathius says *ἧς* (*sc. τῆς βασιλείας*) *αἴνιγμα καὶ ὁ Ζεὺς εἰς νοῦν ποτε μεταλαμβανόμενος, ἔτι δὲ καὶ ὁ τοῦ Διὸς πατὴρ Κρόνος, εἰς νοῦν οὐ τὸν ἁπλῶς ἀλλὰ τὸν καθαρὸν ἀλληγορούμενος, ὡς οἷά τις κόρος νοῦς, ὁ καὶ ἀγκυλομήτης διὰ τὸ κατ' αὐτὸν ἀγκύλον καὶ συνεστραμμένον. οὐ γὰρ ἔξω πλανᾶταί που ὁ τοιοῦτος νοῦς ἀλλ' εἰς ἑαυτὸν ἔστραπται, καὶ μάλισθ' ὅτε νοεῖν ἐθέλει ἑαυτόν,* he does in the last words perhaps use Sallustius iv., p. 4. 25, *ἐπειδὴ νοερὸς ὁ θεός, πᾶς δὲ νοῦς εἰς ἑαυτὸν ἐπιστρέφει, τὴν οὐσίαν ὁ μῦθος αἰνίττεται τοῦ θεοῦ*[16].

[15] Oelmann, xxv.

[16] *ad Il.* II. 207, p. 203. 20. Κρόνος—Χρόνος and Κρόνος—κορόνους are commonplace: yet this point is not. (Eustathius is certainly *not* using Demo: we have her note *ad loc.* in the Scholia.) Another possible trace of the influence of Sallustius occurs in the Ἀλληγορία ἀναγωγική which Joannes Diaconus Galenus wrote on *Il.* IV. 1–4 (Flach, *Glossen und Scholien zur hesiodeischen Theogonie*, 423): it is there stated that myths may be allegorised φυσικῶς, ἠθικῶς, θεολογικῶς: this omits ὑλικῶς, but that fashion was not approved by our author (p. 6, 2). This differs from the schemes of Aphthonius (cf. p. xlv, n. 35) and of Eustathius, *Proem. in Il.*, p. 3. The *Anonymus* printed by Westermann in his *Scriptores poeticae historiae graeci*, 327, gives ἢ πραγματικῶς (=on Euhemerist lines, cf. Flach, 132), ἢ ψυχικῶς ἢ στοιχειακῶς: this lacks the characteristic θεολογικῶς and resembles much Tzetz. *ad* Hes. *Op. et Di.* 1., p. 36. 1 Gaisford. We cannot however well expect evidence of much reading of Sallustius at Byzantium: it is clear from the allegorisation of the myth of Kronos by Psellus (published by C. Sathas, *Annuaire de l'Association pour l'encouragement des études grecques*, IX. (1875), 219 ff.) that Psellus was not acquainted with the treatment of that theme in ch. iv. of our text.

Such a corpus would have served practical ends, since the allegorisation of myths was a regular literary occupation in Byzantine times[17]. But these speculations are in the air: we cannot trace the history of the text of Sallustius with any confidence, and the stemma indicating its possible descent is therefore relegated to a footnote[18].

§ 3. *Editions.*

Of these it is not necessary to speak at length, since Muccio has given full information in *Studi italiani*, III. 24 ff., VII. 45 f. The *editio princeps*, published by Gabriel Naudaeus as the work of Leo Allatius at Rome in 1638[19], was based on the Barberini MS., making certain easy emendations, giving the work its present title, altering the chapter-division, and modifying the κεφάλαια which precede the text in the MSS. (Muccio, 26): instead of the thirty-two chapters of the Barberini MS. (which follows herein Ambrosianus B 99, while the other copy, O 123, substituted a division in thirty-eight chapters[20]), Allatius made twenty-one. Thomas Gale, Fellow

[17] Cf. the *Anonymus* quoted in n. 16: he gives practical advice for the art. Examples are afforded by Psellus, Tzetzes, Anon. *De Ulixis erroribus* (Westermann, 329 ff.), Nicephorus Gregorus in the fourteenth century (Matranga, *Anecdota graeca*, II. 520), and Christophorus Contoleon (*ib.* 479 ff.). The same pursuit in the West produced the *Ouidius moralisatus*: cf. also the moralising scholia on Terence, H. T. Karsten, *Album Herwerden*, 129 ff.

[18]

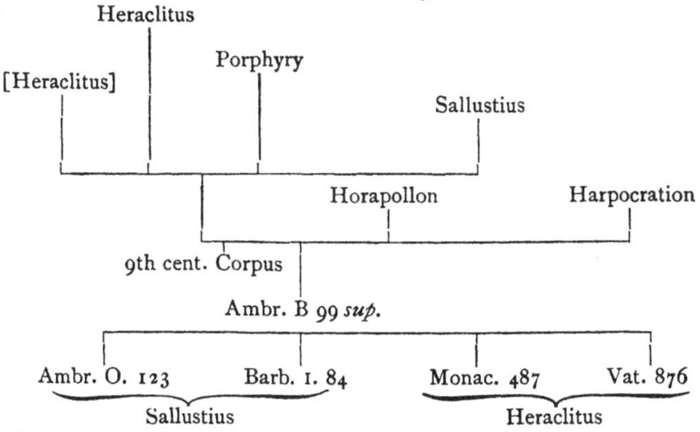

[19] A revised edition appeared at Leyden in 1639.

[20] The chapters in Ambrosianus B 99 are indicated by numerals in the margin:

of Trinity and Regius Professor of Greek in this University, included Sallustius in his *Opuscula Mythologica, Physica, et Ethica*, published at Cambridge in 1671 and at Amsterdam in a revised form in 1688: the text is based on that of Allatius, but includes some good emendations of his own. In the eighteenth century the text was translated into French by J. H. S. Formey, who reprinted the Greek also (Berlin, 1748), into German by J. G. Schultess (*Bibliothek der griechischen Philosophen*, III., Zürich, 1779), and into English by Thomas Taylor, who published this translation in a volume containing also his renderings of the Pythagoric sentences of Demophilus and five hymns of Proclus (London, 1793)[21]. Gale's notes, as also those of the *editio princeps* and some of Formey's, were reproduced by J. C. Orelli in his edition (Zürich, 1821), a work of considerable use by reason of its collection of parallel passages from other Neoplatonists. This in its turn was employed by Mullach for his reprint of the text, *Fragmenta Philosophorum Graecorum*, III., 30–50 (Paris, 1881). All these editions are based on the collation of the Barberini MS. by Allatius. Muccio, by his discovery of Ambrosianus B 99, and by his realisation of its importance (*Studi italiani*, III., 1895, 1 ff.) put the text on a new basis; his projected edition has not appeared, though some conjectures have been put forward by him in *Studi italiani*, VII., 1899, 45 ff.

The bibliography of the treatise in recent years is brief: Zeller, *Die Philosophie der Griechen*[4], III., ii., $793_{1,2}$.

some of these have vanished, while for others it is difficult to determine at which word they mean the break to come. The list which follows is therefore defective. (1) τοὺς μὲν περὶ θεῶν. (2) δεῖ δὲ καὶ τὰς... (?). (3) οἱ δὲ λόγοι.... (4) οὐδὲ ἐκ σωμάτων εἰσί. (5) οὐδὲ τόπῳ περιέχονται. (6) τί δήποτε οὖν τούτους. (7) τῶν δὲ μύθων οἱ μὲν. (8) πρέπουσι δὲ τῶν μύθων. (9) ἀκόλουθον δὲ τούτοις ἐστι. (10) τῶν δὲ θεῶν οἱ μέν. (11) τῶν δὲ ὑπερκοσμίων. (12) καὶ σφαίρας δὲ τούτων. (13) αὐτὸν δὲ τὸν κόσμον. (14) τῶν δὲ ἐν τῷ κόσμῳ σωμάτων (?). (15) τῶν δὲ ψυχῶν αἱ μὲν. (16) ἀθάνατον δὲ αὐτὴν εἶναι ἀνάγκη. (17) τὴν δὲ τῶν θεῶν πρόνοιαν. (18) οἱ δὲ περὶ τῆς ἀρετῆς. (19) καὶ αἱ πολιτεῖαι δὲ (?). (20) ἀλλὰ πῶς θεῶν. (21) περὶ μὲν οὖν θεῶν. (22) ? (23) εἰ δέ τις τὸ μὲν (?). (24) ἄξιον δὲ οἶμαι. (25) τὸν δὲ κόσμον ὅτι μὲν. (26) καὶ μὴν οὐδὲ τὸ ἀθεΐας. (27) καὶ διὰ τοῦτο ὡς ἔοικεν. (28) ? (29) κολάζονται δὲ τοῦ σώματος ἐξελθοῦσαι. (30) αἱ δὲ μετεμψυχώσεις. (31) τὴν δὲ μετεμψύχωσιν. (32) αἱ δὲ κατ' ἀρετὴν ζήσασαι.

[21] I have not seen any of these translations.

F. Cumont, *Salluste le philosophe: Revue de philologie*, XVI. (1892), 49–56.

E. E. Passamonti, *La dottrina dei miti di Sallustio filosofo neoplatonico: Rendiconti accad. Lincei, Ser. quinta*, I. (1892), 643–664: *La dottrina morale e religiosa di Sallustio filosofo neoplatonico, ib.* 712–727.

K. Praechter, *Woch. Klass. Phil.*, 1900, 182–6.

P. Wendland, *Berl. Phil. Woch.*, 1899, 1409–1414 (reviews of Muccio's second paper).

G. Murray, *Four Stages of Greek Religion* (Oxford, 1912), ch. iv. *The Last Protest*, pp. 157–184, and a translation of Sallustius, pp. 187–214, reprinted as *Five Stages of Greek Religion* (Oxford, 1925), ch. v., pp. 211–238 and pp. 241–267.

K. Praechter, *Sallustius* (37) in Pauly-Wissowa, *Real-enzyklopädie*, II. A, 1960. 50 ff. (published 1920).

I have not seen J. Gimazane, *De Salustio Promoto praetorio Galliarum et Orientis praefecto*, a Bordeaux thesis published at Toulouse in 1889: its theory is summarised by Praechter in his article, 1964. 51 ff., and would seem to need no further discussion. It need hardly be said that there is much of value for the interpretation of this text in general works of reference and in monographs dealing with other authors.

SALLVSTIVS

Σαλουστίου φιλοσόφου κεφάλαια τοῦ βιβλίου. οἷον δεῖ εἶναι τὸν ἀκούοντα καὶ περὶ κοινῆς ἐννοίας. ὅτι ὁ θεὸς οὐ μεταβάλλεται. ὅτι πᾶς θεὸς ἀγέννητος καὶ ἀΐδιος. ὅτι πᾶς θεὸς ἀσώματος. ὅτι οὐκ ἐν τόπῳ. περὶ μύθων. ὅτι καὶ θεῖοι οἱ μῦθοι. ὅτι διὰ τί θεῖοι οἱ μῦθοι. ὅτι πέντε εἴδη τῶν μύθων, καὶ ἑκάστου ὑποδείγματα. περὶ τῆς πρώτης 5 αἰτίας. περὶ τῶν ὑπερκοσμίων θεῶν. περὶ τῶν δώδεκα ἐγκοσμίων. ὅτι σφαῖραι δώδεκα. περὶ τῆς φύσεως τοῦ κόσμου καὶ τῆς ἀϊδιότητος. ὅτι γῆ μέση καὶ διὰ τί. περὶ νοῦ καὶ ψυχῆς. ὅτι ἀθάνατος ἡ ψυχή. περὶ προνοίας καὶ εἱμαρμένης καὶ τύχης. περὶ ἀρετῆς καὶ κακίας. περὶ ὀρθῆς πολιτείας καὶ φαύλης. πόθεν τὰ κακὰ καὶ ὅτι κακοῦ φύσις οὐκ 10 ἔστιν. πῶς τὰ ἀΐδια λέγεται γίνεσθαι. πῶς οἱ θεοὶ μὴ μεταβαλλόμενοι ὀργίζεσθαι καὶ θεραπεύεσθαι λέγονται. διὰ τί ἀνενδεεῖς ὄντας τοὺς θεοὺς τιμῶμεν. περὶ θυσιῶν καὶ τῶν ἄλλων τιμῶν, ὅτι θεοὺς μὲν οὐδέν, ἀνθρώπους δὲ ὠφελοῦμεν. ὅτι καὶ φύσει ἄφθαρτος ὁ κόσμος. διὰ τί ἀθεΐαι γίγνονται καὶ ὅτι θεὸς οὐ βλάπτεται. ὅτι αἱ ἀποφράδες 15 διὰ τὸ μὴ δύνασθαι ἀεὶ τοὺς ἀνθρώπους θεραπεύειν ἐγένοντο. διὰ τί οἱ ἁμαρτάνοντες οὐκ εὐθέως κολάζονται. ὅτι διάφοροι αἱ κολάσεις καὶ πᾶσαι μετὰ τῆς ἀλόγου ψυχῆς διὰ τοῦ σκιοειδοῦς σώματος. περὶ μετεμψυχώσεως, καὶ πῶς εἰς ἄλογα λέγονται φέρεσθαι. ὅτι ἀνάγκη μετεμψύχωσιν εἶναι. ὅτι καὶ ζῶντες καὶ τελευτήσαντες εὐδαίμονες οἱ ἀγαθοί. 20

Hunc indicem non a Sallustio profectum esse probauit Muccio, *Studi italiani*, III. 25_2, VII. 46. 14 ὠφελοῦμεν] sic ut uidetur cod.: ὠφελοῦσιν exspectes. 15 ἀθεΐαι] θυσίαι cod.

I τοὺς περὶ θεῶν ἀκοῦσαι ἐθέλοντας δεῖ μὲν ἐκ παίδων ἦχθαι καλῶς καὶ μὴ ἀνοήτοις συντρέφεσθαι δόξαις, δεῖ δὲ καὶ τὴν φύσιν ἀγαθοὺς εἶναι καὶ ἔμφρονας ἵνα ὅμοιόν τι ἔχωσι τοῖς λόγοις. δεῖ δὲ αὐτοὺς καὶ τὰς κοινὰς ἐννοίας εἰδέναι. κοιναὶ δέ εἰσιν ἔννοιαι ὅσας πάντες ἄνθρωποι ὀρθῶς ἐρωτηθέντες 5 ὁμολογήσουσιν, οἷον ὅτι πᾶς θεὸς ἀγαθός, ὅτι ἀπαθής, ὅτι ἀμετάβλητος, πᾶν γὰρ τὸ μεταβαλλόμενον ἢ ἐπὶ τὸ κρεῖττον ἢ ἐπὶ τὸ χεῖρον· καὶ εἰ μὲν ἐπὶ τὸ χεῖρον, κακύνεται, εἰ δὲ

II ἐπὶ τὸ κρεῖττον, τὴν ἀρχὴν ἦν κακόν· καὶ ὁ μὲν ἀκούων ἔστω τοιοῦτος, οἱ δὲ λόγοι τοιοίδε γινέσθωσαν. αἱ τῶν θεῶν 10 οὐσίαι οὐδὲ ἐγένοντο (τὰ γὰρ ἀεὶ ὄντα οὐδέποτε γίνεται· ἀεὶ δὲ ἔστιν, ὅσα δύναμίν τε ἔχει τὴν πρώτην καὶ πάσχειν οὐδὲν πέφυκεν) οὐδὲ ἐκ σωμάτων εἰσὶ (καὶ γὰρ τῶν σωμάτων αἱ δυνάμεις ἀσώματοι) οὐδὲ τόπῳ περιέχονται (σωμάτων γὰρ τοῦτό γε) οὐδὲ τῆς πρώτης αἰτίας ἢ ἀλλήλων χωρίζονται, 15 ὥσπερ οὐδὲ νοῦ αἱ νοήσεις οὐδὲ ψυχῆς αἱ ἐπιστῆμαι οὐδὲ ζῴου αἱ αἰσθήσεις.

III τί δήποτε οὖν τούτους ἀφέντες τοὺς λόγους οἱ παλαιοὶ μύθοις ἐχρήσαντο, ζητεῖν ἄξιον καὶ τοῦτο πρῶτον ἐκ τῶν μύθων ὠφελεῖσθαι τό γε ζητεῖν καὶ μὴ ἀργὸν τὴν διάνοιαν 20 ἔχειν. ὅτι μὲν οὖν θεῖοι οἱ μῦθοι, ἐκ τῶν χρησαμένων ἔστιν εἰπεῖν· καὶ γὰρ τῶν ποιητῶν οἱ θεόληπτοι καὶ τῶν φιλοσόφων οἱ ἄριστοι οἵ τε τὰς τελετὰς καταδείξαντες καὶ αὐτοὶ δὲ ἐν χρησμοῖς οἱ θεοὶ μύθοις ἐχρήσαντο. διὰ τί δὲ θεῖοι οἱ μῦθοι, φιλοσοφίας ζητεῖν. ἐπεὶ τοίνυν πάντα τὰ ὄντα ὁμοιό- 25 τητι μὲν χαίρει ἀνομοιότητα δὲ ἀποστρέφεται, ἐχρῆν καὶ τοὺς περὶ θεῶν λόγους ὁμοίους εἶναι ἐκείνοις, ἵνα τῆς τε οὐσίας αὐτῶν ἄξιοι γίγνωνται καὶ τοῖς λέγουσιν τοὺς θεοὺς

---

3 ἵνα ὅμοιον] ἵν ῞μοιον cod., suppleuit Muccio. 11 οὐδὲ] οὐκ Wendland: fortasse οὐδέποτε. γίνεται] γίνονται cod., corr. Muccio. 12 ἔστιν] εἰσίν cod., corr. Wendland, Praechter. 19 interpunctionem post ἄξιον sustulit Wendland. 22 εἰπεῖν] ἰδεῖν Mullach, collato ix., p. 16. 16.

I Those who would learn about the gods need to have been well educated from childhood and must not be bred up among foolish ideas; they must also be good and intelligent by nature, in order that they may have something in common with the subject. Further, they must be acquainted with universal opinions, by which I mean those in which all men, if rightly questioned, would concur; such opinions are that every god is good and impassive and unchangeable (since whatever changes, changes for better or for worse; if for worse, it becomes bad, if for the better, it proves to have been

II bad in the first place). Such must be the learner, and his instruction should be as follows. The essences of the gods never came into being, for whatever always exists never comes into being, and all things that have first power and are by nature impassive do exist always; they are not formed of bodies, for even of bodies the powers are bodiless; they are not limited by space, for that certainly is an attribute of bodies; and they are never separated from the First Cause or from one another, any more than are thoughts from the mind, sciences from the soul, or the senses from a living creature.

III It is worth our while to enquire why the ancients left the statement of these truths and employed myths, and so to obtain this first benefit from the myths, that we enquire and do not keep our intellects in idleness. Consideration of those who have employed myths justifies us in saying that myths are divine; for indeed the inspired among poets, and the best of philosophers, and the founders of solemn rites, and the gods themselves in oracles, have employed myths. Why myths are divine is a question belonging to philosophy. Since all things in existence rejoice in likeness and turn from unlikeness, it follows that our statements about the gods ought to be like the gods, in order that being worthy of their true nature they may find favour for their narrators

ποιῶσιν εὐμενεῖς, ὅπερ διὰ τῶν μύθων μόνως ἂν γένοιτο. αὐτοὺς μὲν οὖν τοὺς θεοὺς κατὰ τὸ ῥητόν τε καὶ ἄρρητον, ἀφανές τε καὶ φανερόν, σαφές τε καὶ κρυπτόμενον οἱ μῦθοι μιμοῦνται ⟨καὶ⟩ τὴν τῶν θεῶν ἀγαθότητα, ὅτι ὥσπερ ἐκεῖνοι τὰ μὲν ἐκ τῶν αἰσθητῶν ἀγαθὰ κοινὰ πᾶσιν ἐποίησαν τὰ δὲ 5 ἐκ τῶν νοητῶν μόνοις τοῖς ἔμφροσιν, οὕτως οἱ μῦθοι τὸ μὲν εἶναι θεοὺς πρὸς ἅπαντας λέγουσι, τίνες δὲ οὗτοι καὶ ὁποῖοι τοῖς δυναμένοις εἰδέναι. καὶ τὰς ἐνεργείας δὲ μιμοῦνται τῶν θεῶν. ἔξεστι γὰρ καὶ τὸν κόσμον μῦθον εἰπεῖν, σωμάτων μὲν καὶ χρημάτων ἐν αὐτῷ φαινομένων, ψυχῶν δὲ καὶ νῶν 10 κρυπτομένων. πρὸς δὲ τούτοις τὸ μὲν πάντας τὴν περὶ θεῶν ἀλήθειαν διδάσκειν ἐθέλειν τοῖς μὲν ἀνοήτοις διὰ τὸ μὴ δύνασθαι μανθάνειν καταφρόνησιν τοῖς δὲ σπουδαίοις ῥᾳθυμίαν ἐμποιεῖ, τὸ δὲ διὰ μύθων τἀληθὲς ἐπικρύπτειν τοὺς μὲν καταφρονεῖν οὐκ ἐᾷ τοὺς δὲ φιλοσοφεῖν ἀναγκάζει. ἀλλὰ διὰ 15 τί μοιχείας καὶ κλοπὰς καὶ πατέρων δεσμοὺς καὶ τὴν ἄλλην ἀτοπίαν ἐν τοῖς μύθοις εἰρήκασιν; ἢ καὶ τοῦτο ἄξιον θαύματος, ἵνα διὰ τῆς φαινομένης ἀτοπίας εὐθὺς ἡ ψυχὴ τοὺς μὲν λόγους ἡγήσηται προκαλύμματα, τὸ δὲ ἀληθὲς ἀπόρρητον εἶναι νομίσῃ; 20

IV τῶν δὲ μύθων οἱ μέν εἰσι θεολογικοί, οἱ δὲ φυσικοί, ἔτι δὲ ψυχικοί τε καὶ ὑλικοὶ καὶ ἐκ τούτων μικτοί. εἰσὶ δὲ θεολογικοὶ οἱ μηδενὶ σώματι χρώμενοι ἀλλὰ τὰς οὐσίας αὐτὰς τῶν θεῶν θεωροῦντες, οἷον αἱ τοῦ Κρόνου καταπόσεις τῶν παίδων. ἐπειδὴ νοερὸς ὁ θεός, πᾶς δὲ νοῦς εἰς ἑαυτὸν ἐπι- 25 στρέφει, τὴν οὐσίαν ὁ μῦθος αἰνίττεται τοῦ θεοῦ. φυσικῶς δὲ τοὺς μύθους ἔστι θεωρεῖν ὅταν τὰς περὶ τὸν κόσμον ἐνεργείας λέγῃ τις τῶν θεῶν, ὥσπερ ἤδη τινὲς χρόνον μὲν τὸν Κρόνον ἐνόμισαν, τὰ δὲ μέρη τοῦ χρόνου παῖδας τοῦ ὅλου καλέσαντες καταπίνεσθαι ὑπὸ τοῦ πατρὸς τοὺς παῖδάς 30 φασιν. ὁ δὲ ψυχικὸς τρόπος ἐστὶν αὐτῆς τῆς ψυχῆς τὰς ἐνεργείας σκοπεῖν, ὅτι καὶ τῶν ἡμετέρων ψυχῶν αἱ νοήσεις,

---

1 ποιῶσιν] ποιοῦσιν cod., corr. ed. pr. iteratis curis. 3 σαφὲς] σόφον cod., corr. Orelli; idem ⟨καὶ⟩ suppleuit. 10 νῶν] νόων cod., correxi: cf. viii., p. 16. 5, νῷ, xii., 22. 19, νοῖς. 11 πάντας] πᾶσαν Wendland. 21 ἔτι] οἱ cod., correxi: possis et οἱ δὲ ψυχικοί, εἰσι δὲ καὶ.... 29 ὅλου] θεοῦ Vitelli: τοῦ ὅλου idem ualere quod τοῦ ὅλου χρόνου perspexit Wendland.

(and such favour can by myths alone be won). So the myths represent the gods in respect of that which is speakable and that which is unspeakable, of that which is obscure and that which is manifest, of that which is clear and that which is hidden, and represent the goodness of the gods; just as the gods have given to all alike the benefits to be drawn from objects perceptible to the senses while restricting to the wise the enjoyment of those received from objects perceptible to the intellect, so the myths proclaim to all that the gods exist, telling who they are and of what sort to those able to know it. Again, myths represent the active operations of the gods. The universe itself can be called a myth, since bodies and material objects are apparent in it, while souls and intellects are concealed. Furthermore, to wish to teach all men the truth about the gods causes the foolish to despise, because they cannot learn, and the good to be slothful, whereas to conceal the truth by myths prevents the former from despising philosophy and compels the latter to study it. Why, however, have the ancients told in their myths of adulteries and thefts and binding of fathers and other strange things? Is this also admirable, meant to teach the soul by the seeming strangeness at once to think the words a veil and the truth a mystery?

IV Of myths some are theological, some physical; there are also psychical myths and material myths and myths blended from these elements. Theological myths are those which do not attach themselves to any material objects but regard the actual natures of the gods. Such is the tale that Kronos swallowed his children; since the god is intellectual, and all intellect is directed towards itself, the myth hints at the god's essential nature. Again, it is possible to regard myths in a physical way when one describes the activities of the gods in the universe; so some before now have thought Kronos to be Chronos or Time, and calling the parts of Time children of the whole say that the father swallows his children. The psychical interpretation lies in considering the activities of the soul itself: the thoughts of our souls,

κἂν εἰς τοὺς ἄλλους προέλθωσιν, ἀλλ' οὖν ἐν τοῖς γεννήσασι μένουσιν. ὑλικὸς δέ ἐστι καὶ ἔσχατος, ᾧ μάλιστα Αἰγύπτιοι δι' ἀπαιδευσίαν ἐχρήσαντο, αὐτὰ τὰ σώματα θεοὺς νομίσαντες καὶ καλέσαντες [καὶ] Ἶσιν μὲν τὴν γῆν Ὄσιριν δὲ τὸ ὑγρὸν Τυφῶνα δὲ τὴν θερμότητα ἢ Κρόνον μὲν ὕδωρ Ἄδωνιν 5 *δὲ καρποὺς Διόνυσον δὲ οἶνον. ταῦτα δὲ ἀνακεῖσθαι μὲν θεοῖς λέγειν, ὥσπερ βοτάνας καὶ λίθους καὶ ζῷα, σωφρονούντων ἐστὶν ἀνθρώπων, θεοὺς δὲ καλεῖν μαινομένων, εἰ μὴ ἄρα ὥσπερ τοῦ ἡλίου τὴν σφαῖραν καὶ τὴν ἀπὸ τῆς σφαίρας ἀκτῖνα ἥλιον ἐν συνηθείᾳ καλοῦμεν. τὸ δὲ μικτὸν εἶδος τῶν* 10 *μύθων ἐν πολλοῖς μὲν καὶ ἄλλοις ἔστιν ἰδεῖν· καὶ μέντοι καὶ ἐν τῷ συμποσίῳ φασὶ τῶν θεῶν τὴν Ἔριν μῆλον ῥίψαι χρυσοῦν καὶ περὶ τούτου τὰς θεὰς φιλονεικούσας ὑπὸ τοῦ Διὸς πρὸς τὸν Πάριν πεμφθῆναι κριθησομένας· τῷ δὲ καλήν τε φανῆναι τὴν Ἀφροδίτην καὶ ταύτῃ δοῦναι τὸ μῆλον. ἐνταῦθα γὰρ τὸ* 15 *μὲν συμπόσιον τὰς ὑπερκοσμίους δυνάμεις δηλοῖ τῶν θεῶν, καὶ διὰ τοῦτο μετ' ἀλλήλων εἰσί, τὸ δὲ χρυσοῦν μῆλον τὸν κόσμον ὃς ἐκ τῶν ἐναντίων γινόμενος εἰκότως ὑπὸ τῆς Ἔριδος λέγεται ῥίπτεσθαι. ἄλλων δὲ ἄλλα τῷ κόσμῳ χαριζομένων θεῶν, φιλονεικεῖν ὑπὲρ τοῦ μήλου δοκοῦσιν. ἡ δὲ κατ' αἴσθη-* 20 *σιν ζῶσα ψυχή (τοῦτο γάρ ἐστιν ὁ Πάρις) τὰς μὲν ἄλλας ἐν τῷ κόσμῳ δυνάμεις οὐχ ὁρῶσα, μόνον δὲ τὸ κάλλος, τῆς Ἀφροδίτης τὸ μῆλον εἶναί φησι. πρέπουσι δὲ τῶν μύθων οἱ μὲν θεολογικοὶ φιλοσόφοις, οἱ δὲ φυσικοὶ καὶ ψυχικοὶ ποιηταῖς, οἱ δὲ μικτοὶ τελεταῖς, ἐπειδὴ καὶ πᾶσα τελετὴ πρὸς τὸν* 25 *κόσμον ἡμᾶς καὶ πρὸς τοὺς θεοὺς συνάπτειν ἐθέλει. εἰ δὲ δεῖ καὶ ἕτερον μῦθον εἰπεῖν, τὴν μητέρα τῶν θεῶν φασι τὸν Ἄττιν παρὰ τῷ Γάλλῳ κείμενον ἰδοῦσαν ποταμῷ ἐρασθῆναί τε καὶ λαβοῦσαν τὸν ἀστερωτὸν αὐτῷ περιθεῖναι πῖλον καὶ τοῦ λοιποῦ μεθ' ἑαυτῆς ἔχειν· ὁ δὲ νύμφης ἐρασθεὶς τὴν* 30 *θεῶν μητέρα ἀπολιπὼν τῇ νύμφῃ συνῆν. καὶ διὰ τοῦτο ἡ*

---

4 [*καὶ*] secl. Muccio. 14 *καλήν*] non quod forsitan exspectes *καλλίστην*, recte, cf. Lucian. *Dial. deor.* XX. 7, *ἡ καλὴ λαβέτω* (*ib.* 11).

even if they go forth to others, still remain in their creators. The worst explanation, the material, is that which the Egyptians because of their ignorance used most; they regarded and described material things as gods, earth as Isis, moisture as Osiris, heat as Typhon, or water as Kronos, the fruits of the soil as Adonis, wine as Dionysos[1]. To say that these things, as also plants and stones and animals, are sacred to the gods, is the part of reasonable men, to call them gods is the part of madmen, unless by a common figure of speech, as we call the sphere of the sun and the ray coming from that sphere the sun. The blended kind of myths can be seen in numerous examples; one is the tale they tell that at the banquet of the gods Strife threw a golden apple and the goddesses, vying with one another for its possession, were sent by Zeus to Paris to be judged; Paris thought Aphrodite beautiful, and gave her the apple. Here the banquet signifies the supramundane powers of the gods, and that is why they are together, the golden apple signifies the universe, which, as it is made of opposites, is rightly said to be thrown by Strife, and as the various gods give various gifts to the universe they are thought to vie with one another for the possession of the apple; further, the soul that lives in accordance with sense-perception (for that is Paris), seeing beauty alone and not the other powers in the universe, says that the apple is Aphrodite's.

Theological myths suit philosophers, physical and psychical myths poets; blended myths suit solemn rites, since every rite seeks to give us union with the universe and with the gods. If I must relate another myth, it is said that the Mother of the gods saw Attis lying by the river Gallos and became enamoured of him, and took and set on his head the starry cap, and kept him thereafter with her, and he, becoming enamoured of a nymph, left the Mother of the gods and consorted with the nymph. Wherefore the Mother

[1] As Wendland remarks, *Berl. phil. Woch.* 1899, 1411, this sentence, in which Greek gods are named after Egyptian deities, apparently as in the same category, is clumsy, but the clumsiness may well be due to the author.

μήτηρ τῶν θεῶν ποιεῖ μανῆναι τὸν Ἄττιν καὶ τὰ γονιμα ἀποκοψάμενον ἀφεῖναι παρὰ τῇ νύμφῃ, πάλιν δὲ ἀνελθόντα αὐτῇ συνοικεῖν. ἡ μὲν οὖν μήτηρ τῶν θεῶν ζωογόνος ἐστὶ θεά, καὶ διὰ τοῦτο μήτηρ καλεῖται, ὁ δὲ Ἄττις τῶν γινομένων καὶ φθειρομένων δημιουργός, καὶ διὰ τοῦτο παρὰ τῷ 5 Γάλλῳ λέγεται εὑρεθῆναι ποταμῷ· ὁ γὰρ Γάλλος τὸν Γαλαξίαν αἰνίττεται κύκλον, ἀφ' οὗ τὸ παθητὸν ἄρχεται σῶμα. τῶν δὲ πρώτων θεῶν τελειούντων τοὺς δευτέρους ἐρᾷ μὲν ἡ μήτηρ τοῦ Ἄττεως καὶ οὐρανίους αὐτῷ δίδωσι δυνάμεις (τοῦτο γάρ ἐστιν ὁ πῖλος)· ἐρᾷ δὲ ὁ Ἄττις τῆς νύμφης· αἱ 10 δὲ νύμφαι γενέσεως ἔφοροι· πᾶν γὰρ τὸ γινόμενον ῥεῖ· ἐπεὶ δὲ ἔδει στῆναι τὴν γένεσιν καὶ μὴ τῶν ἐσχάτων γενέσθαι τὸ χεῖρον, ὁ ταῦτα ποιῶν δημιουργὸς δυνάμεις γονίμους ἀφεὶς εἰς τὴν γένεσιν πάλιν συνάπτεται τοῖς θεοῖς. ταῦτα δὲ ἐγένετο μὲν οὐδέποτε, ἔστι δὲ ἀεί, καὶ ὁ μὲν νοῦς ἅμα πάντα ὁρᾷ, ὁ δὲ 15 λόγος τὰ μὲν πρῶτα τὰ δὲ δεύτερα λέγει. οὕτω δὲ πρὸς τὸν κόσμον οἰκείως ἔχοντος τοῦ μύθου, ἡμεῖς τὸν κόσμον μιμούμενοι (πῶς γὰρ ἂν μᾶλλον κοσμηθείημεν;) ἑορτὴν ἄγομεν διὰ ταῦτα· καὶ πρῶτον μὲν ὡς καὶ αὐτοὶ πεσόντες ἐξ οὐρανοῦ καὶ τῇ νύμφῃ συνόντες ἐν κατηφείᾳ ἐσμὲν σίτου τε καὶ τῆς 20 ἄλλης παχείας καὶ ῥυπαρᾶς τροφῆς ἀπεχόμεθα (ἑκάτερα γὰρ ἐναντία ψυχῇ)· εἶτα δένδρου τομαὶ καὶ νηστεία ὥσπερ καὶ ἡμῶν ἀποκοπτομένων τὴν περαιτέρω τῆς γενέσεως πρόοδον· ἐπὶ τούτοις γάλακτος τροφὴ ὥσπερ ἀναγεννωμένων. ἐφ' οἷς ἱλαρεῖαι καὶ στέφανοι καὶ πρὸς τοὺς θεοὺς οἷον ἐπάνοδος. 25 μαρτυρεῖ δὲ τούτοις καὶ ὁ τῶν δρωμένων καιρός. περὶ γὰρ τὸ ἔαρ καὶ τὴν ἰσημερίαν δρᾶται τὰ δρώμενα, ὅτε τοῦ μὲν γίνεσθαι παύεται τὰ γινόμενα, ἡμέρα δὲ μείζων γίνεται τῆς νυκτός, ὅπερ οἰκεῖον ἀναγομέναις ψυχαῖς. περὶ γοῦν τὴν ἐναντίαν

---

7 ἄρχεται] ἔρχεται cod., correxi, L. W. Hunterum secutus qui lectione Barberiniani ἔρχεσθαι cognita ἄρχεσθαι coniecit.

of the gods caused Attis to go mad and to cut off his genitals and leave them with the nymph and to return and dwell with her again. Well, the Mother of the gods is a life-giving goddess, and therefore she is called mother, while Attis is creator of things that come into being and perish, and therefore is he said to have been found by the river Gallos: for Gallos suggests the Galaxias Kyklos or Milky Way, which is the upper boundary of matter liable to change. So, as the first gods perfect the second, the Mother loves Attis and gives him heavenly powers (signified by the cap). Attis, however, loves the nymph, and the nymphs preside over coming into being, since whatever comes into being is in flux. But since it was necessary that the process of coming into being should stop and that what was worse should not sink to the worst, the creator who was making these things cast away generative powers into the world of becoming and was again united with the gods. All this did not happen at any one time but always is so: the mind sees the whole process at once, words tell of part first, part second[1]. Since the myth is so intimately related to the universe we imitate the latter in its order (for in what way could we better order ourselves?) and keep a festival therefore. First, as having like Attis fallen from heaven and consorting with the nymph, we are dejected and abstain from bread and all other rich[2] and coarse food (for both are unsuited to the soul). Then come the cutting of the tree and the fast, as though we also were cutting off the further progress of generation; after this we are fed on milk as though being reborn; that is followed by rejoicings and garlands and as it were a new ascent to the gods. This interpretation is supported also by the season at which the ceremonies are performed, for it is about the time of spring and the equinox, when things coming into being cease so to do, and day becomes longer than night, which suits souls rising to life.

[1] As Praechter explains, *W. kl. Ph.* 1900, 184, what is ever present to the *nous* is projected into the succession of historical events.

[2] As for instance pomegranates, dates, fish, pork (H. Hepding, *Attis*, 156 f.).

ἰσημερίαν ἡ τῆς Κόρης ἁρπαγὴ μυθολογεῖται γενέσθαι, ὃ δὴ
κάθοδός ἐστι τῶν ψυχῶν. τοσαῦτα περὶ μύθων εἰποῦσιν
ἡμῖν αὐτοί τε οἱ θεοὶ καὶ τῶν γραψάντων τοὺς μύθους αἱ
ψυχαὶ ἵλεῳ γένοιντο.

V ἀκόλουθον δὲ τούτοις ἐστι τήν τε πρώτην αἰτίαν εἰδέναι 5
καὶ τὰς μετ' ἐκείνην τάξεις τῶν θεῶν καὶ τοῦ κόσμου τὴν
φύσιν, νοῦ τε καὶ ψυχῆς τὴν οὐσίαν, πρόνοιάν τε καὶ εἱμαρμένην καὶ τύχην, ἀρετήν τε καὶ κακίαν καὶ τὰς ἐκ τούτων
γινομένας ἀγαθάς τε καὶ φαύλας πολιτείας ἰδεῖν, καὶ πόθεν
ἄρα τὰ κακὰ εἰς τὸν κόσμον ἀφίκετο. τούτων δὲ ἕκαστον 10
λόγων δεῖται πολλῶν καὶ μεγάλων, ὡς δὲ ἐν βραχέσιν εἰπεῖν
καὶ πρὸς τὸ μὴ παντελῶς ἀνηκόους εἶναι, οὐδὲν ἴσως λέγειν
κωλύει.

τὴν πρώτην αἰτίαν μίαν τε εἶναι προσήκει (παντὸς γὰρ
πλήθους ἡγεῖται μονάς) δυνάμει τε καὶ ἀγαθότητι πάντα 15
νικᾷ, καὶ διὰ τοῦτο πάντα μετέχειν ἐκείνης ἀνάγκη· οὐδὲν
γὰρ αὐτὴν ἄλλο κωλύσει διὰ τὴν δύναμιν οὐδὲ ἑαυτὴν ἀφέξει
δι' ἀγαθότητα· ἀλλ' εἰ μὲν ἦν ψυχή, πάντα ἂν ἔμψυχα ἦν,
εἰ δὲ καὶ νοῦς, παντὰ νοερά, εἰ δὲ οὐσία, πάντα οὐσίας μετ-
εῖχε. τοῦτο δὲ ἐν πᾶσιν ἰδόντες τινὲς ἐκεῖνο οὐσίαν ἐνόμισαν. 20
εἰ μὲν οὖν ἦν μόνον τὰ ὄντα, ἀγαθὰ δὲ οὐκ ἦν, ἀληθὴς ⟨ἂν⟩
ἦν ὁ λόγος· εἰ δὲ δι' ἀγαθότητα ἔστι τε τὰ ὄντα καὶ μετεί-
ληχεν ἀγαθοῦ, ὑπερούσιον μὲν ἀγαθὸν δὲ εἶναι τὸ πρῶτον
ἀνάγκη. σημεῖον δὲ μέγιστον· τοῦ γὰρ εἶναι διὰ τὸ ἀγαθὸν
αἱ σπουδαῖαι καταφρονοῦσι ψυχαί, ὅταν ὑπὲρ πατρίδος ἢ 25
φιλῶν ἢ ἀρετῆς κινδυνεύειν ἐθέλωσι. μετὰ δὲ τὴν οὕτως
ἄρρητον δύναμιν αἱ τῶν θεῶν τάξεις εἰσί.

VI τῶν δὲ θεῶν οἱ μέν εἰσιν ἐγκόσμιοι, οἱ δὲ ὑπερκόσμιοι.
ἐγκοσμίους δὲ λέγω αὐτοὺς τοὺς τὸν κόσμον ποιοῦντας θεούς.
τῶν δὲ ὑπερκοσμίων οἱ μὲν οὐσίας ποιοῦσι θεῶν, οἱ δὲ νοῦν, 30
οἱ δὲ ψυχὰς, καὶ διὰ τοῦτο τρεῖς ἔχουσι τάξεις καὶ πάσας ἐν

---

12 post ἀνηκόους εἶναι ⟨τοὺς ἀκούοντας⟩ suppleuit Muccio. 16 νικᾷ] νικᾶν Muccio. 17 ἀφέξει] ἐφέξει Wendland. 21 ⟨ἂν⟩ suppleui.

Certainly the rape of Kore is said in the myth to have happened near the other equinox, and this signifies the descent of souls. To us who have spoken thus concerning myths may the gods themselves and the spirits of those who wrote the myths be kind.

V Next, the learner should know the First Cause and the classes of the gods subordinated to it and the nature of the universe, the essential characters of mind and soul, Providence too and Fate and Chance, virtue and vice, and should see the good and evil constitutions arising from them, and whence it was that evils came into the universe. Each of these topics requires many long discussions, but there is perhaps no reason why we should not treat them here in a summary way, to prevent readers from being completely ignorant of them.

The First Cause must be one, since the unit is superior to all other numbers, and surpasses all things in power and goodness, for which reason all things must partake of it; because of its power nothing else will bar it, and by reason of its goodness it will not keep itself aloof. Now if the First Cause was soul, everything would be animated by soul, if intelligence, everything would be intellectual, if being, everything would share in being. Some in fact, seeing that all things possess being, have thought that the First Cause was being. This would be correct if things that were in being were in being only and were not good. If, however, things that are are by reason of their goodness and share in the good, then what is first must be higher than being and in fact good. A very clear indication of this is that fine souls for the sake of the good despise being, when they are willing to face danger for country or friends or virtue. After this unspeakable power come the orders of the gods.

VI Of the gods some are mundane, some supramundane. By mundane I mean the gods who make the universe. Of the supramundane some make the essences of the gods, some the intelligence, some the souls[1]: they are therefore divided

[1] So rather than as Murray, 'Of the Hypercosmic gods some create Essences.'

τοῖς περὶ τούτων λόγοις ἔστιν εὑρεῖν. τῶν δὲ ἐγκοσμίων οἱ μὲν εἶναι ποιοῦσι τὸν κόσμον οἱ δὲ αὐτὸν ψυχοῦσιν οἱ δὲ ἐκ διαφόρων ὄντα ἁρμόζουσιν οἱ δὲ ἡρμοσμένον φρουροῦσι. τούτων δὲ ὄντων τεσσάρων πραγμάτων καὶ ἑκάστου πρῶτα ἔχοντος καὶ μέσα καὶ τελευταῖα, καὶ τοὺς διοικοῦντας δώδεκα 5 εἶναι ἀνάγκη. οἱ μὲν οὖν ποιοῦντες τὸν κόσμον Ζεὺς καὶ Ποσειδῶν εἰσι καὶ Ἥφαιστος, οἱ δὲ ψυχοῦντες Δημήτηρ καὶ Ἥρα καὶ Ἄρτεμις, οἱ δὲ ἁρμόζοντες Ἀπόλλων καὶ Ἀφροδίτη καὶ Ἑρμῆς, οἱ δὲ φρουροῦντες Ἑστία καὶ Ἀθηνᾶ καὶ Ἄρης. αἰνίγματα δὲ τούτων ἐν τοῖς ἀγάλμασιν ἔστιν ἰδεῖν. ὁ μὲν 10 γὰρ Ἀπόλλων λύραν ἁρμόζει, ὥπλισται δὲ ἡ Ἀθηνᾶ, γυμνὴ δὲ ἡ Ἀφροδίτη, ἐπειδὴ ἁρμονία μὲν τὸ κάλλος ποιεῖ, ..., τὸ δὲ κάλλος ἐν τοῖς ὁρωμένοις οὐ κρύπτεται. τούτων δὲ πρώτως ἐχόντων τὸν κόσμον, καὶ τοὺς ἄλλους ἐν τούτοις ἡγητέον εἶναι θεούς, οἷον Διόνυσον μὲν ἐν Διὶ Ἀσκληπιὸν δὲ 15 ἐν Ἀπόλλωνι Χάριτας δὲ ἐν Ἀφροδίτῃ. καὶ σφαίρας δὲ τούτων ἔστιν ἰδεῖν, Ἑστίας μὲν γῆν, Ποσειδῶνος δὲ ὕδωρ, Ἥρας ⟨δὲ⟩ ἀέρα, Ἡφαίστου δὲ πῦρ, ἓξ δὲ τὰς ἀνωτέρας ὧν ἔθος νομίζειν θεῶν· Ἀπόλλωνα γὰρ καὶ Ἄρτεμιν ἀνθ' Ἡλίου καὶ Σελήνης ληπτέον. τὴν Κρόνου δὲ Δήμητρι δοτέον, Ἀθηνᾷ 20 δὲ τὸν αἰθέρα, ὁ δὲ οὐρανὸς πάντων κοινός. αἱ μὲν οὖν τάξεις καὶ δυνάμεις καὶ σφαῖραι τῶν δώδεκα θεῶν οὕτως εἴρηνταί τε καὶ ὕμνηνται.

VII αὐτὸν δὲ τὸν κόσμον ἄφθαρτόν τε καὶ ἀγένητον εἶναι ἀνάγκη, ἄφθαρτον μὲν ὅτι ἀνάγκη τούτου φθαρέντος ἢ κρείτ- 25 τονα ἢ χείρονα ποιῆσαι ἢ τὸν αὐτὸν ἢ ἀκοσμίαν. ἀλλ' εἰ μὲν χείρονα, κακὸς ὁ ἐκ κρείττονος χεῖρον ποιῶν, εἰ δὲ κρείττονα, ἀδύνατος ὁ μὴ τὴν ἀρχὴν τὸ κρεῖττον ποιήσας, εἰ δὲ τὸν αὐτόν, μάτην ποιήσει, εἰ δὲ ἀκοσμίαν, ἀλλ' οὐδὲ ἀκούειν τοῦτό γε θέμις. ἀγένητον δὲ ἱκανὰ μὲν δεῖξαι καὶ ταῦτα (εἰ γὰρ μὴ 30 φθείρεται, οὐδὲ γέγονεν, ἐπειδὴ πᾶν τὸ γινόμενον φθείρεται)

---

7 εἰσι] ἐστι cod., correxi: error fortasse ex similitudine compendiorum (·|., ·||.) ortus est. 12 deesse aliquid de Minerua intellexit Wendland. 18 ⟨δὲ⟩ suppleuit Gale. 19 νομίζειν] ὀνομάζειν Vitelli. 21 δὲ] μὲν cod., corr. Boll. 25 ἀνάγκη in codice dispexit Muccio: uestigia obscura quidem sunt, huic uerbo uerum congruunt; uerbum aptum, cf. xiii., p. 22. 18, xvii., p. 32. 13.

into three orders, all of which may be found in treatises on these matters. Of the mundane some cause the universe to exist, others animate it, others harmonise it out of its varied components, others guard it when so harmonised. These are four operations, and each has a beginning, a middle, and an end; their superintendents, therefore, must be twelve in number. The creators of the universe are Zeus, Poseidon, and Hephaestos, the animators Demeter, Hera, and Artemis, the harmonisers Apollo, Aphrodite, and Hermes, and the guardians Hestia, Athena, and Ares. Hints of these functions may be seen in their images: Apollo strings a lyre, Athena is armed, and Aphrodite is naked because harmony causes beauty, ..., and beauty in things seen is not concealed. While these gods possess the universe in a primary way, the other gods must be supposed to be contained in them, as for instance Dionysos in Zeus, Asklepios in Apollo, and the Graces in Aphrodite. Further, we can see their spheres, earth as Hestia's, water as Poseidon's, air as Hera's, fire as that of Hephaestos, and six spheres, those higher, belonging to the gods to whom they are usually assigned; for we must regard Apollo and Artemis as Sun and Moon. We must give the sphere of Kronos to Demeter, the ether again to Athena, while the firmament is common to them all. So in this manner have the orders and powers and spheres of the twelve gods been set forth and hymned.

VII The universe itself must be imperishable and uncreated, imperishable because if it perishes God must necessarily make either a better or a worse or the same or disorder: (if He made a worse, then He is bad in that He makes what is worse from what is better; if He made a better, He must have been deficient in power not to have made the better thing in the first place; if the same, that will be a purposeless creation; if disorder, why, that will not bear hearing). That it is uncreated even what I have said suffices to show, because if it does not perish, neither did it come into being, since whatever comes into being perishes, coupled with the fact that,

καὶ ὅτι ἀνάγκη διὰ τὴν τοῦ θεοῦ ἀγαθότητα ὄντος τοῦ κόσμου
ἀεί τε τὸν θεὸν ἀγαθὸν εἶναι καὶ τὸν κόσμον ὑπάρχειν ὥσπερ
ἡλίῳ μὲν καὶ πυρὶ συνυφίσταται φῶς, σώματι δὲ σκιά. τῶν
δὲ ἐν τῷ κόσμῳ σωμάτων τὰ μὲν νοῦν μιμεῖται καὶ κύκλῳ
κινεῖται, τὰ δὲ ψυχὴν καὶ ἐπ' εὐθείας· καὶ τῶν μὲν ἐπ' 5
εὐθείας πῦρ μὲν καὶ ἀὴρ ἄνω γῆ δὲ καὶ ὕδωρ κάτω, τῶν δὲ κύκλῳ
ἡ μὲν ἀπλανὴς ἀπ' ἀνατολῆς, αἱ δὲ ἑπτὰ ἐκ δύσεως φέρονται·
αἰτίαι δὲ τούτου πολλαὶ μὲν καὶ ἄλλαι καὶ τὸ μὴ ταχείας
τῆς περιόδου τῶν σφαιρῶν γινομένης ἀτελῆ τὴν γένεσιν εἶναι.
διαφόρου δὲ τῆς κινήσεως οὔσης διαφέρειν καὶ τὴν φύσιν τῶν 10
σωμάτων ἀνάγκη καὶ μήτε καίειν μήτε ψύχειν τὸ οὐράνιον
σῶμα μηδὲ ἄλλο τι ποιεῖν ἃ τῶν τεσσάρων στοιχείων. σφαίρας δὲ οὔσης τοῦ κόσμου (ὁ γὰρ ζῳδιακὸς δείκνυσι τοῦτο),
ἐπειδὴ σφαίρας πάσης τὸ κάτω μέσον ἐστὶν (πανταχόθεν
γὰρ πλεῖστον ἀφέστηκε) τά τε βάρεα φέρεται κάτω φέρεται 15
δὲ εἰς γῆν, ⟨ἀνάγκη μέσην εἶναι τοῦ κόσμου τὴν γῆν⟩. ταῦτα
δὲ πάντα ποιοῦσι μὲν θεοί, τάττει δὲ νοῦς, κινεῖ δὲ ψυχή.
καὶ περὶ μὲν θεῶν ἤδη προείρηται.

VIII ἐστὶ δὲ νοῦς δύναμις οὐσίας μὲν δευτέρα ψυχῆς δὲ πρώτη,
ἔχουσα μὲν ἐκ τῆς οὐσίας τὸ εἶναι, τελειοῦσα δὲ τὴν ψυχὴν 20
ὥσπερ ἥλιος τὰς ὄψεις. τῶν δὲ ψυχῶν αἱ μέν εἰσι λογικαὶ
καὶ ἀθάνατοι, αἱ δὲ ἄλογοι καὶ θνηταί, καὶ αἱ μὲν ἐκ τῶν
πρώτων αἱ δὲ ἐκ τῶν δευτέρων παράγονται θεῶν. πρῶτον δὲ
ὅτιπέρ ἐστι ψυχὴ ζητητέον. ᾧ τοίνυν διαφέρει τὰ ἔμψυχα
τῶν ἀψύχων, τοῦτό ἐστι ψυχή· διαφέρει δὲ κινήσει αἰσθήσει 25
φαντασίᾳ νοήσει. ἐστὶν ἄρα ψυχὴ ἄλογος μὲν ζωὴ αἰσθη-
τικὴ καὶ φανταστική, λογικὴ δὲ αἰσθήσεως καὶ φαντασίας
ἄρχουσα καὶ λόγῳ χρωμένη, καὶ ἡ μὲν ἄλογος τοῖς σωμα-
τικοῖς ἕπεται πάθεσιν (ἐπιθυμεῖ γὰρ ἀλόγως καὶ ὀργίζεται),
ἡ δὲ λογικὴ τοῦ τε σώματος μετὰ λόγου καταφρονεῖ καὶ πρὸς 30
τὴν ἄλογον μαχομένη κρατήσασα μὲν ἀρετὴν ἡττηθεῖσα δὲ
κακίαν ποιεῖ. ἀθάνατον δὲ αὐτὴν εἶναι ἀνάγκη ὅτι τε γινώ-

---

1 ὅτι] fortasse ἔτι; conferas tamen, xviii., p. 32. 29, ὅτι τε...καὶ διὰ τὸ...: alterum fortasse additur argumentum ὅτι...σκιά. 2 ἀεὶ... κόσμον] ἀεί τε τοῦ θεοῦ ἀγαθοῦ ὄντος ἀεὶ καὶ τὸν κόσμον Praechter, ubi offendit τε. 16 suppleuit Muccio. 19 νοῦς] τις cod., corr. Vitelli: ἐ. δὲ ὁ νοῦς δ. τις Muccio: ἐ. δὲ τ. δ. ὁ νοῦς Wendland. 24 ἔμψυχα] ἄψυχα cod., corr. Gale.

since the universe exists because of God's goodness, it follows that God is ever good and the universe ever exists, as light accompanies the existence of sun and fire, and shadow that of body.

Of the bodies in the universe some imitate mind and have a circular motion, while others imitate soul and have a rectilinear motion. Of the latter, fire and air move upwards, earth and water downwards: of the former the sphere of the fixed stars moves from East to West, and the seven planetary spheres move from West to East: among the many reasons for this is the need of preventing the process of creation from being imperfect if the rotation of the spheres is rapid. This difference of motion implies a difference in the nature of the bodies; the heavenly body cannot scorch or chill or perform any other function of the four elements. Since the universe is a sphere (as is shown by the zodiac), and the lowest part of a sphere, being furthest distant from all points on its circumference, is its centre[1], and heavy bodies move downwards and move towards the earth, it follows that the earth is the centre of the universe. All these things are made by the gods, ordered by mind, and set in motion by soul. Concerning the gods I have spoken earlier.

VIII Mind is a power inferior to being and superior to soul, deriving existence from being and perfecting soul (as the sun perfects sight). Of souls some are rational and immortal, others irrational and mortal: the former are derived from the primary gods, the latter from the secondary. We must first investigate the nature of soul. It is that whereby animate differs from inanimate, and the difference lies in motion, perception, imagination, and intelligence. Irrational soul is life with perception and imagination, rational is life controlling perception and imagination and employing reason. Irrational soul is subject to the feelings of the body, it desires and is angered unreasonably. Rational soul despises the body reasonably and fights against the irrational; if it is successful, it produces virtue, if it is worsted, vice.

[1] That is, as Murray renders, "in every sphere 'down' means 'towards the centre.'"

σκει θεούς (θνητὸν δὲ οὐδὲν ἀθάνατον οἶδε) τῶν τε ἀνθρωπίνων πραγμάτων ὡς ἀλλοτρίων καταφρονεῖ καὶ τοῖς σώμασιν ὡς ἀσώματος ἀντιπέπονθε. καλῶν μὲν γὰρ καὶ νέων ὄντων ἁμαρτάνει, γηρώντων δὲ ἐκείνων ἀκμάζει, καὶ πᾶσα μὲν σπουδαία ψυχὴ κέχρηται νῷ, νοῦν δὲ οὐδὲν σῶμα γεννᾷ· πῶς γὰρ 5 ἂν τὰ ἀνόητα νοῦν γεννήσαι; ὀργάνῳ δὲ χρωμένη τῷ σώματι οὐκ ἔστιν ἐν τούτῳ, ὥσπερ οὐδὲ ὁ μηχανοποιὸς ἐν τοῖς μηχανήμασι· καίτοι πολλὰ τῶν μηχανημάτων οὐδενὸς ἁπτομένου κινεῖται. εἰ δὲ ὑπὸ τοῦ σώματος παρατρέπεται πολλάκις, θαυμάζειν οὐ δεῖ· καὶ γὰρ αἱ τέχναι τῶν ὀργάνων βλαβέν- 10 των ἐνεργεῖν οὐκ ἂν δύναιντο.

IX τὴν δὲ τῶν θεῶν πρόνοιαν ἔστι μὲν καὶ ἐκ τούτων ἰδεῖν· πόθεν γὰρ ἡ τάξις τῷ κόσμῳ εἴπερ μηδὲν ἦν τὸ τάττον; πόθεν δὲ τὸ πάντα τινὸς ἕνεκα γίνεσθαι, οἷον ἄλογον μὲν ψυχὴν ἵνα αἴσθησις ᾖ, λογικὴν δὲ ἵνα κοσμῆται ἡ γῆ; ἔστι 15 δὲ καὶ ἐκ τῆς περὶ τὴν φύσιν προνοίας ἰδεῖν. τὰ μὲν γὰρ ὄμματα διαφανῆ πρὸς τὸ βλέπειν κατεσκεύασται, ἡ δὲ ῥὶς ὑπὲρ τὸ στόμα διὰ τὸ κρίνειν τὰ δυσώδη, τῶν δὲ ὀδόντων οἱ μὲν μέσοι ὀξεῖς διὰ τὸ τέμνειν οἱ δὲ ἔνδον πλατεῖς διὰ τὸ τρίβειν τὰ σίτια. καὶ πάντα δὲ ἐν πᾶσιν οὕτω κατὰ λόγον 20 ὁρῶμεν. ἀδύνατον δὲ ἐν μὲν τοῖς ἐσχάτοις τοσαύτην εἶναι τὴν πρόνοιαν, ἐν δὲ τοῖς πρώτοις μὴ εἶναι. αἵ τε ἐν τῷ κόσμῳ μαντεῖαι καὶ θεραπεῖαι σωμάτων γιγνόμεναι τῆς ἀγαθῆς προνοίας εἰσὶ τῶν θεῶν. τὴν δὲ τοιαύτην περὶ τὸν κόσμον ἐπιμέλειαν οὐδὲν βουλευομένους οὐδὲ πονοῦντας τοὺς θεοὺς 25 ἡγητέον ποιεῖσθαι, ἀλλ' ὥσπερ τῶν σωμάτων τὰ δύναμιν ἔχοντα αὐτῷ τῷ εἶναι ποιεῖ ἃ ποιεῖ, οἷον ἥλιος φωτίζει καὶ θάλπει αὐτῷ μόνῳ τῷ εἶναι, οὕτω πολὺ μᾶλλον ἡ τῶν θεῶν πρόνοια αὐτῇ τε ἀπόνως καὶ τοῖς προνοουμένοις ἐπ' ἀγαθῷ γίνεται. ὥστε καὶ αἱ τῶν Ἐπικουρείων λέλυνται ζητήσεις· 30 τὸ γὰρ θεῖόν φασιν οὐδὲ αὐτὸ πράγματα ἔχειν οὐδὲ ἄλλοις παρέχειν. καὶ ἡ μὲν ἀσώματος περί τε τὰ σώματα καὶ τὰς

6 γεννήσαι] γεννήσοι cod., corr. Mullach. 7 μηχανήμασι] μηχανοποιήμασι, cod., corr. Wendland. 20 ⟨κατεσκευασμένα⟩ κατὰ λόγον Wendland. 25 πονοῦντας] ποιοῦντας cod., corr. Gale. 29 αὐτῇ] αὐτῇ cod., correxi. 31 οὐδὲ...οὐδὲ] οὔτε...οὔτε Wendland: sed cf. *Proll.*, cviii.

Immortal it must be, because it knows the gods (and nothing mortal knows what is immortal), and despises human affairs as not affecting itself, and, not being of the nature of body, has an experience which is the opposite of the body's; when the body is beautiful and young, the soul errs, when the body is ageing, the soul is at its prime. Again, every good soul has employed mind, and mind is created by no body; how indeed could things lacking in mind create mind? The soul uses the body as an instrument, but is not within it, just as the engineer is not within the engine, and in fact many engines move without any one touching them. If the soul is often caused by the body to err, we must not be surprised: even so the arts cannot do their work if their instruments are spoiled.

IX The providence of the gods can be seen even from these facts which have been stated[1]. Whence comes the order of the universe if there is nothing that sets it in order? Why is it that everything comes into being for a purpose, as, for instance, irrational soul that there may be perception, rational soul that the earth may be adorned? Providence can be seen again from its application to our bodies. The eyes were made transparent that we might see, the nose put over the mouth that we might distinguish evil-smelling food; of the teeth those in front are sharp, to cut the food, those within flat, to grind it. In this way we see that every detail in every part is in accordance with reason. But it is impossible that there should be providence to such an extent in mean details, and not at all in first things. The oracles and healings which happen in the universe also belong to the good providence of the gods. We must consider that the gods bestow all this attention on the universe without any deliberation or toil: just as bodies with a function do what they do merely by existing, as the sun lights and warms merely by existing, in this way and much more so does the providence of the gods benefit its objects without involving toil for itself. Hence the questions of the Epicureans are answered: their contention is that what is divine neither is itself troubled nor troubles others. Such is the incorporeal providence of

[1] The first question which follows looks back to ch. VII., the second to ch. VIII.

ψυχὰς πρόνοια τῶν θεῶν ἐστι τοιαύτη, ἡ δὲ ἐκ τῶν σωμάτων καὶ ἐν τοῖς σώμασιν ἑτέρα τε ταύτης ἐστὶ καὶ εἱμαρμένη καλεῖται, διὰ τὸ μᾶλλον ⟨ἐν⟩ τοῖς σώμασι φαίνεσθαι τὸν εἱρμόν, περὶ ἣν καὶ ἡ μαθηματικὴ εὕρηται τέχνη. τὸ μὲν οὖν μὴ μόνον ἐκ θεῶν ἀλλὰ καὶ ἐκ τῶν θείων σωμάτων διοικεῖσθαι 5 *τὰ ἀνθρώπινα πράγματα καὶ μάλιστα τὴν σωματικὴν φύσιν εὔλογόν ἐστι καὶ ἀληθές, καὶ διὰ τοῦτο ὑγίειάν τε καὶ νόσον, εὐτυχίας τε καὶ δυστυχίας κατ' ἀξίαν ἐκεῖθεν γίνεσθαι ὁ λόγος εὑρίσκει, τὸ δὲ ἀδικίας τε καὶ ἀσελγείας †ἐκ τῆς εἱμαρμένης διδόναι ἡμᾶς μὲν ἀγαθοὺς τοὺς δὲ θεοὺς ποιεῖν ἐστι* 10 *κακούς, εἰ μὴ ἄρα ἐκεῖνο λέγειν ἐθέλοι τις ὡς ὅλῳ μὲν τῷ κόσμῳ καὶ τοῖς κατὰ φύσιν ἔχουσιν ἐπ' ἀγαθῷ γίνεται πάντα, τὸ δὲ τραφῆναι κακῶς ἢ τὴν φύσιν ἀσθενεστέρως ἔχειν τὰ παρὰ τῆς εἱμαρμένης ἀγαθὰ εἰς τὸ χεῖρον μεταβάλλει, ὥσπερ τὸν ἥλιον, ἀγαθὸν ὄντα πᾶσι, τοῖς ὀφθαλμιῶσιν ἢ πυρέττουσι* 15 *βλαβερὸν εἶναι συμβαίνει. διὰ τί γὰρ* Μασσαγέται *μὲν τοὺς πατέρας ἐσθίουσιν,* Ἑβραῖοι *δὲ περιτέμνονται,* Πέρσαι *δὲ τὴν εὐγένειαν σώζουσιν ⟨ἐκ μητέρων παιδοποιούμενοι⟩; πῶς δὲ* Κρόνον *τε καὶ* Ἄρην *κακοποιοὺς λέγοντες πάλιν ποιοῦσιν ἀγαθοὺς φιλοσοφίαν τε καὶ βασιλείαν, στρατηγίας τε καὶ* 20 *θησαυροὺς εἰς ἐκείνους ἀνάγοντες; εἰ δὲ τρίγωνα καὶ τετράγωνα λέξουσιν, ἄτοπον τὴν μὲν ἀνθρωπίνην ἀρετὴν πανταχοῦ τὴν αὐτὴν μένειν, τοὺς δὲ θεοὺς ἐκ τῶν τόπων μεταβάλλεσθαι. τὸ δὲ καὶ πατέρων εὐγένειαν ἢ δυσγένειαν προλέγειν ὡς οὐ πάντα ποιούντων τινὰ δὲ σημαινόντων μόνον τῶν* 25 *ἄστρων διδάσκει. πῶς γὰρ ἂν τὰ πρὸ τῆς γενέσεως ἐκ τῆς γενέσεως γένοιτο; ὥσπερ τοίνυν πρόνοια καὶ εἱμαρμένη ἐστι*

---

3 ⟨*ἐν*⟩ suppleuit Orelli. 9 *ἐκ τῆς εἱμαρμένης διδόναι*] cod., quod uix ferendum est (sensu 'affirmare dari illi'): *ἐκ τ. εἱ. διοικεῖσθαι* A. C. Pearson: *ἐ. τ. εἱ. διδόσθαι* patruelis Orellii. 15 *πᾶσι τοῖς*] *πᾶσι* ⟨*τοῖς ἄλλοις*⟩, *τοῖς* Wendland. 16 *Μασσαγέται*] *μασαγέται* cod. 18 *σώζουσιν*] *σώζουσι* cod., mutauit Praechter qui locum suppleuit: *εὐγένειαν* non sollicitandum est, collato loco Philonis *De spec. leg.* III. 3, § 13, p. 153. 13 ed. Cohn (=p. 301 Mangey) *μητέρας γὰρ οἱ ἐν τέλει Περσῶν τὰς ἑαυτῶν ἄγοντας καὶ τοὺς φύντας ἐκ τούτων εὐγενεστάτους νομίζουσι καὶ βασιλείας, ὡς λόγος, τῆς μεγίστης ἀξιοῦσιν*, quod monuit benigne Franciscus Cumont. De sententia, cf. *Proll.* lxxii. 25 *μόνον*] *μόνων* cod., corr. Gale. 26 *διδάσκει*] *διδάσκειν* cod., corr. Mullach: cf. *Proll.* cviii.

the gods for bodies and souls. Their providence exercised from bodies upon bodies is different from this and is called Heimarmene, because the Heirmos or chain appears more clearly in bodies. It is with reference to this Heimarmene that the art of astrology has been invented. It is reasonable and correct to believe that not only the gods but also the divine heavenly bodies govern human affairs, and in particular our bodily nature. Hence reason discovers that health and disease and good and evil fortune come as deserved from this cause. On the other hand, to suppose that acts of injustice and wantonness come thence is to make us good and the gods bad, unless what is meant thereby is that everything happens for the good of the universe as a whole and of all things in a natural condition, but that evil education or weakness of nature changes the blessings of Heimarmene to evil, as the sun, good as it is for all, is found to be harmful to those suffering from inflammation of the eyes or from fever. Otherwise, why do the Massagetae eat their fathers and the Jews circumcise themselves and the Persians preserve their nobility by begetting children on their mothers? How, when astrologers call Saturn and Mars maleficent, do they again make them beneficent, ascribing philosophy and kingship, commands in war and finding of treasures to them? If they talk of trines and squares, it is strange that human virtue should remain the same everywhere, but the gods change their natures with their positions. The mentioning in horoscopes of good birth or evil birth of ancestors shows that the stars do not cause all things, but do no more than indicate some. How indeed could events before the moment of birth be produced by the conjunction of heavenly bodies at that moment?

So then, as Providence and Heimarmene exist for tribes

μὲν περὶ ἔθνη καὶ πόλεις, ἔστι δὲ καὶ περὶ ἕκαστον ἄνθρωπον, οὕτω καὶ τύχη, περὶ ἧς καὶ λέγειν ἀκόλουθον. ἡ τοίνυν τὰ διάφορα καὶ τὰ παρ' ἐλπίδα γινόμενα πρὸς ἀγαθὸν τάττουσα δύναμις τῶν θεῶν τύχη νομίζεται, καὶ διὰ τοῦτο μάλιστα κοινῇ τὰς πόλεις τὴν θεὸν προσήκει τιμᾶν. πᾶσα γὰρ πόλις ἐκ 5 διαφόρων πραγμάτων συνίσταται. ἐν σελήνῃ δὲ τὴν δύναμιν ἔχει, ἐπειδὴ ὑπὲρ σελήνην οὐδὲ ἓν ἐκ τύχης ἂν γένοιτο. εἰ δὲ κακοὶ μὲν εὐτυχοῦσι, ἀγαθοὶ δὲ πένονται, θαυμάζειν οὐ δεῖ· οἱ μὲν γὰρ πάντα, οἱ δὲ οὐδὲν ὑπὲρ πλούτων ποιοῦσι. καὶ τῶν μὲν κακῶν ἡ εὐτυχία οὐκ ἂν ἀφέλοι τὴν κακίαν, τοῖς δὲ 10 ἀγαθοῖς ἡ ἀρετὴ μόνον ἀρκέσει.

X οἱ δὲ περὶ τῆς ἀρετῆς καὶ τῆς κακίας λόγοι πάλιν τῶν περὶ ψυχῆς δέονται. τῆς γὰρ ἀλόγου ἰούσης εἰς τὰ σώματα καὶ θυμὸν εὐθὺς καὶ ἐπιθυμίαν ποιούσης ἡ λογικὴ τούτοις ἐφεστηκυῖα τριμερῆ ποιεῖ τὴν ψυχήν, ἐκ λόγου καὶ θυμοῦ καὶ 15 ἐπιθυμίας. ἀρετὴ δὲ λόγου μὲν φρόνησις, θυμοῦ δὲ ἀνδρεία, ἐπιθυμίας δὲ σωφροσύνη, ὅλης δὲ τῆς ψυχῆς δικαιοσύνη. δεῖ γὰρ τὸν μὲν λόγον κρῖναι τὰ δέοντα, τὸν δὲ θυμὸν λόγῳ πειθόμενον τῶν δοκούντων δεινῶν καταφρονεῖν, τὴν δὲ ἐπιθυμίαν μὴ τὸ φαινόμενον ἡδὺ ἀλλὰ τὸ μετὰ λόγου διώκειν. 20 τούτων δὲ οὕτως ἐχόντων ὁ βίος γίνεται δίκαιος. ἡ γὰρ περὶ χρήματα δικαιοσύνη μικρόν τι μέρος ἐστὶν ἀρετῆς. καὶ διὰ τοῦτο ἐν μὲν τοῖς πεπαιδευμένοις πάσας ἔστιν ἰδεῖν, ἐν δὲ τοῖς ἀπαιδεύτοις ὁ μέν ἐστιν ἀνδρεῖος καὶ ἄδικος ὁ δὲ σώφρων καὶ ἀνόητος ὁ δὲ φρόνιμος καὶ ἀκόλαστος, ἅσπερ οὐδὲ ἀρετὰς 25 προσήκει καλεῖν λόγου τε ἐστερημένας καὶ ἀτελεῖς οὔσας καὶ τῶν ἀλόγων τισὶ παραγινομένας. ἡ δὲ κακία ἐκ τῶν ἐναντίων θεωρείσθω, λόγου μὲν ἄνοια, θυμοῦ δὲ δειλία, ἐπιθυμίας δὲ ἀκολασία, ὅλης δὲ τῆς ψυχῆς ἀδικία. γίνονται δὲ αἱ μὲν ἀρεταὶ ἐκ πολιτείας ὀρθῆς καὶ τοῦ τραφῆναι καλῶς 30 καὶ παιδευθῆναι, αἱ δὲ κακίαι ἐκ τῶν ἐναντίων.

---

1 μὲν in cod. dispexit Muccio, recte mea quidem sententia.
6 ἐν σελήνῃ δὲ cod.: in margine manu fortasse posteriore additum est μήποτε ἐν τοῖς ὑπὸ σελήνην ὀφείλει γράφεσθαι. Hoc uero ἐν τοῖς ὑπὸ σελήνην mera coniectura est. Fortasse legendum est ἕως δὲ εἰς σελήνην, uel μέχρι σελήνης δὲ. Fieri tamen potest, quod monuit D. S. Robertson, ut ἐν σελήνῃ uerum sit, cf. *Proll.* lxxv. n. 161, Macrob. *Sat.* I. 19. 17, *luna* τύχη (sc. *creditur*) *quia corporum praesul est, quae fortuitorum uarietate iactantur*, Roscheri *Lex.* V. 1331. 9 πλούτων] fort. πλούτου. 13 ἰούσης] οὔσης cod., corr. Gale.

and cities and exist also for each individual, in like manner does Fortune, about which I must next speak. The power of the gods that orders for the good diverse and unexpected happenings is considered to be Fortune: and for this reason in particular cities ought to pay corporate worship to this goddess, since every city is composed of diverse components. Fortune's power rests in the moon[1], since above the moon nothing whatsoever could happen because of her. If the bad prosper and the good suffer poverty, we must not be surprised. The former do anything to obtain wealth, the latter nothing: from the bad prosperity cannot take their badness, while the good will be content with virtue alone.

X This discussion of virtue and vice requires again a discussion of the soul. When the irrational soul enters bodies and at once produces spirit and desire, the rational soul, presiding over these, causes the entire soul to consist of three parts, reason, spirit, and desire. The excellence of reason is wisdom, of spirit courage, of desire temperance, of the whole soul justice. Reason must make a right judgment, spirit must, in obedience to reason, despise seeming dangers, and desire must pursue not seeming pleasure but reasonable pleasure. When these conditions are fulfilled life becomes just (justice in money matters is but a small part of virtue). For this reason in the educated all virtues may be seen, while among the uneducated one is brave and unjust, one temperate and imprudent, one prudent and intemperate, and indeed it is not right to call these qualities virtues when shorn of reason and imperfect and occurring in certain unreasoning creatures. Vice must be considered by examining the opposites; the vice of reason is folly, of spirit cowardice, of desire intemperance, and of the whole soul injustice. Virtues are the products of a rightly constituted state and of good upbringing and education, vices of their opposites.

[1] Or 'Fortune's power extends to the moon,' if *ἕως δὲ εἰς σελήνην* or *μέχρι σελήνης* is read. That view is perhaps supported by *ἐπειδὴ... γένοιτο*, which then follows logically.

XI καὶ αἱ πολιτεῖαι δὲ κατὰ τὴν τριμέρειαν γίνονται τῆς ψυχῆς. ἐοίκασι γὰρ οἱ μὲν ἄρχοντες τῷ λόγῳ οἱ δὲ στρατιῶται τῷ θυμῷ οἱ δὲ δῆμοι ταῖς ἐπιθυμίαις. καὶ ὅπου μὲν κατὰ λόγον πράττεται πάντα καὶ ὁ πάντων ἄριστος ἄρχει, βασιλεία γίνεται, ὅπου δὲ κατὰ λόγον τε καὶ θυμόν, καὶ 5 πλείους ἑνὸς ἄρχουσιν, ἀριστοκρατίαν εἶναι συμβαίνει, ὅπου δὲ κατὰ ἐπιθυμίαν πολιτεύονται καὶ αἱ τιμαὶ πρὸς τὰ χρήματα γίγνονται, τιμοκρατία ἡ τοιαύτη πολιτεία καλεῖται. ἐναντία δὲ βασιλείᾳ μὲν τυραννίς, ἡ μὲν γὰρ μετὰ λόγου πάντα, ἡ δὲ οὐδὲν κατὰ λόγον ποιεῖ, ἀριστοκρατίᾳ δὲ ὀλιγ- 10 αρχία, ὅτι οὐχ οἱ ἄριστοι ἀλλ' ὀλίγοι κάκιστοι ἄρχουσι, τιμοκρατίᾳ δὲ δημοκρατία, ὅτι οὐχ οἱ τὰς οὐσίας ἔχοντες ἀλλ' ὁ δῆμος κύριός ἐστιν ἁπάντων.

XII ἀλλὰ πῶς θεῶν ἀγαθῶν ὄντων καὶ πάντα ποιούντων τὰ κακὰ ἐν τῷ κόσμῳ; ἢ πρῶτον μὲν αὐτὸ τοῦτο ῥητέον ὅτι 15 θεῶν ἀγαθῶν ὄντων καὶ πάντα ποιούντων κακοῦ φύσις οὐκ ἔστιν, ἀπουσίᾳ δὲ ἀγαθοῦ γίγνεται ὥσπερ καὶ σκότος αὐτὸ μὲν οὐκ ἔστιν, ἀπουσίᾳ δὲ φωτὸς γίγνεται; ἀνάγκη δέ, εἴπερ ἔστιν, ἢ ἐν θεοῖς ⟨εἶναι⟩ ἢ νοῖς ἢ ψυχαῖς ἢ σώμασιν. ἀλλ' ἐν μὲν θεοῖς οὐκ ἔστιν, ἐπειδὴ πᾶς θεὸς ἀγαθός. εἰ δὲ νοῦν τίς 20 φησι κακόν, νοῦν ἀνόητον λέγει· εἰ δὲ ψυχήν, χείρονα ποιήσει σώματος (πᾶν γὰρ σῶμα καθ' ἑαυτὸ κακίαν οὐκ ἔχει), εἰ δὲ ἐκ ψυχῆς καὶ σώματος, ἄλογον κεχωρισμένα μὲν μὴ εἶναι κακὰ συνελθόντα δὲ κακίαν ποιεῖν. εἰ δὲ δαίμονάς τις λέγοι κακούς, εἰ μὲν ἐκ θεῶν τὴν οὐσίαν ἔχουσιν, οὐκ ἂν εἶεν κακοί, 25 εἰ δὲ ἀλλαχόθεν, οὐ πάντα ποιοῦσι θεοί· εἰ δὲ μὴ πάντα ποιοῦσιν, ἢ βουλόμενοι οὐ δύνανται ἢ δυνάμενοι οὐ βούλονται, ὧν οὐδέτερον πρέπει θεῷ. ὅτι μὲν οὖν οὐδὲν ἐν τῷ κόσμῳ φύσει κακὸν ἐκ τούτων ἔστιν ἰδεῖν, περὶ δὲ τὰς τῶν ἀνθρώπων ἐνεργείας καὶ τούτων οὐ πάντων οὐδὲ ἀεὶ φαίνεται 30 τὰ κακά. ταῦτα δὲ εἰ μὴν δι' αὐτὸ τὸ κακὸν ἡμάρτανον ἄνθρωποι, αὐτὴ ἂν ἦν ἡ φύσις κακή· εἰ δὲ ὁ μὲν μοιχεύων τὴν μὲν μοιχείαν ἡγεῖται κακὸν τὴν δὲ ἡδονὴν ἀγαθόν, ὁ δὲ

---

3 δῆμοι] fortasse δημόται legendum est. 4 ad καὶ ὁ πάντων... in mg. adscriptum est ζή (=ζήτησις) περὶ ἀρχῆς. 7 χρήματα] χρήσιμα cod., corr. Orelli. 19 ⟨εἶναι⟩ suppleuit Gale.

XI Constitutions also correspond to the triple division of the soul: the rulers resemble reason, the soldiers spirit, and the commoners desire. Where everything is done in accordance with reason, and the best man of all rules, monarchy results; where everything is done in accordance with reason and spirit, and more than one rule, the product is aristocracy; where men regulate their political life by desire, and honours go by wealth, the constitution is called timocracy. The opposite of monarchy is tyranny, since monarchy acts always in accordance with reason, tyranny never; of aristocracy oligarchy, since not the best but a few and the basest rule; of timocracy democracy, since not men of property but the commons control the state.

XII But how is it, if the gods are good and make everything, that there are evils in the universe? Perhaps we must first say that, since the gods are good and make everything, evil has no objective existence, and comes into being through the absence of good, just as darkness has no absolute existence, and comes into being through the absence of light. If evils exist, they must be in gods or in minds or in souls or in bodies. But in gods they cannot be, since every god is good, and if anyone says that mind is evil, he represents it as the negation of itself, if soul, he will make it worse than the body, since every body in itself is free from evil; if he asserts that evil arises from the soul and the body, it is unreasonable that they should not be evil when separate but should, when combined, create evil. If again spirits are called evil, they, if they owe their existence to the gods, cannot be evil; if they owe it to some other source, it follows that the gods do not make everything, and if they do not make everything, either they wish to do so but cannot, or they can but will not; neither supposition is suitable to a god. From these considerations it can be perceived that there is nothing naturally evil in the universe; evils appear in connection with the activities of men, and not of all men or at all times. Now, if men caused these evils for the evil's sake, Nature itself would be evil; but if the adulterer thinks adultery evil, but pleasure good, or the

φονεύων τὸν μὲν φόνον ἡγεῖται κακὸν τὰ δὲ χρήματα ἀγαθά, ὁ δὲ ἐχθρὸν κακῶς ποιῶν τὸ μὲν κακῶς ποιῆσαι κακὸν τὸ δὲ τὸν ἐχθρὸν ἀμύνασθαι ἀγαθόν, καὶ πάντα οὕτως ἁμαρτάνει ἡ ψυχή, δι' ἀγαθότητα γίνεται τὰ κακὰ [ὥσπερ διὰ τὸ φῶς μὴ εἶναι γίνεται σκότος φύσει μὴ ὄν]. ἁμαρτάνει μὲν οὖν 5 ψυχὴ ὅτι ἐφίεται ἀγαθοῦ, πλανᾶται δὲ περὶ τὸ ἀγαθὸν ὅτι μὴ πρώτη ἐστὶν οὐσία. ὑπὲρ δὲ τοῦ μὴ πλανᾶσθαι καὶ πλανηθεῖσαν θεραπεύεσθαι πολλὰ παρὰ θεῶν γινόμενα ἔστιν ἰδεῖν· καὶ γὰρ τέχναι καὶ ἐπιστῆμαι καὶ †ἀρεταί, εὐχαί τε καὶ θυσίαι καὶ τελεταί, νόμοι τε καὶ πολιτεῖαι, δίκαι τε καὶ 10 κολάσεις διὰ τὸ κωλύειν ψυχὰς ἁμαρτάνειν ἐγένοντο, καὶ τοῦ σώματος ἐξελθούσας θεοὶ καθάρσιοι καὶ δαίμονες τῶν

XIII ἁμαρτημάτων καθαίρουσιν. περὶ μὲν οὖν θεῶν καὶ κόσμου καὶ τῶν ἀνθρωπίνων πραγμάτων τοῖς μήτε διὰ φιλοσοφίας ἀχθῆναι δυναμένοις μηδὲ τὰς ψυχὰς ἀνιάτοις ἀρκέσει ταῦτα. 15 περὶ δὲ τοῦ μὴ γενέσθαι ταῦτά ποτε μηδὲ ἀλλήλων χωρίζεσθαι λείπεται λέγειν, ἐπειδὴ καὶ ἡμεῖς ἐν τοῖς ⟨προτέροις⟩ λόγοις ὑπὸ τῶν πρώτων τὰ δεύτερα εἴπομεν γίνεσθαι.

πᾶν τὸ γινόμενον ἢ τέχνῃ ἢ φύσει ἢ κατὰ δύναμιν γίγνεται. τὰ μὲν οὖν κατὰ τέχνην ἢ φύσιν ποιοῦντα πρότερα 20 εἶναι τῶν ποιουμένων ἀνάγκη. τὰ δὲ κατὰ δύναμιν μεθ' ἑαυτῶν συνίστησι τὰ γινόμενα, ἐπειδὴ καὶ τὴν δύναμιν ἀχώριστον ἔχει ὥσπερ δὴ ἥλιος μὲν φῶς, πῦρ δὲ θερμότητα, χιὼν δὲ ψυχρότητα. εἰ μὲν οὖν τέχνῃ τὸν κόσμον ποιοῦσι θεοί, οὐ τὸ εἶναι τὸ δὲ τοιόνδε εἶναι ποιοῦσι· πᾶσα γὰρ τέχνη τὸ 25 εἶδος ποιεῖ· πόθεν οὖν τὸ εἶναι τῷ κόσμῳ; εἰ δὲ φύσει, πᾶν τὸ φύσει ποιοῦν ἑαυτοῦ τι δίδωσι τῷ γινομένῳ. ἀσωμάτων δὲ τῶν θεῶν ὄντων ἐχρῆν καὶ τὸν κόσμον ἀσώματον εἶναι. εἰ δὲ τοὺς θεοὺς σώματα λέγοι τις, πόθεν τῶν ἀσωμάτων ἡ δύναμις; εἰ δὲ τοῦτο συγχωρήσαιμεν, φθειρομένου 30 τοῦ κόσμου τὸν ποιήσαντα φθείρεσθαι ἀνάγκη εἴπερ κατὰ φύσιν ποιεῖ. εἰ δὲ μὴ τέχνῃ μηδὲ φύσει τὸν κόσμον ποιοῦσι

---

4 codicem virgulam tantum, non siglum quod significat *καί*, ante *δι' ἀγαθότητα* habere testatur Ceriani *ap.* Muccio *S. I.* VII., p. 59 sq. *ὥσπερ...ὄν* secl. Orelli tanquam ex p. 22 l. 17 inlatum. 7 *πρώτη... οὐσία*] *πρώτης...οὐσίας* D. S. Robertson, fortasse recte. 9 *ἀρεταί*] *μελέται* Muccio. 17 suppleui ex. gr.: ⟨*ἔμπροσθεν*⟩ Muccio: ⟨*περὶ τούτων*⟩ Praechter. 23 *δὴ*] *δὲ* cod., corr. Orelli.

murderer murder bad, but money good, or he who harms an enemy harm bad, but vengeance good, and all the soul's sins happen in this way, evil arises because of goodness. In fact, the soul sins because, though desiring good, it errs in respect of what is good through not being of First Being. That it may not err, and that if it errs it may be cured, is the object of many things which the gods have created and we can see; arts and sciences and virtuous deeds, prayers and sacrifices and solemn rites, laws and constitutions, trials and punishments came into being to prevent souls from sinning, and when souls have left the body they are purged of their sins by gods and spirits of purification. Of the gods and of the universe and of human affairs this account will suffice for those who neither can be steeped in philosophy nor are incurably diseased in soul. It remains that we should discuss the fact that all these things never came into existence nor are separated from one another, since I have spoken earlier of second things proceeding from first things.

XIII

Everything that comes into being is created by technical skill or by natural process or in virtue of a function. Creators by skill or by a natural process must be prior to their creations: creators in virtue of a function bring their products into existence with themselves, since their function, like the sun's light, fire's heat, snow's cold, cannot be separated from them. If then the gods make the universe by skill, they make its character but not its existence, since form is what technical skill always makes. Whence in that case does the universe derive its existence? If the gods create by nature, we know that what creates by nature must give of itself to its creation. So, as the gods are incorporeal, the universe ought to be incorporeal; and if it is maintained that the gods are corporeal, whence comes the power of things incorporeal? If we accepted this view, the destruction of the universe involves also the destruction of its creator, if he created by natural process. If, however, the gods make the universe neither by technical skill nor by nature, the re-

θεοί, δυνάμει λείπεται μόνον. πᾶν δὲ τὸ δυνάμει γινόμενον τῷ τὴν δύναμιν ἔχοντι συνυφίσταται. καὶ οὐδὲ ἀπολέσθαι ποτὲ τὰ οὕτως γινόμενα δύναται εἰ μὴ τοῦ ποιοῦντος ἀφέλοι τις τὴν δύναμιν. ὥστε οἱ τὸν κόσμον φθείροντες θεοὺς μὴ εἶναι λέγουσιν, ἢ θεοὺς εἶναι λέγοντες τὸν θεὸν ποιοῦσιν 5
ἀδύνατον. δυνάμει μὲν οὖν πάντα ποιῶν ἑαυτῷ συνυφίστησι πάντα. μεγίστης δὲ δυνάμεως οὔσης οὐκ ἀνθρώπους ἔδει καὶ ζῷα μόνα ποιεῖν ἀλλὰ θεούς τε καὶ †ἀνθρώπους καὶ δαίμονας. καὶ ὅσῳ τῆς ἡμετέρας φύσεως ὁ πρῶτος διαφέρει θεός, τοσούτῳ πλείους εἶναι τὰς μεταξὺ ἡμῶν τε κἀκείνου 10
δυνάμεις ἀνάγκη. πάντα γὰρ πλεῖστον ἀλλήλων κεχωρισμένα πολλὰ ἔχει τὰ μεταξύ.

XIV *εἰ δέ τις τὸ μὲν θεοὺς μὴ μεταβάλλεσθαι εὔλογόν τε ἡγεῖται καὶ ἀληθές, ἀπορεῖ δὲ πῶς ἀγαθοῖς μὲν χαίρουσι κακοὺς δὲ ἀποστρέφονται καὶ ἁμαρτάνουσι μὲν ὀργίζονται* 15
θεραπευόμενοι δὲ ἵλεῳ γίνονται, ῥητέον ὡς οὐ χαίρει θεὸς (τὸ γὰρ χαῖρον καὶ λυπεῖται) οὐδὲ ὀργίζεται (πάθος γὰρ καὶ τὸ ὀργίζεσθαι) οὐδὲ δώροις θεραπεύεται (ἡδονῆς γὰρ ἂν ἡττηθείη) οὐδὲ θέμις ἐκ τῶν ἀνθρωπίνων πραγμάτων οὔτε καλῶς οὔτε κακῶς ἔχειν τὸ θεῖον, ἀλλ' ἐκεῖνοι μὲν ἀγαθοί τέ 20
εἰσιν ἀεὶ καὶ ὠφελοῦσι μόνον βλάπτουσι δὲ οὐδέποτε, κατὰ τὰ αὐτὰ ὡσαύτως ἔχοντες, ἡμεῖς δὲ ἀγαθοὶ μὲν ὄντες δι' ὁμοιότητα θεοῖς συναπτόμεθα κακοὶ δὲ γενόμενοι δι' ἀνομοιότητα χωριζόμεθα, καὶ κατ' ἀρετὰς μὲν ζῶντες ἐχόμεθα τῶν θεῶν κακοὶ δὲ γενόμενοι ἐχθροὺς ἡμῖν ποιοῦμεν ἐκείνους, 25
οὐκ ἐκείνων ὀργιζομένων ἀλλὰ τῶν ἁμαρτημάτων θεοὺς μὲν οὐκ ἐώντων ἐλλάμπειν δαίμοσι δὲ κολαστικοῖς συναπτόντων. εἰ δὲ εὐχαῖς καὶ θυσίαις λύσιν τῶν ἁμαρτημάτων εὑρίσκομεν

---

3 *δύναται*] *δύνανται* cod., corr. Gale. 8 *ἀνθρώπους*] coniecerim *ἀγγέλους*, cl. Iambl. *De myst.* II. 6, p. 81. 11 sq., *θεῶν...ἀρχαγγέλων...ἀγγέλων...δαιμόνων...ἡρώων...ἀρχόντων*, *ap.* Stob. I. 49. 39, p. 378, *θεῶν, ἀγγέλων, δαιμόνων, ἡρώων*, Psell. *Hypotyp. orac. Chald.*, § 21 (quod edidit Kroll, *De oraculis Chaldaicis*, 75). De angelis Neoplatonicorum adhibendus est Andres, *P. W. Suppl.* III. 111 sqq. *ἀνθρώπους* ex priore *ἀνθρώπους* inlatum esse in promptu est. *ἀνθρώπους* damnauit Murray. 15 *κακοὺς*] *κακοῖς* cod., corr. Gale. 18 *ἡδονῆς*] *ἡδονῇ* cod., ut uidetur; correxi. 25 *γενόμενοι*] *γινόμενοι* cod., corr. ed. pr.

maining view is that they make it by a function. Everything made in virtue of a function comes into being with the possessor of the function, and things so made cannot ever perish, unless their maker is deprived of the functional power. Accordingly, those who suppose that the universe perishes deny the existence of gods, or, if they assert that existence, make the Creator powerless. Therefore, as He makes everything in virtue of a functional power, He makes all things coexistent with Himself. So, as He had the greatest power, it was necessary that He should make not only men and animals, but also gods and angels (?) and spirits, and the wider the gap is between our nature and the first god, the more powers must there be between us and Him, since all things furthest removed have many intermediate points.

XIV If any man thinks it a reasonable and correct view that the gods are not subject to change, and then is unable to see how they take pleasure in the good and turn their faces away from the bad, are angry with sinners and propitiated by service, it must be replied that a god does not take pleasure (for that which does is also subject to pain) or feel anger (for anger also is an emotion), nor is he appeased by gifts (that would put him under the dominion of pleasure), nor is it right that the divine nature should be affected for good or for evil by human affairs. Rather, the gods are always good and do nothing but benefit us, nor do they ever harm us: they are always in the same state. We, when we are good, have union with the gods because we are like them; if we become bad, we are separated from them because we are unlike them. If we live in the exercise of virtue, we cling to them; if we become bad, we make them our enemies, not because they are angry but because our sins do not allow the gods to shed their light upon us and instead subject us to spirits of punishment. If by prayers and sacrifices we obtain release from our sins, we do not serve the gods nor

οὔτε τοὺς θεοὺς θεραπεύομεν οὔτε μεταβάλλομεν, ἀλλὰ διὰ τῶν δρωμένων καὶ τῆς πρὸς τὸ θεῖον ἐπιστροφῆς τὴν ἡμετέραν κακίαν ἰώμενοι πάλιν τῆς τῶν θεῶν ἀγαθότητος ἀπολαύομεν. ὥστε ὅμοιον τοὺς θεοὺς λέγειν τοὺς κακοὺς ἀποστρέφεσθαι καὶ τὸν ἥλιον τοῖς ἐστερημένοις τῶν ὄψεων κρύπτεσθαι.

XV ἐκ δὲ τούτων καὶ ἡ περὶ θυσιῶν καὶ τῶν ἄλλων τῶν εἰς θεοὺς γινομένων τιμῶν λέλυται ζήτησις. αὐτὸ μὲν γὰρ τὸ θεῖον ἀνενδεές· αἱ δὲ τιμαὶ τῆς ἡμετέρας ὠφελείας ἕνεκα γίνονται. καὶ ἡ μὲν πρόνοια τῶν θεῶν διατείνει πανταχοῦ ἐπιτηδειότητος δὲ μόνον πρὸς ὑποδοχὴν δεῖται· πᾶσα δὲ ἐπιτηδειότης μιμήσει καὶ ὁμοιότητι γίνεται. διὸ οἱ μὲν ναοὶ τὸν οὐρανὸν οἱ δὲ βωμοὶ μιμοῦνται τὴν γῆν τὰ δὲ ἀγάλματα τὴν ζωήν, καὶ διὰ τοῦτο ζῴοις ἀπείκασται, αἱ δὲ εὐχαὶ τὸ νοερόν, οἱ δὲ χαρακτῆρες τὰς ἀρρήτους ἄνω δυνάμεις, βοτάναι δὲ καὶ λίθοι τὴν ὕλην, τὰ δὲ θυόμενα ζῷα τὴν ἐν ἡμῖν ἄλογον ζωήν. ἐκ δὲ τούτων ἁπάντων τοῖς μὲν θεοῖς πλέον οὐδέν (τί γὰρ ἂν πλέον γένοιτο θεῷ;), ἡμῖν δὲ πρὸς ἐκείνοις γίνεται συναφή.

XVI ἄξιον δὲ οἶμαι περὶ θυσιῶν βραχέα προσθεῖναι. πρῶτον μὲν ἐπειδὴ πάντα παρὰ θεῶν ἔχομεν δίκαιον δὲ τοῖς διδοῦσι τῶν διδομένων ἀπάρχεσθαι, χρημάτων μὲν δι' ἀναθημάτων, σωμάτων δὲ διὰ κόμης, ζωῆς δὲ διὰ θυσιῶν ἀπαρχόμεθα. ἔπειτα αἱ μὲν χωρὶς θυσιῶν εὐχαὶ λόγοι μόνον εἰσὶν αἱ δὲ μετὰ θυσιῶν ἔμψυχοι λόγοι, τοῦ μὲν λόγου τὴν ζωὴν δυναμοῦντος τῆς δὲ ζωῆς τὸν λόγον ψυχούσης. ἔτι παντὸς πράγματος εὐδαιμονία ἡ οἰκεία τελειότης ἐστίν, οἰκεία δὲ τελειότης ἑκάστῳ ἡ πρὸς τὴν ἑαυτοῦ αἰτίαν συναφή, καὶ διὰ τοῦτο ἡμεῖς εὐχόμεθα συναφθῆναι θεοῖς· ἐπεὶ τοίνυν ζωὴ μὲν πρώτη ἡ τῶν θεῶν ἐστι, ζωὴ δέ τις καὶ ἡ ἀνθρωπίνη βούλεται δὲ αὕτη συναφθῆναι ἐκείνῃ, μεσότητος δεῖται (οὐδὲν γὰρ τῶν πλεῖστον διεστώτων ἀμέσως συνάπτεται) ἡ δὲ μεσότης ὁμοία

---

1 οὔτε τοὺς θεοὺς θεραπεύομεν οὔτε] καὶ τ. θ. θ. καὶ cod., corr. Mullach, Schultessium secutus, qui οὐδὲ...οὐδὲ coniecit. 17 τοῖς μὲν θεοῖς] τοὺς μὲν θεοὺς cod., corr. ed. pr. in *erratis*. 23 κόμης] κόμ cod., addito supra σ et ȣ, manu, ni fallor, recentiore, quod efficit κοσμȣ, id est κόσμου: κόμης, quod κομς saepe scribitur, restitui. 29 post ἡμεῖς rasura in cod.

change them, but by the acts we perform and by our turning to the divine we heal our vice and again enjoy the goodness of the gods. Accordingly, to say that the gods turn their faces away from the bad is like saying that the sun hides himself from those bereft of sight.

XV These considerations settle also the question concerning sacrifices and the other honours which are paid to the gods. The divine nature itself is free from needs; the honours done to it are for our good. The providence of the gods stretches everywhere and needs only fitness for its enjoyment. Now all fitness is produced by imitation and likeness. That is why temples are a copy of heaven, altars of earth, images of life (and that is why they are made in the likeness of living creatures), prayers of the intellectual element, letters of the unspeakable powers on high, plants and stones of matter, and the animals that are sacrificed of the unreasonable life in us. From all these things the gods gain nothing (what is there for a god to gain?), but we gain union with them.

XVI I think it worth while to add a few words about sacrifices. In the first place, since everything we have comes from the gods, and it is just to offer to the givers first fruits of what is given, we offer first fruits of our possessions in the form of votive offerings, of our bodies in the form of hair, of our life in the form of sacrifices. Secondly, prayers divorced from sacrifices are only words, prayers with sacrifices are animated words, the word giving power to the life and the life animation to the word. Furthermore, the happiness of anything lies in its appropriate perfection, and the appropriate perfection of each object is union with its cause. For this reason also we pray that we may have union with the gods. So, since though the highest life is that of the gods, yet man's life also is life of some sort, and this life wishes to have union with that, it needs an intermediary (for objects most widely separated are never united without a middle term), and the intermediary ought to be like the objects being united. Accordingly, the

εἶναι τοῖς συναπτομένοις ὀφείλει, ζωῆς οὖν μεσότητα ζωὴν ἐχρῆν εἶναι, καὶ διὰ τοῦτο ζῷα θύουσιν ἄνθρωποι οἵ τε νῦν εὐδαίμονες καὶ πάντες οἱ πάλαι, καὶ ταῦτα οὐχ ἁπλῶς ἀλλ' ἑκάστῳ θεῷ τὰ πρέποντα, μετὰ πολλῆς τῆς ἄλλης θρησκείας. καὶ περὶ μὲν τούτων ἱκανά. 5

XVII τὸν δὲ κόσμον ὅτι μὲν οὐκ [ἂν] θεοὶ φθεροῦσιν εἴρηται· ὅτι δὲ καὶ τὴν φύσιν ἄφθαρτον ἔχει, λέγειν ἀκόλουθον. πᾶν γὰρ τὸ φθειρόμενον ἢ ὑφ' ἑαυτοῦ φθείρεται ἢ ὑπὸ ἄλλου. εἰ μὲν οὖν ὑφ' ἑαυτοῦ ὁ κόσμος φθείρεται, ἔδει καὶ τὸ πῦρ ἑαυτὸ καίειν καὶ τὸ ὕδωρ ἑαυτὸ ξηραίνειν. εἰ δὲ ὑπὸ ἄλλου, 10 ἢ σώματος ἢ ἀσωμάτου. ἀλλ' ὑπὸ μὲν ἀσωμάτου ἀδύνατον (τὰ γὰρ ἀσώματα σώζει τὰ σώματα, οἷον φύσις καὶ ψυχή, οὐδὲν δὲ ὑπὸ τοῦ φύσει σώζοντος φθείρεται), εἰ δὲ ὑπὸ σωμάτων, ἢ ὑπὸ τῶν ὄντων ἢ ὑπὸ ἑτέρων. καὶ εἰ μὲν ὑπὸ τῶν ὄντων, ἢ ὑπὸ τῶν κύκλῳ κινουμένων τὰ ἐπ' εὐθείας ἢ ὑπὸ 15 τῶν ἐπ' εὐθείας τὰ κύκλῳ· ἀλλ' οὐδὲ τὰ κύκλῳ φθαρτικὴν ἔχει φύσιν. διὰ τί γὰρ μηδὲν ὁρῶμεν ἐκεῖθεν φθειρόμενον; οὐδὲ τὰ ἐπ' εὐθείας ἐκείνων ἅψασθαι δύναται. διὰ τί γὰρ ἄχρι νῦν οὐκ ἠδυνήθη; ἀλλ' οὐδὲ τὰ ἐπ' εὐθείας ὑπ' ἀλλήλων φθείρεσθαι δύναται· ἡ γὰρ ἄλλου φθορὰ ἄλλου γένεσίς 20 ἐστι, τοῦτο δὲ φθείρεσθαι μὲν οὔκ ἐστι, μεταβάλλεσθαι δέ· εἰ δὲ ὑπ' ἄλλων σωμάτων ὁ κόσμος φθείρεται, πόθεν γενομένων ἢ ποῦ νῦν ὄντων οὐκ ἔστιν εἰπεῖν. ἔτι πᾶν τὸ φθειρόμενον ἢ εἴδει ἢ ὕλῃ φθείρεται· ἐστὶ δὲ εἶδος μὲν τὸ σχῆμα, ὕλη δὲ τὸ σῶμα. καὶ τοῦ μὲν εἴδους φθειρομένου τῆς δὲ ὕλης 25 μενούσης ἕτερα ὁρῶμεν γινόμενα. εἰ δὲ ὕλη φθείρεται, πῶς ἐν τοσούτοις ἔτεσιν οὐκ ἐπέλιπεν; εἰ δὲ ἀντὶ τῆς φθειρομένης ἑτέρα γίγνεται, ἢ ἐκ τῶν ὄντων ἢ ἐκ τῶν μὴ ὄντων γίγνεται. ἀλλ' εἰ μὲν ἐκ τῶν ὄντων, τῶν ὄντων μενόντων ἀεὶ καὶ ἡ ὕλη ἔστιν ἀεί. εἰ δὲ καὶ τὰ ὄντα φθείρεται, οὐ τὸν κόσμον μόνον 30 ἀλλὰ καὶ πάντα λέγουσι φθείρεσθαι. εἰ δὲ ἐκ τῶν μὴ ὄντων ἡ ὕλη, πρῶτον μὲν ἀδύνατον ἐκ τῶν μὴ ὄντων εἶναί τι, εἰ δὲ καὶ

---

6 ἂν seclusi, cf. *Proll.* cvi. 10 καίειν] exspectes σβεννύναι.

intermediary between life and life should be life, and for this reason living animals are sacrificed by the blessed among men to-day and were sacrificed by all the men of old, not in a uniform manner, but to every god the fitting victims, with much other reverence. Concerning this subject I have said enough.

XVII That the gods will not destroy the universe has been stated; that its nature is immortal must now be set forth. Whatever is destroyed is destroyed either by itself or by something else. If the universe is destroyed by itself, fire ought to burn itself and water dry itself. If the universe is destroyed by something else, that something must be either corporeal or incorporeal. Incorporeal it cannot be, since things incorporeal, as nature and soul, preserve things corporeal, and nothing is destroyed by what naturally preserves it. If corporeal, it must be one of existents or of non-existents; if the first then bodies moving in circles must destroy bodies moving in straight lines or bodies moving in straight lines must destroy bodies moving in circles. But bodies moving in circles do not possess a destructive nature; otherwise, why do we see nothing perishing thence? Nor can bodies moving in straight lines touch bodies moving in circles; otherwise, why have they hitherto been unable to do so? Nor, again, can bodies moving in straight lines be destroyed by one another, since the destruction of one is the creation of another, and this is not destruction but change.

If the universe is destroyed by other bodies, whence they come or where they now are cannot be said. Further, whatever perishes, perishes either in form or in matter, form being the shape, matter the body. If the form perishes and the matter remains we see other things being produced; if matter perishes, why has it not failed in all these years? If matter perishes, and other matter takes its place, the latter must come either from existents or from non-existents; if from existents, so long as they remain for ever, matter is for ever, and if existents perish, this means the destruction not merely of the universe but of everything; if from non-existents, firstly, it is impossible that anything should come

τοῦτο γένοιτο καὶ δυνατὸν ἐκ τῶν μὴ ὄντων εἶναι τὴν ὕλην, ἕως ἂν ᾖ τὰ μὴ ὄντα ἔσται καὶ ἡ ὕλη· οὐ γὰρ δήποτε καὶ τὰ μὴ ὄντα ἀπόλλυται. εἰ δὲ ἀνείδεον λέγουσι μένειν τὴν ὕλην, πρῶτον μὲν διὰ τί οὐ κατὰ μέρη ἀλλ' ἐν ὅλῳ τοῦτο γίνεται τῷ κόσμῳ; ἔπειτα οὐ τὸ εἶναι τῶν σωμάτων τὸ δὲ κάλλος φθείρουσι μόνον. ἔτι πᾶν τὸ φθειρόμενον ἢ ἀφ' ὧν ἐγένετο εἰς ἐκεῖνα λύεται ἢ εἰς τὸ μὴ ὂν ἀφανίζεται. ἀλλ' εἰ μὲν ἀφ' ὧν ἐγένετο εἰς ἐκεῖνα λυθείη, πάλιν γίνεται ἕτερα· διὰ τί γὰρ τὴν ἀρχὴν ἐγένετο; εἰ δὲ εἰς τὸ μὴ ὂν ἄπεισι τὰ ὄντα, τί κωλύει καὶ τὸν θεὸν τοῦτο παθεῖν; εἰ δὲ ἡ δύναμις κωλύει, οὐκ ἐστὶ δυνατοῦ ἑαυτὸν μόνον σώζειν. καὶ ὁμοίως δὲ ἀδύνατον ἐκ τῶν μὴ ὄντων γίγνεσθαι τὰ ὄντα καὶ τὰ ὄντα εἰς τὸ μὴ ὂν ἀφανίζεσθαι. ἔτι ἀνάγκη τὸν κόσμον εἰ φθείρεται ἢ κατὰ φύσιν φθείρεσθαι ἢ παρὰ φύσιν, ⟨ἀλλ' εἰ μὲν κατὰ φύσιν, παρὰ φύσιν συνέστη καὶ μέχρι τοῦδε συνείχετο. ἀλλ' οὐδὲν γίνεται παρὰ φύσιν,⟩ οὐδὲ τὸ παρὰ φύσιν πρότερον ἔχει τῆς φύσεως. εἰ δὲ παρὰ φύσιν, δεῖ ἑτέραν εἶναι φύσιν τὴν μεταβάλλουσαν τοῦ κόσμου τὴν φύσιν, ὅπερ οὐ φαίνεται. ἔτι πᾶν τὸ φύσει φθειρόμενον καὶ ἡμεῖς φθείρειν δυνάμεθα, τοῦ δὲ κόσμου τὸ μὲν κυκλικὸν σῶμα οὔτε ἔφθειρέ τίς ποτε οὔτε μετέβαλε, τῶν δὲ στοιχείων ⟨ἕκαστον⟩ μεταβάλλειν μὲν δυνατὸν φθείρειν δὲ ἀδύνατον. ἔτι πᾶν τὸ φθειρόμενον ὑπὸ χρόνου μεταβάλλεται καὶ γηρᾷ, ὁ δὲ κόσμος ἐν τοσούτοις ἔτεσιν ἀμετάβλητος μένει. τοσαῦτα καὶ πρὸς τοὺς ἰσχυροτέρων ἀποδείξεων δεομένους εἰπόντες αὐτὸν ἡμῖν εὐχόμεθα ἵλεων τὸν κόσμον γενέσθαι.

XVIII καὶ μὴν οὐδὲ τὸ ἀθεΐας περί τινας τόπους τῆς γῆς γενέσθαι πολλάκις δὲ ὕστερον ἔσεσθαι ἄξιον ταράττειν τοὺς ἔμφρονας, ὅτι τε οὐκ εἰς θεοὺς γίνεται ταῦτα, ὥσπερ οὐδὲ αἱ τιμαὶ ἐκείνους ὠφελοῦσαι ἐφάνησαν, καὶ διὰ τὸ ἀδυνατεῖν μέσης οὐσίας οὖσαν τὴν ψυχὴν ἀεὶ κατορθοῦν καὶ τὸ μὴ δύνασθαι πάντα

---

14 suppleuit Praechter ex. gr.: alii alia, uelut ⟨εἰ μὲν παρὰ φύσιν,⟩ οὐδὲν τὸ παρὰ φύσιν πρότερον ἔχει τῆς φύσεως· εἰ δὲ κατὰ φύσιν Muccio, qui etiam φύσιν ante τὴν μεταβάλλουσαν secludit, ut ed. pr. iteratis curis. 17 ἔχει] ἐστι Wendland. 21 ⟨ἕκαστον⟩ suppleuit Muccio, collato loco Philonis *De mundi aeternitate* XVI. § 82, εἰ μὲν ἕκαστον ἐν μέρει τῶν στοιχείων ἐφθείρετο μεταβολὴν ἐδύνατο τὴν εἰς ἕτερον δέχεσθαι.

from non-existents, and secondly, if this should happen and it should be possible for matter to come from non-existents, so long as non-existents are, matter also will be: for surely non-existents do not also perish. But if they say that matter remains without form, firstly, why does this happen to the whole universe and not to parts? Secondly, they deprive bodies of beauty alone, not of being.

Further, whatever perishes either is resolved into its components or disappears into nothingness. If it is resolved into its elements, other things are again produced; if this were not so, why were the components made in the first place? If, however, existents will disappear into nothingness, what prevents this from happening to God too? But if His functional power prevents it, such power does not belong to one able only to preserve himself. It is equally impossible for existents to be produced out of non-existents and for existents to vanish into nothingness.

Then too, the universe, if it perishes, must perish either in accordance with nature or contrary to nature. ⟨If it perishes in accordance with nature, then the making and continuance till now of the universe prove to be unnatural, and yet nothing is made contrary to nature⟩, nor does what is contrary to nature take precedence over nature. If it perishes contrary to nature, there must be another nature changing the nature of the universe, and this we do not see. Further, whatever perishes naturally we too can destroy: but the circular body of the universe no one has ever destroyed or changed, while the elements can be changed, but not destroyed. Moreover, whatever perishes is changed by time and grows old, but the universe remains unchanged by all the lapse of time. Having said so much in answer to those who require stronger proofs, I pray that the universe may itself be propitious to me.

XVIII Again, the fact that unbelief has arisen in certain parts of the earth and will often occur hereafter should not disturb men of sense. Such neglect does not affect the gods, just as we saw that honours do not benefit them: further, the soul, being of a middle nature, cannot always judge aright,

τὸν κόσμον τῆς τῶν θεῶν προνοίας ἀπολαύειν ὁμοίως, ἀλλὰ τὰ μὲν αἰωνίως τὰ δὲ κατὰ χρόνον καὶ τὰ μὲν πρώτως τὰ δὲ δευτέρως μετέχειν ἐκείνης, ὥσπερ καὶ τῶν αἰσθήσεων πασῶν μὲν ἡ κεφαλὴ μιᾶς δὲ ὅλον τὸ σῶμα αἰσθάνεται. καὶ διὰ τοῦτο ὡς ἔοικεν οἱ τὰς ἑορτὰς καταστησάμενοι καὶ ἀπο- 5 φράδας ἐποίησαν ἐν αἷς τὰ μὲν ἤργει τῶν ἱερῶν τὰ δὲ ἐκλείετο τῶν δὲ καὶ τὸν κόσμον ἀφῄρουν πρὸς τὴν ἀσθένειαν τῆς ἡμετέρας ἀφοσιούμενοι φύσεως. καὶ κολάσεως δὲ εἶδος εἶναι ἀθεΐαν οὐκ ἀπεικός· τοὺς γὰρ γνόντας θεοὺς καὶ καταφρονήσαντας εὔλογον ἐν ἑτέρῳ βίῳ καὶ τῆς γνώσεως στέρεσθαι, 10 καὶ τοὺς ἑαυτῶν βασιλέας ὡς θεοὺς τιμήσαντας ἔδει τὴν Δίκην αὐτῶν ποιῆσαι τῶν θεῶν ἐκπεσεῖν.

XIX εἰ δὲ μηδὲ τούτων μηδὲ τῶν ἄλλων ἁμαρτημάτων εὐθὺς αἱ δίκαι τοῖς ἁμαρτήσασιν ἕπονται, θαυμάζειν οὐ δεῖ· ὅτι τε οὐ δαίμονές εἰσι μόνον οἱ κολάζοντες τὰς ψυχὰς ἀλλὰ καὶ 15 αὐτὴ ἑαυτὴν ὑπάγει τῇ δίκῃ καὶ ὅτι μένουσι τὸν ἅπαντα χρόνον, οὐκ ἐχρῆν ἐν ὀλίγῳ πάντων τυχεῖν καὶ διὰ τὸ δεῖν ἀνθρωπίνην ἀρετὴν εἶναι. εἰ γὰρ τοῖς ἁμαρτήσασιν εὐθὺς ἠκολούθουν αἱ δίκαι φόβῳ δικαιοπραγοῦντες ἄνθρωποι ἀρετὴν οὐκ ἂν εἶχον. κολάζονται δὲ τοῦ σώματος ἐξελθοῦσαι, 20 αἱ μὲν ἐνταῦθα πλανώμεναι αἱ δὲ εἴς τινας τόπους τῆς γῆς θερμοὺς ἢ ψυχρούς, αἱ δὲ ὑπὸ δαιμόνων ταραττόμεναι· πάντα δὲ μετὰ τῆς ἀλόγου ὑπομένουσι, μεθ' ἧσπερ καὶ ἥμαρτον· δι' ἣν καὶ τὸ σκιοειδὲς σῶμα ὑφίσταται, ὃ περὶ τοὺς τάφους καὶ μάλιστα τῶν κακῶς ζησάντων ὁρᾶται. 25

XX αἱ δὲ μετεμψυχώσεις, εἰ μὲν εἰς λογικὰ γένοιντο, αὐτὸ τοῦτο ψυχαὶ γίγνονται σωμάτων· εἰ δὲ εἰς ἄλογα, ἔξωθεν ἕπονται ὥσπερ καὶ ἡμῖν οἱ εἰληχότες ἡμᾶς δαίμονες. οὐ γὰρ μήποτε λογικὴ ἀλόγου ψυχὴ γένηται. τὴν δὲ μετεμψύχωσιν

---

7 πρὸς secl. Orelli. Quae protulerunt exempla constructionis ἀφοσιοῦσθαι πρὸς Wernsdorfius ad Himer. *Ecl.* v. 24, Praechter, *W. k. Ph.* 1900, 186, huc non pertinent ut in quibus sensus sit *satisfacere alicui homini uel rei.* ἀφοσιοῦσθαι tamen absolute positum est etiam cum significat *neglegenter rem perficere* (uelut Isae. *Or.* VII. 38); nihil igitur fortasse mutandum est. 12 Δίκην ut Iustitiam ipsam intellegendam esse perspexit Wendland. 28 οὐ γὰρ μήποτε λ. ἀ. ψ. γένηται] sic Muccio, cf. *Proll.* cvi.: γένοιτο cod.: οὐκ ἄν ποτε λ. ἀ. ψ. γένοιτο Mullach.

and the entire universe cannot equally enjoy the providence of the gods: some sections can always participate therein, some at times, some in the first degree, some in the second degree, just as the head possesses all the senses, the body as a whole, one only. For this reason, it seems, the founders of festivals established also banned days, on which some temples[1] were idle, some shut, some even stripped of their ornaments: this perfunctory service was done in view of the weakness of human nature. It is, moreover, not unlikely that unbelief is a kind of punishment: it is reasonable that those who have known the gods and despised them should in another life be deprived of this knowledge, and that Justice should cause those who honoured kings of their own as gods to be banished from the true gods.

XIX But if neither for these sins nor for others the punishment follows directly on the offence, we must not be surprised, because not only are there spirits that punish souls but also the soul brings itself to judgment, and because, since souls survive through eternity, they ought not in a short time to bear all their chastisement, and because there must be human virtue; for if punishments followed directly on offences, men would do right from fear and would not have virtue. Souls are punished after leaving the body, some wandering here, others to hot or cold places in the earth, others being tormented by spirits; all these things they endure together with the unreasonable soul, in whose company they sinned: because of this the shadowy form seen about tombs, especially of evil livers, comes into being.

XX If transmigration of a soul happens into a rational creature, the soul becomes precisely that body's soul, if into an unreasoning creature, the soul accompanies it from outside as our guardian spirits accompany us; for a rational soul could never become the soul of an irrational creature. The reality of transmigration can be seen from the existence of

[1] Muccio, *Studi italiani*, VII. 70, makes ἱερά mean 'ceremonies': this seems less probable.

ἐκ τῶν ἐκ γενετῆς παθῶν ἔστιν ἰδεῖν (διὰ τί γὰρ οἱ μὲν τυφλοὶ οἱ δὲ παρειμένοι οἱ δὲ καὶ αὐτὴν τὴν ψυχὴν κακῶς ἔχοντες τίκτονται;) καὶ ἐκ τοῦ φύσει ἐχούσας ἐν σώματι πολιτεύεσθαι τὰς ψυχὰς μὴ δεῖν ἅπαξ ἐξελθούσας τὸν πάντα αἰῶνα μένειν ἐν ἀργίᾳ· εἰ γὰρ μὴ πάλιν αἱ ψυχαὶ εἰς σώματα 5 φέροιντο ἀνάγκη ἀπείρους εἶναι ἢ τὸν θεὸν ἀεὶ ἑτέρας ποιεῖν. ἀλλ' οὐδὲ ἄπειρόν τι ἐν τῷ κόσμῳ· ἐν γὰρ πεπερασμένῳ ἄπειρόν τι οὐκ ἂν γένοιτο. οὐδὲ ἄλλας γίνεσθαι δυνατόν· πᾶν γὰρ ἐν ᾧ τι γίγνεται καινόν, καὶ ἀτελὲς εἶναι ἀνάγκη. τὸν δὲ κόσμον ἐκ τελείου γενόμενον τέλειον εἶναι προσήκει. 10

XXI αἱ δὲ κατ' ἀρετὴν ζήσασαι ψυχαὶ τά τε ἄλλα εὐδαιμονοῦσαι καὶ τῆς ἀλόγου χωρισθεῖσαι καὶ καθαραὶ παντὸς γενόμεναι σώματος θεοῖς τε συνάπτονται καὶ τὸν ὅλον κόσμον συνδιοικοῦσιν ἐκείνοις. καίτοι καὶ εἰ μηδὲν αὐτοῖς τούτων ἐγένετο, αὐτή γε ἡ ἀρετὴ καὶ ἡ ἐκ τῆς ἀρετῆς ἡδονή τε καὶ 15 δόξα ὅ τε ἄλυπος καὶ ἀδέσποτος βίος εὐδαίμονας ⟨ἂν⟩ ἤρκει ποιεῖν τοὺς κατ' ἀρετὴν ζῆν προελομένους καὶ δυνηθέντας.

---

3 φύσει] φύσεως cod., corr. Muccio (qui φύσιν quoque coniecit): φύσεως seruato τῆς pro τοῦ reposuit Gale. 4 δεῖν] cod.: δεῖ Mullach. ἐξελθούσας] ἐλθούσας cod., corr. Mullach. 7 οὐδὲ] οὐδὲν cod., corr. ed. pr. 10 ἐκ τελείου γενόμενον] cod.: ἐκ τελείων γενόμενον Muccio, cf. Julian, p. 139 B, τέλειον ἐκ μερῶν τελείων, Herm. Trismeg. *ap.* Stob. III. 11. 31, p. 436 Hense (=p. 382 Scott), ζῷον ἀτελὲς ἐξ ἀτελῶν συγκείμενον μερῶν (sic Scott pro μελῶν). 11 εὐδαιμονοῦσαι] fortasse εὐδαιμονοῦσι. 16 ⟨ἂν⟩ suppleui. 17 post δυνηθέντας habet cod. τ, id est τέλος.

congenital complaints (else why are some born blind, some born paralysed, some born diseased in soul?) and from the fact that souls which are naturally qualified to act in the body must not, once they have left it, remain inactive throughout time. Indeed, if souls do not return into bodies, they must either be unlimited in number or God must continually be making others. But there is nothing unlimited in the universe, since in what is ordered by limit there cannot be anything unlimited. Nor is it possible that other souls should come into being, for everything in which something new is produced must be imperfect, and the universe, as proceeding from what is perfect, should be perfect.

XXI Souls that have lived in accordance with virtue have as the crown of their happiness that freed from the unreasonable element and purified from all body they are in union with the gods and share with them the government of the whole universe. Yet, even if they attained none of these things, virtue itself and the pleasure and honour of virtue, and the life free from pain and from all other tyrants, would suffice to make happy those who had chosen to live in accordance with virtue and had proved able.

APPENDIX

Variants of Cod. Barb. I 84.

Title. ἡρακλείτου ὁμηρικῶν προβλημάτων εἰς ἃ περὶ θεῶν | σαλουστίου φιλοσόφου κεφάλαια τοῦ βιβλίου, with a marginal note in the same hand[1] after περὶ θεῶν: ἐν τῷ τέλει τοῦ | προηγουμένου ἐγέγρ(α)πτο· ἄδηλον δὲ εἴτε ἀρχὴ εἴτε τέλος τοῦτο.

List of Contents, l. 1 τὸν ἀκροάτην ὄντα. 4 μῦθοι | διὰ τί θεῖοι[2]. 5 ἀποδείγματα. 8 μέση ’στι.

I 2. 3 after ἔμφρονας a gap of 12 or 13 letters at end of line. l. 5 *om.* ὀρθῶς.

II 2. 16 *om.* οὐδὲ ζῴου αἱ αἰσθήσεις.

III 2. 24 χρη(σμοῖς), with indications of alteration. 4. 1 καὶ διὰ. 4. 7 οἱ ποῖοι.

IV 4. 27 ἀνεργείας (—αι Cum.). 4. 29 τοὺς ὅλους. l. 30 καταπίνεσθαι δὲ ὑπὸ. 6. 6 ἐναρκεῖσθαι (ἀνακει above) μὲν θεους (οις above). 6. 31 τὴν νύμφην. 8. 7 ἔρχεσθαι. 8. 9 ἀττεἶθαι (=ἀττεωσθαι, the σθαι being deleted) καὶ. l. 19 *om.* ὡς.

V 10. 11 *om.* δέ.

VI 12. 14 πρωτως (ους above). l. 17 ἔστίμεν (μεν deleted) ας μεν. l. 20 ληπτέους.

VII 12. 24 ἀγέννητον, as below 30, where *om.* καὶ. l. 25 οὐκ ἔστι (underlined, in place of A’s faintly-written ἀνάγκη).

VIII 14. 24 ζητέον. l. 30 καταφρονήσει corrected to καταφρονεῖ. 16. 3 ἀσωμάτοις corrected to ἀσώματος.

IX 16. 19 μεσοι μὲν. l. 22 *om.* τὴν. l. 26 τὴν δύναμιν ἐχόντων. l. 29 αὐτῇ καὶ, καὶ being altered to τε. 18. 14 περα (α above). l. 15 πυρρέσσουσι. 20. 6 ἔν τε πελήνῃ δέ. l. 8 ἀτυχοῦσι altered to εὐτυχοῦσι.

XI 22. 5 *om.* καὶ before πλείους. l. 10 πάντως.

XII 22. 15 after κακὰ is written ἔνεστιν, later deleted. l. 21 κακόν written over an erasure (perhaps οὐ καλόν was first written). l. 26 οἱ (?) δὲ ἀλλαχόθεν. l. 27 erasure of about 6 letters before ἢ βουλόμενοι.

[1] Cumont thinks in another hand, Muccio, *Studi* III. 9, in the same; my notes are silent on the point.

[2] Cumont’s collation gives θεοί, and in l. 15 ὁ καὶ ἁ.

XIII 24. 19 γίνεσθαι altered to γίνεται. 26. 2 συνιφίσταται. 26. 9 φύσεως διαφέρει ὁ πρῶτος θεός (a reading inferred *ex silentio*).

XIV 28. 1 δίχα τῶν δρωμένων. Note before this the placing of a question-mark after μεταβάλλομεν, which we may regard as an attempt to make sense of the sentence.

XVI 28. 21 περὶ θ. (due to a misunderstanding of πᵉ, = παρά, in A).

XVII 32. 3 μέν for μένειν (μέν″). l. 4 *om.* ἐν. l. 5 οὐδὲ (δὲ deleted later). l. 19 ἢ altered into καὶ. l. 24 καὶ over an erasure.

XVIII 32. 30 τοῦ corrected to τὸ. 34. 10 before εὔλογον add. ἔδει τὴν δίκην αὐτῶν ποιῆσαι, then deleted.

XIX 34. 14 *om.* τοῖς. l. 22 πάντως.

XX 36. 5 χρόνον before αἰῶνα, then deleted.

I infer from the silence of Cumont's notes that this MS. gives πῶς in p. 24. 26 in place of πᾶν, as the editions have: the reading necessitates the insertion of οὐχ before ἑαυτοῦ, as Schultess proposed. It is no doubt due to a misreading of the compendium used in the Ambrosian MS.

INDEX

§ I. SUBJECTS

INDEX

§ II. THE GREEK OF SALLUSTIUS

§ III. GREEK

Other texts emended or explained.